The Good Child

The Good Child

Moral Development in a Chinese Preschool

Jing Xu

Stanford University Press
Stanford, California

Stanford University Press
Stanford, California

Printed in the United States of America on acid-free, archival-quality paper

Library of Congress Cataloging-in-Publication Data

Names: Xu, Jing, 1983- author.
Title: The good child : moral development in a Chinese preschool / Jing Xu.
Description: Stanford, California : Stanford University Press, 2017. |
   Includes bibliographical references and index.
Identifiers: LCCN 2016049914 | ISBN 9780804799263 (cloth : alk. paper) |
   ISBN 9781503602434 (pbk. : alk. paper) | ISBN 9781503602472 (e-book)
Subjects: LCSH: Moral development—China—Shanghai. | Preschool
   children—China—Shanghai—Conduct of life. | Moral education
   | Preschool—China—Shanghai. | Child development—China—Shanghai.
Classification: LCC BF723.M54 X8 2017 | DDC 155.4/18250951132—dc23 LC record
available at https://lccn.loc.gov/2016049914

ISBN 9780804799263 (cloth); 9781503602434 (paper)

Typeset by Dovetail Publishing Services in 10/14 Minion

To my parents, Tu Meifang, and Xu Shuiping,
who have supported me in every possible way,
and to my son Felix (Wandou),
who opened my eyes to the mysterious world of child development.

Contents

Illustrations and Tables

Acknowledgments

This book began as ethnographic research at Washington University in St. Louis and took shape more than two years at the University of Washington, Seattle. Many people have helped me in this book writing process, and words cannot express all that I wish to say to them.

Pascal Boyer introduced me to the fascinating interdisciplinary field of culture and cognition. His wisdom in thinking beyond disciplinary boundaries inspired me to situate my inquiry of culture and moral development within a broader intellectual network. He gave me the best possible support and advice throughout my research at Washington University.

James Wertsch has been an extraordinary mentor. He was always there for me when I needed advice on research, writing, career, and life in general. He was the one who constantly reminded me that I needed to get the book out as soon as possible and that solid empirical evidence was enormously important in academic works. Jim, together with his wife, Mary Wertsch, gave me the warmest encouragement and strongest support throughout this book writing process, amid the darkest time of my life. I am really lucky to have Jim and Mary as my "American parents."

Many other teachers have generously given me advice and support in various ways. I owe many thanks to Xiaojun Zhang at Tsinghua University, Beijing. Since 2005, he has always offered me intellectual guidance and encouraged me to pursue my true academic interests. Jun Jing introduced me to the field of cultural anthropology at Tsinghua University. Geoff Childs helped me to formulate a solid fieldwork methodology prior to fieldwork and to overcome my post-fieldwork procrastination. Priscilla Song gave me invaluable suggestions on situating my research in China anthropology literatures. Lori

Markson brought me into the field of cognitive development; such warm encouragement from Lori, a mainstream developmental psychologist, meant a lot to me. Bob Canfield patiently listened to my many frustrations and difficulties with research and writing, and kindly encouraged me about the unique value of my project. Bambi Chapin generously shared with me her book prospectus. Stevan Harrell introduced me to the community of anthropology and China studies at University of Washington. I presented my book manuscript for the first time and got helpful feedback in the China Anthropology Seminar that Steve organized. Steve also thoroughly read through the main part of my book manuscript and offered wonderful suggestions and humorous comments. Jessica Sommerville from University of Washington's psychology department offered insights on how to sharpen my argument and present my main findings to a broader audience outside anthropology. I also thank William Jankowiak, who invited me to present my book manuscript at University of Nevada, Las Vegas, and offered insightful comments. I am also grateful for the questions and comments I received when I presented portions of this book at meetings of the American Anthropological Association, the Association of Asian Studies, and the Society for Psychological Anthropology, from the discussants Rubie Watson, Ann Anagnost, and James Wilce, as well as the audience.

Many colleagues and friends have animated this journey. I am thankful to Helina Solomon-Woldekiros, Chaoxiong Zhang, Yang Zhan, Xia Zhang, Chen Chen, Ge Jian, Juan Luo, Jie Lie, Xiang He, Bin Li, Xiameng Tian, and Lucie Saether, and many other people who have offered valuable comments and suggestions to me. My "sister" Lihong Shi gave me unwavering support throughout the various phases of this project, from preparing for fieldwork to the last stage of my book writing. She is both a wonderful friend and an excellent role model.

A thousand thanks to the families and teachers at Biyun Preschool, Shanghai, who kindly allowed me to become part of their community and opened their hearts to me. As a new parent in a new city, I came to Shanghai with a depressing sense of insecurity and disorientation. It was the connections with these people that made my research possible and my fieldwork experience meaningful.

I owe many thanks to Vanessa Fong and two anonymous reviewers with the Stanford University Press. My editor, Jenny Gavacs, guided me through the book revision process, and reminded me to think about the big picture. Thank you also to Kate Wahl, editor in chief at Stanford University Press, who explained things to me in great clarity. James Holt was an excellent editorial assistant, always there to promptly answer my questions. I also appreciate the support from all the staff and editors who have worked on the final production of my book.

My deepest gratitude goes to my family. As the only child of my family, I have enjoyed all the love and support from my parents. I am forever thankful to my mother for always being kind and encouraging, for instilling in me a strong curiosity in children's world, and for setting up a wonderful exemplar of living an authentic life. My lovely son, Felix (Wandou), inspired me to humble myself, put aside my adult prejudices, and learn to see the world through children's eyes. He gave me a sense of purpose and strength at the most difficult time in my life. My husband Lorenzo's love, patience, and kindness sustained me when I was trapped in senses of insecurity and failure. I dedicate this book to them.

Introduction

Becoming a Moral Child in China

The "Traffic Light" Story

On a sunny morning in a crowded neighborhood in urban Shanghai, China, two mothers were sitting on a bench, chatting about the vicissitudes of child-rearing. Lulu was a native Shanghainese mother of a bright four-year-old daughter, Weijian. The other mother was me, who had just come back to China from the United States with a two-year-old son, to conduct my ethnographic fieldwork on Chinese children's moral development. I had met Lulu a few months earlier at Biyu Preschool, my field-site and the school of my son and her daughter. Lulu was very concerned about her child growing up in the unwholesome Chinese environment, like many other mothers I met in Shanghai, and told me this "traffic light" story:

> Lulu: One day my daughter told her paternal grandfather: "Grandma took me across the street while there was a red light." What her grandma did was the opposite of what she learned from her preschool teachers and me. I feel bad about it. The educational environment in China is terrible! You came back from America. I heard that people in the Western countries obey the traffic rules very well, right?

> Jing: In the United States, it seemed so natural for everyone to observe the traffic rules. Although I'm Chinese, it still took time for me to readjust back to the reality here.

> Lulu: The Western parents set up such a good example for their children. So should we! Even if this broader social environment is really bad, we should still help the child to learn the correct rules. My daughter first got to learn about the rules of traffic lights "stop at the red light, walk at the green light"

(*hongdeng ting, lüdeng xing*), in the popular cartoon *Smart Tiger* (*qiao hu*). When I took her to the street, I intentionally avoided the intersection with a green light and chose the one with a red light. This was to teach her to wait patiently and obey the traffic rules. I told her, "If now I take you across the street when the light is still red, then those behind us will follow us, and it will be a messy situation and the traffic rules won't work. But if I tell you to wait at the red light, then those behind us will also wait. We all obey the traffic rules, which is great.

Beneath its literal meaning, this "traffic light" story has profound metaphorical significance. As Lulu explained to me later in our conversation, this story was not so much about obeying traffic rules, *per se*; rather, it was about instilling moral norms and beliefs among the younger generation, an urgent and challenging mission in contemporary China. Anxieties over moral development of China's only children are greatly heightened for Chinese families and the general public. In addition, the cultivation of moral values has become particularly challenging because socializers all worry that Chinese society is a terribly bad educational environment in which no one observes rules. The scene of violating traffic lights is merely a microcosm of the perceived chaotic social and moral reality in China today.

Such concerns are built upon assumptions, estimations, and imaginaries of the "child" in relation to the "adult," "Chinese society" in relation to "Western society," and "morality" in relation to "immorality." In particular, such concerns indicate two interlocking logics popular in Chinese thinking from ancient times until today, in the Confucian and neo-Confucian moral and educational traditions that connect self-cultivation (*xiu shen*) to bringing peace to the whole world (*ping tianxia*) (Ivanhoe, 2000): one is the positive link between edifying the child/human and bettering society (Bakken 2000): when the child develops the "correct" beliefs and acts in righteous ways, our society has a promising future; the other is the negative link between the deteriorating society and the victimized child: the moral decay of the society will endanger children's moral cultivation.

Although apparently highlighting children's significance in society, such concerns actually overlook children's own subjectivities. Lulu's comments reflect a popular view that emphasize the critical importance of educators/socializers in child development: the "wrong" message from the grandparent would cause the child to stumble while the "correct" teachings from the mother would pull the child back to the right track and motivate more people to follow.

Although these perspectives suggest the role of multiple voices—sometimes in conflict and contradiction—in Chinese society, the voices of children themselves are nonetheless obscured.

As Jon L. Saari, a historian on Chinese childhood perceptively points out, however: "We must posit not the mind as tabula rasa but the world as tabula rasa, and see it through the eyes and emotions of a developing child" (Saari 1990: 76). My book aims to answer this central question: How are Chinese children, born under the one-child policy and often seen as self-centered "little emperors," navigating this tense social world and constructing their own moral universe, at the height of China's "moral crisis"? From 2011 to 2012, I conducted fieldwork in a middle-class preschool community in Shanghai, a city that encapsulates the most dramatic social transformations in China. My son was admitted to that preschool, and we lived in a nearby neighborhood. Through everyday interactions with children, teachers, parents, grandparents, and other people living in the community, I was immersed in this community and gained understanding of the lived experiences of children, their socializers, and other Chinese people, which also enriched my own lived experiences as a researcher, a mother, and a Chinese woman. Drawing from different kinds of data, including ethnographic field observations, interviews, questionnaire surveys, field experiments, and media texts, this book reveals how children's nascent moral dispositions are selected, expressed or repressed, and modulated in specific cultural and educational processes in China.

Morality and Child Development: Conversations between Anthropology and Psychology

My book is situated within the larger theoretical adventure of bridging anthropology and psychology in studying child development. All human behavior is driven by various psychological forces that are, on the one hand, generated in particular historical and sociocultural dynamics, and, on the other hand, shaped by these particular cultural dynamics in multiple and profound ways. In recent years, anthropologists have called for a re-engagement with trends in the psychological sciences, emphasizing that anthropology has important lessons to offer in understanding human behavior in its fullest sense (Astuti and Bloch 2010, 2012; Bloch 2005, 2012; Sahlins 2011; Sperber 1996). More generally, scholars in both fields realize the need for in-depth conversations in which both anthropologists and psychologists appreciate human beings' intertwined psychological-social nature (Bender, Hutchins, and Medin 2010; Luhrmann 2006; Quinn 2006). Child development is a central "test field" in this exciting endeavor. Leading scholars in psychological anthropology have discovered common features of child-rearing across cultures that are based on universal psychological mechanisms (Quinn 2005). Anthropologists and psychologists have worked together to combine experimental methods with ethnographic fieldwork to investigate conceptual development (Astuti, Solomon, and Carey 2004). Moreover, anthropologists have taken on the role of critically engaging with and reassessing influential psychological theories, such as attachment theory (Bowlby 1969, 1982; Ainsworth 1979), using ethnographic evidence from multiple sociocultural contexts (Quinn and Mageo 2013). My research is greatly inspired by these conversations. In what follows, I will present the bodies of literatures from both anthropology and psychology that substantially informed my study of moral development in early childhood.

First, my project joins the newly emerging trend of the anthropology of morality (or moral anthropology), in which morality is made the explicit focus of empirical analysis and theoretical argumentation (Fassin 2012). My book embraces an inclusive understanding of morality, including the level of everyday bodily practice as well as that of public and institutionally articulated discourse (Zigon 2008). My Chinese informants actually talk about "morality" on both levels, and these two levels generate, inform, and complement each other, like that of *yin* and *yang*.

One important issue with which the new field of moral anthropology (or the anthropology of morality) is grappling is the opposition between "morality" and "ethics." For example, Jarrett Zigon (2008: 17–18) argues that morality is about the "unreflective/unreflexive" and ethics is about the "reflective/reflexive." Other scholars emphasize the dichotomy of structure (morality) versus agency (ethics) (Lambek 2010; Stafford 2013a). My book chooses to use the terms *morality* and *moral*, instead of *ethics* and *ethical* for two reasons. First, in line with the understanding of cultural values (Robbins 2012), moral sentiments (Throop 2012), moral reasoning (Sykes 2012), and the like, my book focuses on the psychological workings of morality, instead of "an anthropology of ethics" (Faubion 2011; Laidlaw 2002) under the Foucauldian tradition that aims to dissect the political (in a broad sense) workings of morality. Second, in Chinese, *morality* (*dao de*) is a broader category that can refer to both moral codes (structure) and moral dispositions/sentiments/reasoning/actions (agency), and it is used in both official and vernacular language, whereas *ethics* (*lun li*) refers to the narrower domains of ethical rules. My informants used the term *morality* (*dao de*) much more frequently than *ethics* (*lun li*), as the making of moral personhood and moral society became a central concern in their life.

Moreover, psychological literatures on moral domains inspire me to carve out the basic analytical themes for this book. The quest to map out "moral domains" is born out of the impetus to go beyond the ethnocentric Western obsession with the domain of justice alone, in order to accommodate and explain cultural diversity and achieve a more comprehensive view of morality. Major Western theoretical frameworks include the "big three" of morality (autonomy, community, and divinity), also known as the "three ethics" theory (Shweder et al. 1997); the moral foundations theory (MFT), which postulates five foundational domains (like five taste buds): harm/care, fairness/reciprocity, in-group/loyalty, authority/respect, and purity/sanctity (Haidt 2012; Haidt and Graham 2007); and the evolving relational models theory (RMT) (Fiske 1991; Fiske 1992; Fiske and Haslam 2005; Rai and Fiske 2011), which identifies four fundamental relational structures underlying all social coordination and corresponding moral motivations: community sharing; unity, authority ranking; hierarchy, equality matching; balanced reciprocity, market pricing; and proportionality (Fiske 1991; Fiske 1992).

This book, however, does not mechanically map any such categorization onto my field data, for the following reasons. First, there are intricate connections between different moral domain categories within and across the moral domain theories. For example, the motive to care for others and the motive of achieving or restoring fairness are sometimes intertwined in children's moral judgments and emotions. The calculus of fairness is also a complex combination of different factors, such as the motive of equality and that of proportionality, rather than being reducible to a singular formula. The motive of "unity" underlying the relation of community sharing is also multifaceted: "unity" is manifested in caring and empathizing with others, or loyalty to the group, and these can be mixed together in what Victor Turner called "communitas" (Turner 1995). Moreover, these theories do not address some important themes in children's social life, for example, ownership. Understandings of ownership permeate children's play time and often cause conflicts. Children's understandings of ownership are closely intertwined with reasoning about fairness in real-life social interactions. Last but not the least, there are distinct Chinese cultural concepts that cannot be accurately and adequately captured by these moral categories. For example, the unique Chinese socialization concept of *guanjiao* integrates the meanings of both discipline and care, and the oppressive and the supportive dimension constitute two sides of the same coin. Based on such considerations, my own analytical framework emerged at the conjunction of the deductive and the inductive, between abstract moral categories and "what behaviors and attitudes were socially important, frequently repeated, and widely understood" (Briggs 1999: 11) in my fieldwork. Thus, instead of analyzing isolated moral domains, I decided to examine the tensions emerging between and within different moral domains/motives in everyday life in the Chinese cultural context. The main themes in my book include empathy and altruism, ownership and fairness, generosity and reciprocity, and *guanjiao*. Analyses of these themes are built on and critically expanded from the moral-domain theories, and more details on the structure of these analyses are provided at the end of this chapter.

Moreover, morality does not come from nowhere. The origins of human morality and cooperation have been an intriguing topic in various social science disciplines (Baumard, André, and Sperber 2013; Bowles and Gintis 2011; Henrich 2004; Tomasello 2009; Tomasello et al. 2012). Recent experimental studies provide evidence that humans' moral dispositions in a variety of domains, such as empathy and care, fairness, and justice and ownership, emerge early in life (Bloom 2013), much earlier than what is assumed in classic theories such as those of Piaget ([1932] 1997) and Kohlberg (1984),[1] which predicated stage-like development.

Scholars have noted, "Ontogenic studies of how culture interacts with developing human individuals are more anthropologically acceptable, though the bulk of such research is still the domain of psychologists" (Whitehead 2012: 50). In order to fully understand the psycho-cultural processes in human development, ethnographic studies are much needed (Weisner 1997). In anthropology, it has long been acknowledged that socialization and enculturation in childhood play a crucial role in the formation of human morality. Moral discourse "saturates the everyday lives of families" (Ochs and Kremer-Sadlik 2007: 9), and moral evaluative force is imbued in child-rearing practices (Quinn 2005). Psychological anthropologists have devoted great efforts to documenting and explaining the complexity and diversity of moral socialization processes, such as different moral values, the socializability of moral values, agents and institutions involved, and techniques and strategies (Fung and Smith 2010: 263).

Although psychologists have yet to pay attention to ethnographic works on the everyday moral socialization in diverse cultures, however, anthropologists have yet to engage with the recent progress in developmental psychology that provides fine-grained clues as to how various prosocial motivations emerge in infancy and early childhood. My research aims to redress this critical disconnect between anthropology and psychology in studying the emergence of different prosocial dispositions in specific cultural dynamics.

My research also highlights the importance of documenting and contextualizing children's own experiences and agency. Anthropologists have realized the need to examine closely the developing children's own subjective experiences and agency in moral socialization (Stafford 2013a). Ethnographic studies are ideally positioned to provide a space where children are seen as social actors who play a unique and active role in shaping their own social world (James 2007). Efforts to contextualize children's "voices" are crucial to exploring how and what children's own perspectives can provide with regard to our theorizing of human sociality.

To sum up, this book draws on anthropological and psychological literature on morality to study a crucial phase for moral development, early childhood, where nascent moral dispositions generate a variety of cooperative behaviors. It integrates ethnographic and field experimental methods in a mutually informative way. And it places children themselves at the center of the analysis, reveals how young children construct their own moral world, and contextualizes their moral practices and understandings within their daily experiences.

Moral Development in China: The Past and the Present

China provides a unique testing ground to examine children's moral development because "morality" had become a central topic in Chinese social life and penetrates familial, educational, and public discussions. First, there is a widespread sense that China is in the midst of a "moral crisis," often phrased in terms of lost, supposedly traditional, moral values. Second, education is seen by most as a crucial element in the project of building a better, more moral China. Third, the one-child policy of the last decades has resulted in a generation of single children with distinctive moral experiences. Taken together, these factors contribute to establish children's moral development as a contested and strategic domain in China.

Chinese educational traditions take *zuo ren* (becoming/acting human), self-fulfillment in terms of moral cultivation, as the ultimate goal:

> A very ancient Chinese expression, *tso jen*,[2] defined the landscape of ideal Chinese behavior. I would translate it into English as the "struggle to be fully human." It mapped the valleys of shame, the plains of decency, and the slopes of virtuous achievement. It pointed to a pathway trod by millions of Chinese youngsters who upon reaching the age of six or seven years were exhorted by nurses, parents, and elders to *ch'eng jen*,[2] to become human, to realize their nature, to bring their innate humanity to expression and completion.

This quote from historian Jon L. Saari (1990: vi) provides an excellent summary of what *zuo ren* (literally, "acting human") means for the Chinese. Peeking into the historical roots of this idea helps us to understand the deep cultural background behind why discussions about *zuo ren* are still central in the vernacular and official discourse of contemporary Chinese social and moral life.

The emphasis on moral cultivation during infancy and childhood, and the linkage between early moral cultivation and overall societal quality, can be traced back to early Confucians such as Confucius himself, Mencius, and Xunzi (Cline 2015). In the Han dynasty (206 BC–220 AD), largely due to the ascendancy of Confucian philosophies, early moral education was at least included in Chinese philosophical and historical discussion (Kinney 1995). Such discussions featured the significance of moral development and emphasized the role of education in molding children into ideal moral persons. To this day, the idea of "teaching-transforming" (*jiao hua*) is still an essential part of educational belief. Ming dynasty neo-Confucian master Wang Yangming revived the Mencian notions that human nature was good, as everyone, even including the "petty people" (*xiao ren*), was naturally equipped with "bright virtues" (Ivanhoe 2009). But according to Wang's follower Li Zhi, the purity of a child's heart would be corrupted once "polluted and contaminated by 'false' book learning, pretentious social customs, ordinary worldly evil . . ." (Hsiung 2005: 225).

On the one hand, the prototypical "image of the individual moral hero against the backdrop of an often corrupted society and polity" (Saari 1990: 27) from the neo-Confucianism thinking was recurrent in later times of social crises, for example, at the turn of the twentieth century. On the other hand, intellectuals and educators also began to question the neo-Confucian system in the turmoil of social reforms and movements since the late Qing dynasty, amid China's quest for modernity. For example, filial piety (*xiao*) was the virtue accused by the cultural reformers of the May Fourth era[3] as killing children's vitality and independence. Such reflections, criticisms, and innovations occurred at a critical time when Chinese intellectuals were exposed to "alien" ideas from the West. This history provides an invaluable referential framework for understanding contemporary discourses and experiences revolving around children's moral development. The accusations of the May Fourth intellectuals concerning various social ills, such as the oppressive family, the callous, self-righteous group, and the national characteristic of apathy and indifference toward one's compatriots,[4] sound very familiar to Chinese parents, educators, and observers today.

Although Chinese moral education traditions were harshly attacked as a declining Chinese civilization clashed with modern Western visions at the turn of the twentieth century, today's Chinese people are lamenting the nation's moral decay/vacuum, both as a loss of traditional values and as the failure to build new values. Amid rapid and profound social transformations, Chinese people are moving "almost desperately in a fast-forward mode" (Siu 2006: 389), their lived experiences characterized by high degrees of uncertainty and inequality; in addition, negative sentiments, such as a sense of insecurity, distrust, and injustice, pervade the society (Wang and Yang 2013). In both public discourse and daily conversations, these problems are typically moralized, in the sense that personal moral qualities and collective moral norms are seen as the ultimate roots and solutions of social crises and governmental problems. Yunxiang Yan analyzes some "immoral" behaviors that perceptions of a looming moral crisis focus on, such as cases in which the Good Samaritan is the target of extortion by the person being helped (Yan 2009). He argues that these perceptions actually reflect the "changing moral landscape" amid China's rapid social transformations—that the Chinese individual is forced into "situations of difficult and sometimes self-contradictory moral reasoning and divided actions" (Yan 2011: 71–72).

The interest in studying China's "changing moral landscape" (Yan 2011) emerged in the broader wave of China anthropologists' recent inquiries into the psychological transformations of Chinese individuals living through the profound structural and social transformations of the reform era (Kleinman et al. 2011; Zhang 2008). Anthropologists present various different visions about the nature of such inner transformations of the Chinese individual amid China's quest for modernity. For example, Li Zhang and Aihwa Ong (2008) argue that the Chinese individual in the post-Mao era lives under the competing forces of the neoliberal logic of entrepreneurs and the socialist elements of the Chinese state. Yunxiang Yan (2009, 2011) posits that the modern Chinese individual is the product of the individualization of the collectivistic society, as these individuals are departing from the responsibility-centered collective ethics in the socialist era and instead embracing rights-centered individualistic ethics. Some cautions are also registered against this linear picture: "We see no simple linear relation between modernity and individuality whereby humans become more and more individualized as their societies become more and more modern" (Kipnis 2012a: 7). Andrew Kipnis (2012d) and his colleagues call for understanding the complexity of the entanglement between Chinese modernity and individual subjectivity, and especially the influence of premodern mechanisms such as the Confucian tradition of governing.

Moral development in early childhood is critical to the understanding of the moral transformations of individual lives in China. Under the widely perceived "moral crisis," socializers are faced with complex challenges in cultivating morality in early childhood. Anthropologists have just started to examine the specific moral negotiations and contradictions in educational settings (Hansen 2013, 2014). However, scholars have yet to closely examine moral development in early childhood, a critical realm where deeply entrenched historical traditions meet new, unique challenges.

Throughout waves of Chinese historical movements, the assumption remains that cultivating the moral child has the potential for addressing the moral crisis and shaping a better society in the future, deriving from the fundamental belief that self-perfection is possible through education, a belief with its deep historical roots in Chinese philosophy and social theory (Tu 1985). As Børge Bakken perceptively observes, morality focusing on personal virtue, education as self-cultivation, and the politics of disciplining people are seen as an integrated whole in Chinese traditions, much more so than in other cultures (Bakken 2000). Such observations converge with empirical research on Chinese education and learning. According to Jin Li (2012: 15), a distinctive feature of Chinese learning and education is that "learning and knowing are geared not to the external world, but to one's self as a goal of personal striving," based on the Confucian cultural foundations of perfecting self/self-cultivation socially and morally in order to take the world upon oneself (*yi tianxia wei ji ren*).

Early education was seen as crucial to the cultivation of a full-fledged moral personhood, and traces of this tradition are still visible in contemporary education policies, beliefs, and practices. On the policy level, moral education is seen as the ultimate goal of basic education, and standard tests of educational achievement include a moral dimension, that is, standardized questions on morality (Cheng 2000). On the practice level, Chinese moral inculcation emphasizes didactic narratives in personal story telling (Miller et al. 1997), as well as salient concepts and values such as training (*guan*) (Chao 1994; Wu 1996a), shame (Fung 1999; Li, Wang, and Fischer 2004), and filial piety (Wu 1996b) as parenting goals. In addition, the literature on the "Chinese learner" demonstrates that the cultural belief in moral development and growth as the central purpose of learning and teaching is still prevalent in China today (Chan and Rao 2009; Watkins and Biggs 2001) and emerges early on in preschool years (Li 2010).

Practices regarding moral education, and the meanings and prioritization of different cultural values, however, are inevitably shaped by particular social and historical changes and structural dynamics (for a review, see Fong and Kim 2011). In particular, as China has undergone rapid social transformations, new individualistic values have emerged in moral education policies, raising controversies and conflicts (Li 1993; Cheung and Pan 2006). Related ambivalence and contradiction in expectations and in the internalization of values surface in child-rearing practices (Fong 2007a; Naftali 2010; Fong et al. 2012).

One crucial factor in the transformation of contemporary Chinese children's lives is the one-child policy launched in 1979. Education of the "child" is closely intertwined with future development of the "nation" in China (Anagnost 1997; Fong 2004; Greenhalgh 2008). Chinese singleton children, seen as the country's "only hope" (Fong 2004), are also denounced as "little emperors" (*xiao huangdi*) who enjoy excessive attention and resources from the whole family (Anagnost 1997; Han 1986). As an aftermath, the moral development of Chinese children has become a critical national challenge, bringing with it heightened concerns and controversies. Anxiety focuses on whether singleton children will become overly self-centered (*ziwo zhongxin*) and socially incapable. Although the latest research reports that this policy has produced significantly less trusting, less trustworthy, and less conscientious young adults (Cameron et al. 2013), no consensus has been achieved among scholars regarding this issue (for a review, see Settles et al. 2013). In recent years, concerns about the "little emperors" have been exacerbated under the newly emerging "4:2:1" family structure, that is, four grandparents, two parents, and one child, as singleton children reach reproductive age (Wang and Fong 2009). Within the broader context of the one-child policy, another index of the perceived national importance of children's moral development is the recent focus of China anthropologists on the education for quality (*suzhi jiaoyu*) movement starting in the 1990s. Studies on this discourse and the impacts of this policy have generated fruitful insights on the relationships between Chinese governmentality and child-rearing practices (Anagnost 2004; Fong 2007a; Kipnis 2006, 2007; Kuan 2008; Woronov 2003, 2009; Zhu 2008), but little is known about young children's own moral experiences.

These tensions in the literature make it even more imperative to explore how the changing moral landscape in China transforms socializers' attitudes and perspectives on young children's moral development and how children themselves navigate in a changing world at a time of a moral crisis.

Fieldwork Settings and Methodology

Biyu Preschool

This book is based on data collected during my twelve months of fieldwork (August 2011 to July 2012) at Biyu Preschool in the megacity Shanghai. Once the frontier of China's modernization in the republican era (1912–1948), Shanghai underwent major social changes in the socialist era, and three decades of reform have again put it in the vanguard of China's economic growth and globalization. During China's "opening-up" processes, the pervasive motivation of seeking wealth has been "highlighted as a source of moral crisis" in Shanghai (Farrer 2002: 17). Shanghai is also one of the cities leading in China's basic education, being famous for its top test scores on international standardized tests and resources devoted to education (Dillon 2010). By 2009, the preschool enrollment rate in Shanghai had reached 98 percent, the highest in the nation, and compared with a 50.9 percent average rate nationwide (Yu 2010).

Biyu Preschool is located in a middle-class neighborhood in Pudong district, near Shanghai's financial hub. Most children live close to the school, some from the same neighborhood where the school is located and others from some nearby neighborhoods within walking distance or an average fifteen-minute drive.[5] The school has eight classes in four grades, with a total of 120 children, ages two to six. Geographical origin is an important matter in Shanghai, not only due to the presence of native Shanghai people's widely known regional pride (Nie and Wyman 2005), but also because of the fact that origin is related to socio-economic status (Pan 2011). The twenty teachers at the preschool are all young women in their twenties, none of them native Shanghainese.[6] In addition, there is a group of helpers called "aunties" (*Ayi*), who perform lower-level tasks to assist the teachers, such as cleaning the classrooms, helping keep the class in order, and assisting children during meal time, bedtime, bathroom time, and so on. Most of these "aunties" are native Shanghai people who retired from menial-labor jobs and work in the preschool for extra income. Parents of Biyu Preschool children come from a diverse population. More than half of the families are "new Shanghainese" (*xin Shanghairen*), highly skilled people from other regions who managed to obtain secure jobs in Shanghai and have settled there. Of the "old (native) Shanghainese" (*lao Shanghai*) families, some are well-educated upper-middle class, whereas others are relatively less educated lower-income people who have benefited from a government housing-compensation project aimed at developing Pudong district. The majority of the couples work full time and live with in-laws who help with childcare. Some even hire a nanny to complement the grandparents' help. A few families have only a nanny to help with childcare. In some families, the mother has quit her job and become a housewife to take care of the child.

This preschool advertises itself as an elite school and uses a variety of strategies to attract students. Compared to good public preschools where each classroom is packed with thirty or more children, Biyu had a higher teacher/student ratio: two teachers, two helpers, and sixteen students in each of the lowest grade classrooms (Class 1A and 1B) and two teachers, one helper, and twenty students in the higher grade classrooms (Class 2A, 2B, 3A, 3B, 4A, and 4B). Because Shanghai parents value English language learning, Biyu has hired a foreign teacher to offer children English classes every day. In addition, it offers other extracurricular classes such as piano, dancing, Chinese painting, and crayon drawing. Parents pay RMB 1600–2700 ($250–$430) per month for a child's tuition, and these extracurricular classes are charged separately.

Biyu Preschool has a three-floor building and a big playground (Figure I.1). The two nursery classes are on the first floor, for the convenience of young children, and the other classes are on the second and third floors. Each class has four rooms, a big activity room where most educational activities take place, a restroom, a dining room, and a bedroom where the children take a noon nap

Figure I.1 Biyu Preschool Main Building and Playground

Figure I.2 Class 1A Activity Room

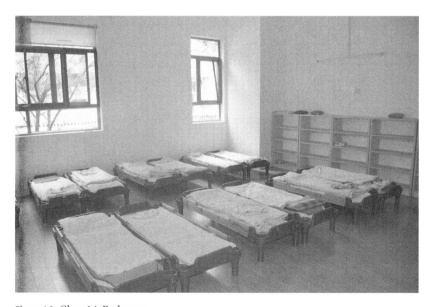

Figure I.3 Class 1A Bedroom

(Figure I.2–I.3). English class is offered in the multimedia classroom on the second floor.

Methodological Reflections

Anthropological fieldwork is surely tough if one has to travel to an exotic island in the Pacific Ocean. It is not easy either for those whose fieldwork is conducted in their home country. The cultural insider's positionality can be a double-edged sword. Although the intimate cultural knowledge one has developed since childhood could play a unique role in gaining an in-depth understanding of the targeted cultural community and social issues, the native anthropologist's own comfortable cultural horizons might obscure him or her from the many meaningful discoveries a nonnative scholar might readily discern with a cross-cultural gaze. Before setting out for fieldwork, I was deeply concerned about the embarrassing possibility that, being Chinese, I might see everything as too familiar and banal, like a fish ignorant of water, and fail to capture what is really significant and interesting through an anthropological lens.

It turned out I had been too naive in assuming that everything in China would seem transparent to me. Among many other eye-opening realities, the heightened attention among Chinese socializers and the general public to children's moral development and its perceived potential ramifications for the future of Chinese society deeply impressed me. Several years after I had left China to study anthropology in the United States, I brought back not only years of American academic training and lived experiences, but also a son who was yet to embark on a challenging journey in a new city. I grew up in central-south China and went to college in Beijing. We had never lived in Shanghai before. I asked myself anxiously: "What is growing up in Shanghai like? What are the aspirations and challenges with which Shanghai parents and teachers are preoccupied?" Being simultaneously an anthropologist interested in child development and a mother anxious about my son's adjustment to the new Chinese life, I found myself absorbing new insights from my Chinese informants, including children, teachers, parents, grandparents, and other people in the community and in the city of Shanghai at large.

We lived in a neighborhood close to Biyu Preschool—approximately a ten-minute walk. My son, Wandou, nineteen months old when I arrived in Shanghai, was admitted to Biyu as its youngest student. Every morning, I went to the school with Wandou at about 8:30 a.m., sent him to the nursery class, and went to other classrooms. I then spent the whole day observing in the classrooms, until school was dismissed at 4:30 in the afternoon. I sometimes went out to the nearby farmer's market to buy fresh food and groceries, where I would often-times run into other parents, mostly grandmothers and mothers, and conversations with them started with ease. Lunchtime was another great opportunity to build my relationships and conduct informal interviews with the teachers, as we often dined together, getting the same food from the school's cafeteria, and then chatting as we ate in the classroom or in the teacher's lounge. After school was over, some children would stay and play in the playground, while parents chatted with teachers or among themselves. I normally would stay a little bit longer in the playground, chatting with teachers and other parents, observing children playing; my son, Wandou, always hoped to stay forever, never wanting to go home.

In addition to conducting participant observation and informal interviews on a daily basis in various settings including the classroom, the playground, school parties, and special school events, I incorporated other methods into my fieldwork. I conducted in-depth interviews with forty parents, teachers, grandparents, and nannies, regarding specific issues in child-rearing and children's moral education, as well as broader topics on Chinese social and moral life. I administered a child-rearing questionnaire to ninety-two families (77 percent of all the families of Biyu Preschool at that time, based on voluntary participation). This questionnaire consists of three sections with a total of twenty questions, and some of the questions include sub-questions. The three sections are: (1) Family SES (socio-economic status) information; (2) reproductive information and values; and (3) children's social moral development. This book also includes data from two field experiments with eighty children: The first is the social investment experiment, consisting of three studies pitching equality against reciprocity in children's decisions to share earned rewards with hypothetical targets. The other one is the fairness experiment, which examines the emerging principle of merit in children's understanding of fairness, in contrast with the principle of equality. The detailed protocols and results of the field experiments are provided in the respective chapters.

The combination of naturalistic ethnography and controlled experiment fits well with studying children's subjective experiences and moral cognition. First of all, compared to the spontaneous, anecdotal episodes of children's daily life I collected through participant observation, the field experiments gave me a sense of structure over my fieldwork time span and provided great opportunities for me to become familiar with the children. For example,

I conducted the first study of the field experiment on social investment in September 2011. When I began my fieldwork, it took me time to familiarize myself with the setting, and it was difficult to gain theoretical insights from the mundane, sometimes random flow of children's life. A field experiment in the early phase of my fieldwork opened up opportunities for me to talk to children on a structured basis, as my field experiment was mainly asking children questions systematically. Also, I gained grounded knowledge on children's moral development in specific domains, which enabled me to ask further questions in my participant observation and interviews. The other experimental studies, scattered through different months and phases, also helped to structure my fieldwork and to refresh myself after the sometimes-clueless observations of children's everyday life.

Second, the experimental data uncover regularities and patterns of children's moral motivations and behaviors, which are otherwise hard to detect through naturalistic observation. Controlled experiments elicited children's behavioral responses that complemented children's limited verbal responses through informal and formal interviews. The regularities and patterns in experimental results, based on carefully designed experimental protocols driven by specific theoretical questions, further helped me to frame my research and direct my attention to particular clusters of issues in my ethnographic observations and interviews. For example, I was interested in Chinese children's sharing behavior, and thus designed an experiment to understand whether young children shared goods equally or strategically based on cues about social distance or reciprocity. I conducted this experiment during the first few months of my fieldwork and found that these preschool children did take into consideration reciprocity and other cues when making a decision on sharing. This finding led me to pay more attention during my participant observation at the preschool and interviews with teachers and parents to how these children came to understand ideas of reciprocity, and interesting stories emerged from this process.

Third, the intimate knowledge I developed through observations and interviews with children and their caregivers enabled me to contextualize how the experimental concepts were related to children's own lived experiences and to interpret and reflect on the experimental procedure and results in reference to the vicissitudes of children's daily life. As an ethnographer spending time with the children and teachers in their classrooms, I was always driven to reflect on what the details of the experimental processes mean to the children. Instead of seeing the experiments as isolated pieces, I was able to re-incorporate them into the natural flow of fieldwork, constantly monitoring and adjusting the details: the experimental settings, the task, the materials, the framing of an experiment as a "fun game," the previous connections I had already established with the children, the ways I interacted with them verbally and nonverbally, the way my "subjects" saw me, the meanings of their utterances, the intentions behind their behaviors, their moods at particular times, and the activities they were engaged in right before or after the experiment. All these constitute an ongoing intersubjective process that the children and I constructed together.

The duality of my identities as a researcher and a mother is also worth closer examination and reflection. As a parent, I had unique opportunities to establish connections and trust with parents, teachers, and children. During my fieldwork, I developed strong friendships with some of the teachers, staff, and parents. Throughout my fieldwork, the director, Ms. Yu, and the vice director, Ms. Su, treated me very generously. For example, they allowed me to have free lunch at school as the teachers did, use the teachers' office, join teachers' and parents' meetings, observe, interview, and run experiments in all the classrooms. I ate lunch with other teachers every day and chatted in the classrooms, playground, and teachers' lounge. We sometimes went to dinner and hung out together after school or during the weekends. From the teachers, I got to know many inside stories of their own and children's life both at school and home.

My role as a parent helped me to gain rapport with other parents to a great extent, and we got to share thoughts, concerns, and stories with one another. To me, these parents were far more than typical "informants," merely providing information I needed. They were more like a support group that I was part of: We talked about our parenting concerns to one another and shared information on parenting issues. Although they saw me as an "expert" in child development, most of the time I felt like I was the one being helped and they were the helpers, as they were much more experienced and resourceful than me in raising children in Shanghai. Sometimes I chatted with Biyu parents and teachers online through the popular Chinese social media QQ and joined their online forums. Our friendship extended from Shanghai to the United States, as now we still exchange messages on child-rearing through Chinese social media.

The school director initially introduced me to the children as "Teacher Xu" (*Xu Laoshi*). In Chinese, *teacher* is a general designation for teachers of all levels, from preschool teachers to university professors. Because young children respect and admire teachers very much, they treated me politely and nicely from the very beginning. They probably had no idea why I was hanging around in their classrooms without doing any of the serious things that a real teacher would do, but that didn't keep me from developing a genuine relationship with them. They were curious about me precisely because of the ambiguity of my identity. Also, I did not get involved in disciplining them as a real teacher would do. Instead, I had the opportunity to comfort those who were disheartened by teachers' disciplinary measures. So I was always the nice and friendly "Teacher Xu," which helped me to get to know each and every one of them.

I am grateful for all of these relationships that I developed in the course of my fieldwork. The school directors accepted me from the very beginning, introduced me to others, and provided me all kinds of conveniences for doing research. The teachers in Shanghai gave me generous support in everyday school life and became my good friends. The parents were willing to share their parenting experiences and concerns with me because I was a child development researcher as well as a mother. The children trusted Teacher Xu and brought me into their own world, a world that inspired my intellectual imagination and enriched my parenting sensitivities. These relationships nurtured my otherwise lonely life in Shanghai, sustained me during the ups and downs of my fieldwork, and made this very research possible.

Entering the Field/School: Sociality and Morality in a Liminal Phase

This section is an embodied narrative of the entanglement between my own experiences of "entering the field" complicated by my struggles as a mother as well as the children's experiences of starting a school life that was new to them. During these days, I had the opportunity to closely explore the initial dynamics of social moral development: How do self-centered "little emperors" become good students who follow teachers' commands and construct a collective social life? How does moral inculcation unfold in daily school activities? What moral values are instilled in these young children? How do children themselves receive and transform moral messages and produce moral actions? By presenting a collection of stories and reflections on the flow of intersubjective encounters, I intend to initiate a discussion of the emerging sociality and morality in the liminal phase and space of children entering a brand new social world. This effort sets the tone for the main themes and arguments of this book.

Nursery Class (Tuo Ban): A Brave New World

September 1, 2011, the first day of the school year, was quite a significant day for the nursery class (*tuo ban*) children—the youngest cohort of children at Biyu Preschool—including my then nineteen-month-old son, Wandou. It was also my official first day of participant observation at this school. I was very excited initially, waiting for powerful theoretical arguments decorated by colorful ethnographic vignettes to come out and embrace me spontaneously. This very first day turned out to be all too dramatic, however. I was not ready to confront the following scenario, where helpless toddlers were separated from their mothers, almost forcefully, and left with complete strangers on their own. These toddlers burst out crying, of course, one after another. Amid waves of crying, their fear, despair, and anger spread out in the classroom like germs, frustrating the teachers and helpers, and breaking the mothers' hearts. A brave new world for these young children and me, the researcher/mother!

Before entering the school, children in this youngest cohort were happy "little emperors" in their own families, served by parents, grandparents, or nannies. Most of them are the only children in the family, who had had little regular peer interaction experiences. Thrown into a school setting all of a sudden, they were expected to act like students and interact, on a daily basis, with adults and children who they hadn't known before. On this very first day, I just couldn't picture how, starting from a dramatic and traumatic moment, such a mess of crying children, frustrated teachers, and heartbroken parents would ever evolve into a real community, with their intentions and emotions related to one another.

Class 1A and Class 1B are called nursery class (*tuo ban*) because of their intermediate nature: Nursery is somewhere between day care, aiming merely at providing basic care to infants, and preschool, providing young children with structured educational activities. The formal cutoff age for preschool is three by August 31, and the nursery class is for children younger than that, normally two-year-olds. It is popular for preschools in Shanghai to have a nursery class, in order to attract more families who want to prepare their children for school life in advance. Most families of Biyu Preschool nursery class already had grandparents or nannies to help with childcare at home, so they didn't necessarily need institutional support for childcare.

With that being the case, then why do parents send their young children to nursery class? Most of the parents are motivated by educational aspirations. They want the children to learn, develop social skills, and experience what they call the "collective life" (*jiti shenghuo*), a term originally referring to communal life in the socialist era. A lot of parents emphasize their child's social development and view preschool life as an important way to combat the negative sides of being an only child. Nuanced negative meanings are associated with the image of the single child: loneliness, no discipline, no social skills, and selfishness. Parents have the expectation that the one year of nursery class will prepare their children with skills and knowledge they would otherwise not acquire and put them in an advantageous position when they enter preschool at age three, compared with those who did not get into nursery class. As more and more parents want to secure a spot for their children at preschool in advance, sending children to nursery class has become a popular trend, and nursery class enrollment has become increasingly competitive in Shanghai (Xu 2012).

One might wonder: How do children's, parents', and teachers' experience in this private middle-class preschool in urban Shanghai relate to the broader picture of China? Actually, exceedingly high educational ambition is pervasive in today's Chinese society, as a product of both deep cultural-historical roots and contemporary institutional, political, and economic forces (Kipnis 2011). Detailed ethnographies find such a trend in many parts of China (Kipnis 2011; Kuan 2015). The competitive mentality associated with child-rearing starts as early as pregnancy, as the slogan "winning at the starting line" indicates (Zhu 2008). Caregivers and educators also used this slogan to justify their decisions to send infants, toddlers, and preschoolers into quality early education centers (*zaojiao zhongxin*) and preschools. Biyu Preschool nursery class provides an interesting case for examining the layers of tensions underlying the competitive mentality that is universally perceived and is being discussed across the nation.

From Babies to Students: Embarking on a Collective Journey

The first few weeks of the nursery class constitute a perfect, liminal phase to investigate how these children together create a collective life for the first time in their lives. In the beginning, the situation was nothing but chaotic. Infants cried desperately, screaming out "I want mother/I want to go home," having no sense of what was going on. Mothers worried, sneaking to the window just to hear waves of screaming. But these mothers, including myself, underestimated at least one thing: children's amazing capacity to survive in and create new social environments. After the first couple of chaotic days, I witnessed the critical, "synergetic" phase transition (Haken 2004) of their lives: under the guidance of teachers, these infants build an orderly collective world within a few weeks and march toward the journey of formal school life. In this new collective setting, children embark on the transition from infants to students who are defined by a complex set of obligations and roles.

Table I.1 summarizes the standard schedule and routine activities of nursery class 1A.

Table I.1 Standard Schedule and Routine Activities of Class 1A

Time	Activities	Location
8:00–8:30 a.m.	Greeting/morning checkup/free play	School main entrance/activity room
8:30–9:00	Breakfast	Dining room
9:00–9:20	English class	Multimedia classroom
9:20–9:30	Water drink/potty time	Dining room/restroom
9:30–9:50	Morning exercise	School playground
9:50–10:00	Water drink/potty time	Dining room/restroom
10:00–10:20	Outdoor activity/free play	School playground/activity room
10:20–10:30	Water drink/potty time	Dining room/restroom
10:30–11:00	"Colorful reasoning" (*duocai siwei*) class	Activity room
11:00–11:30	Lunch	Dining room
11:30 a.m.–12:00 p.m.	Cartoon movie watching/quiet time	Activity room
12:00–2:30	Noon nap	Bedroom
2:30–3:00	Fruit/water drink/potty time	Dining room/restroom
3:00–3:30	Language/math/arts class	Activity room
3:30–4:00	Afternoon snack	Dining room
4:00–4:30	Cartoon movie watching/prepare to leave	Activity room
4:30–5:00	Leave school	School main entrance/playground

The child is trained to follow classroom rules and teacher's commands to act as a group in every activity. During educational activities, children have to sit in their own chairs in a line, facing the teacher, and listen to the teacher carefully. When it is time to go out of the classroom, for English class, outdoor activities, or leaving school, the whole class must stand in line, which is called the "small train" (*xiao huoche*), and walk in a line. This rigid collectiveness penetrates even the most mundane activities such as hand washing, dining, and potty training. Teachers use a set of rhymes to facilitate the learning of detailed prescriptions for collective life. Different rhymes target specific procedures, including sitting, walking, hand washing, and so on. These rhymes are easy for the child to remember, fun to practice, and they feature teacher-child interaction. Most children successfully remembered and internalized these collective scripts in the first couple of weeks.

The following scenario of standing in a straight line demonstrates the degree of rule observance and group-mindedness these young children have achieved, as well as the effectiveness of the teacher's persistent pedagogy.

On September 10, 2011, during noontime, Fanglin, the head teacher of 1A, said to me: "I think my kids (students) are doing a good job. They now have the awareness that they belong to a group. But somehow I think they can be pushed even more. For example, they now know they need to walk in a line, but I think I can train them to walk in a *straight* line. I believe they have this potential." After lunch, she had all the children stand in a line before the class door: "Today, we will have a little walk after lunch. You need to walk in a straight line, so that the small train (children's queue) is running on track. If I see anyone stepping out of the straight line, I will have all of you do it again." She opened the door and led the whole class on a walk in the long hallway. She carefully watched the children walk, especially when they turned at the corner of the hallway. Several children broke the rule, and the line was not straight. She criticized those particular children and had the whole class walk all the way again. She emphasized: "Now, it is because of you that the whole class has to suffer." This was repeated a few times, and the line became straighter and straighter. I was following the whole process, and Fanglin smiled to me proudly: "See? They can make it!" I asked: "How did you make it?" She answered: "You need to understand their psychology (*xinli*, literally means 'principles of the heart'). They don't want to lose face/be shamed in front of their peers and teacher. If one of them breaks the rule, he or she has to take responsibility for the whole group, and the other children will monitor him or her. I just utilize this principle and let them monitor each other. Isn't it easy?" Although I think it was a somewhat cruel experience for these two- and three-year-olds, I was indeed amazed at how much "potential" they had to discipline themselves as a group.

The fact that a new collective order emerges so quickly is a result of effective interactions between children and teachers. First, children are experiencing something similar to what anthropologist Victor Turner (1995) theorizes as "liminality." They are thrown into an environment with no familiar people or things. No preexisting structures are available to them. It is precisely in this situation that new possibilities and structures can be implemented without much obstruction. Second, a new order and its predictabilities are already available in the environment, under teachers' guidance. Third, children are predisposed to learn some of the key lessons of living collectively and socially. Consciously or not, teachers rely on effective universals of child-rearing (Quinn 2005) that correspond to children's psychological needs and characteristics, such as constancy of teaching and evaluation of the child as approved of (reward) or disapproved of (punishment).

Between Self and Other: Becoming a Moral Person

The "entering-the-school" days opened a window through which to observe how children began to engage in social interactions and how such social interactions were imbued with moral messages. Apparently, successful collective training is closely related to, and to some extent dependent on, using children's inner dispositions, especially moral motivations. The preschool classroom is not only a *social* space where children begin to navigate the social world of peers and authorities. It is also a *moral* space where messages about "good" and "bad" are produced, circulated, internalized, and transformed, intentionally or unintentionally. In the collective context, one who follows teachers' commands and complies with classroom rules is defined as the "good baby" (*hao baobao/ guai baobao*).[7] In Chinese culture, it is a deeply ingrained educational principle to use models and exemplars to cultivate ideal personhood and discipline people (Bakken 2000; Munro 2000), and this principle is still alive in today's educational settings (Kuan 2012). It is a key feature of Biyu Preschool's moral pedagogy. Teachers use various methods to reward children who exemplify this ideal and set them as a good example, a model for others to learn from.

Mealtime provides a good occasion to observe moral inculcation. As Ochs and Shohet argue, mealtime is an important cultural site "for the production of sociality, morality, and local understandings of the world" (2006: 35). In Class 1A, this specific lunchtime setting marked a distinct social space saturated with moral meanings. These meanings were produced in a top-down fashion, embedded in the hierarchical structure pertaining to teachers and students.

For example, one day at 11:00 a.m., Teacher Fanglin assigned each child in Class 1A a seat at the table. The fifteen children were divided into three tables. They sat down and waited for *Ayi* Zhang to bring their lunch from the kitchen. Teacher Fanglin announced: "Now we are going to listen to a story from the tape recorder: Dongdong & Lanlan. Please remain seated and listen carefully, and I'll ask you questions." This story featured the contrast between two children: Dongdong eats carefully and finishes all the food in his bowl, while Lanlan doesn't focus on eating and wastes a lot of rice and vegetables. After the story was over, Fanglin asked: "Of these two children, which do you want to be like,

Dongdong who finishes all his food or Lanlan who wastes a lot food?" The children answered in a loud voice: "Dongdong!" Fanglin commented: "Great! You are good children (*hao baobao*)! Yes, we should not waste our food." Shortly after, the food was ready, and teachers and helpers distributed the food into each child's bowl and plate. But they still could not start eating. Teacher Fanglin told them to wait until the others are sitting properly and quietly. Then, Fanglin announced: "OK. Please help yourself, little friends (*xiao pengyou*, a general term referring to small children)." As a response, children said to their classmates: "Please help yourself, everyone." Only then is eating authorized and initiated. Every child was encouraged to eat on his or her own and finish in twenty minutes. During eating, they were not allowed to talk to others because talking was seen as interfering with others' eating and breaking the quietness of the setting. After a child finished eating, he or she was required to push the chair under the table, for others' safety and convenience.

Fanglin explained to me why she insisted on adopting such a rigid procedure: "These children are spoiled. At home they are the center of their families, with everything provided and served to them, and they know nothing about the real world. Literally, they only have to hold out their hands to be dressed and open their mouths to be fed (*yi lai shen shou, fan lai zhang kou*). They are never required to do any labor, always fed by parents or grandparents, and they seldom eat on their own. That's why I need to train them. They have this capacity or potential to carry their own chair and eat on their own. Also, at home, their needs are usually immediately satisfied, and they don't need to respect others. Now I want them to learn waiting and respect for others. They are sent to school to learn things, and it's my responsibility to teach them the rules (*guiju*) and make sure they follow the rules. It's better to learn it sooner than later."

Fanglin stood out as a really skillful teacher in training these young children. She intentionally conveyed the moral messages in every detail of the mealtime procedure. The first part was story learning, and she used this narrative tool to teach children to differentiate the morally good from the morally bad. The virtue being instilled was frugality,[8] a common theme in Chinese moral education (Chan 2006), and its significance was emphasized in educators' concerns about the overindulged only children. The second part was collective eating, with the core moral message of reminding children not to be self-centered, but to have other children in mind. It is with the coordination of teachers and children, and in the details of classroom education, that the "moral conceptions of the good" (Ochs and Kremer-Sadlik 2007) are cultivated and transformed into bodily practices. This illustrates how the collective journey of the nursery class creates a space in which children's moral sensibilities are activated and nurtured in culturally specific ways.

The Emergence of Sociality and Morality

This critical period was a liminal phase for the nursery class children and for me as well. The process of these children entering the school was intertwined with the process of me entering the field as a mother/researcher. Both the children and I were thrown into a strange place and were grappling with a new world, longing for a sense of security and belongingness. Like the teachers, I was eager to be known, accepted, and trusted by these children. Regarding the parents, I *was* one of them, and we were going through the tormenting process of separation anxiety from our children, building trust with teachers, and coming to terms with this big transition in our children's life, which, to some extent, was also a big transition in our own lives. The complexity of human morality and sociality emergent in this liminal process is to be seriously appreciated, from an anthropological as well as an existential perspective. I was deeply impressed by what I witnessed during that time: the nuanced sociality burgeoning in children's world, the complex moral sensibilities manifest in their interpersonal interactions, and the powerful capacity for forming, maintaining, and changing the order of their social lives. In this important transformative process, a new collective life was generated through the synergetic coordination of these children's psychological potentials and their socializers' culturally loaded guiding and regulatory efforts.

Anthropologists Elinor Ochs and Olga Solomon define *human sociality* as "a range of possibilities for social coordination with others" (2010: 71). The emergence of social coordination in a liminal phase—as these children left their self-centered life and entered the new social world of "collective life"—reveals the power and fundamental features of human sociality. In the various ways in which children get to build their social world in this liminal phase, one can see the traces and forces of moral motivations directing and channeling the social coordination processes. Through the various stories in this liminal phase, one gets a glimpse of the fascinating moral world of young children, such as how they bind to a group, follow authority, and learn to respect others. In the remainder of this book, I will elaborate on how different moral motivations, judgments, and emotions emerge in their developmental experiences, sometimes in tension with one another.

Research Questions and Chapters

Based on twelve months of ethnographic fieldwork in a middle-class preschool in Shanghai, China's frontier of globalization and education, this book investigates the following questions: How do Chinese children, born under the one-child policy and often seen as selfish "little emperors," navigate a tense social world and construct their own moral world in the flux of daily practices at the time of a perceived "moral crisis" amid China's profound social transformations? What kinds of moral domains and norms are negotiated and contested by children and socializers in the processes of moral development and education under China's changing moral landscape? How are such developmental processes of children's emerging moral dispositions shaped by the familial, educational, and broader cultural dynamics in contemporary China?

Chapter 1 explores socializers' educational aspirations and anxieties under the one-child policy in an era of "moral crisis," thus providing an overview of the experiences of child-rearing and moral education. This chapter contextualizes Chinese children's moral development in specific historical, cultural, and educational settings, through closely examining educators and caregivers' perspectives and experiences in moral education. Following the line of inquiry on the making and remaking of moral personhood under China's changing moral landscape (Kleinman et al. 2011; Yan 2011), this chapter looks at the dreams and struggles of Chinese parents and teachers in cultivating a moral child—their "only hope"—in an increasingly competitive educational environment. Specifically, it examines the various quandaries of moral cultivation in which socializers are caught in the particular moral ecology of Shanghai educational settings amid China's shifting ethical grounds.

As Chapter 1 paints a general picture of moral education and its dilemmas in this specific Chinese community, the following three chapters delve into children's own developmental experiences in three moral domains, with a focus on the various tensions emerging as children construct their own moral universe. I arrange these three chapters in this order: Chapter 2 examines the education and development of empathy and care, an important foundation for human morality in both ancient Chinese thinking and contemporary empirical research. Because empathy is perceived as compromised in Chinese social interactions today, how to cultivate it among young children becomes a great challenge.

Chapter 3 focuses on the emergence of ownership and fairness understandings, the foundational moral dispositions that govern children's property distribution, exchange, and disputes. Similar to the emphasis on a natural capacity for empathy and a genuine concern and care for others, educators highlight children's natural and genuine disposition toward claiming ownership and fairness. In educators' eyes, however, such natural dispositions are contested and even distorted in a social environment with diverse and competing demands and constraints. Such tensions and dynamics in property distribution and disputes constitute another important domain of moral development in the Chinese context.

In contrast to the fantasy of natural dispositions in the "genuine" child and the liberating potentials for the society, Chapter 4 features socializers' concerns over the darker side of the "genuine" child—the selfish "only child," in the daily ideological inculcation of sharing and generosity, and how children's own practices and beliefs contradict such ideological work in many ways. This chapter investigates children's world of sharing with the tension between egalitarian and strategic cooperative dispositions—a tension that has not only become a focus in recent debates on the nature of human morality, but also reflects key cultural concepts in Chinese social interactions.

The particular topics in these three chapters are chosen for the following reasons. First, these topics have received heightened attention recently in developmental psychology and the broader literature on the origins of human cooperation and morality. Cultural anthropologists, however, have yet to engage with these issues, and in-depth ethnographic documentation is needed in order to gain a fuller picture of the psycho-cultural processes of moral development. Second, the selection of these topics is not only inspired by important categories in influential moral domain theories, but also driven by examining the connections and tensions among these moral categories. Third, these topics are the key themes in Chinese children's everyday social and moral life that emerge in my fieldwork and reflect broader issues and concerns in contemporary Chinese culture and society. Throughout these three chapters, my theoretical aim is to examine how children's psychological dispositions are expressed and modulated in contemporary Chinese cultural dynamics.

After zooming into children's developmental experiences in specific moral domains, in Chapter 5 I turn to the concept of *guanjiao* (literally meaning "govern-educate"), an all-encompassing Chinese concept of child-rearing, and explore the complex beliefs and practices having to do with how parents, grandparents, and teachers raise the "little emperors"—children born under the one-child policy. *Guanjiao* is constructed as a salient cultural concept of

Chinese child-rearing and socialization in the cultural psychology/psychological anthropology literature, and this chapter aims to reveal the layers of tensions emerging in *guanjiao* beliefs and practices, as Chinese socializers are navigating the shifting grounds of moral values and facing the complex child-rearing challenges of raising only children. This chapter not only echoes the broader picture of moral education dilemmas in Chapter 1, but also complements the chapters on moral development in specific domains by providing a systematic view on the socialization beliefs, strategies, and techniques that underpin moral education in general.

To sum up, this book investigates the processes through which young Chinese children, most of whom are only children, become moral persons during a time of a perceived moral crisis and profound social transformation. My research reveals two conflicting sets of motivations amid China's changing moral landscape: the motivation of cultivating a moral child—originated in China's longstanding Confucian educational traditions and undergoing confusing turmoil today, and the motivation of raising a successful only child in a perceived immoral, competitive society. These conflicting motivations create profound quandaries for caregivers and educators and have impacts on the development of children's nascent moral dispositions in various domains. By examining how children's moral dispositions are expressed and modulated in cultural dynamics, this study aims to engage with key issues in psychological anthropology, moral anthropology, the anthropology of children and childhood, and more broadly the anthropology of China.

1   Cultivating Morality:
Educational Aspirations and Anxieties

"Little Emperors," Education, and Morality: What Is at Stake for Parents?

> Father: He (Tiantian) is the one and only. What kind of costs are unafford-
> able for us? That is the failure of (Tiantian's) education. We are anxious about
> his future. Both of us (mother and father) have a kind of elite consciousness/
> aspiration (*jingying yishi*). Perhaps eighty or ninety percent of Chinese parents
> have this elite consciousness/aspiration (*jingying yishi*).

> Mother: What does "society" mean? It means individuals living in their
> own ways. It is now our one and only chance to influence my son when he is
> very young. We don't know if we will succeed or fail. If the society is "whole-
> some" and the general direction where people are going is good, then no
> matter how we educate him, he will not likely go the wrong way. However, the
> worst case is when the society is bad. Then how we educate him really matters,
> and the consequence will loom large.

These two quotes reflect parental aspirations and anxieties regarding the
interplay between education and morality in the project of raising the "little
emperors." Tiantian, a boy in Class 3A, lives with his parents and maternal
grandparents in the neighborhood where Biyu Preschool is located. Both of
his parents are native Shanghainese who graduated from top universities in
Shanghai and got good secure jobs, the father in the government sector and the
mother in a national corporation. Tiantian is the only child of the family; he
was born when his parents were in their early thirties. For this "post-seventies"[1]
couple, the most salient difference between parenting today and parenting in
the last generation was that compared to their own parents, they were much

more focused on the child and much more anxious about child-rearing. These comments from Tiantian's father and mother point to the key theme and main argument of this chapter: Chinese socializers today are caught up in profound quandaries, as they live with extraordinary aspirations for their children's future success and tremendous anxieties regarding child-rearing, amid China's rapid social transformations, including the ramifications of the one-child policy and the perceived "moral crisis."

The one-child policy definitely weighs in here. In contrast to the previous generations, when parents had to take care of several children at the same time and thus didn't have that much energy to devote to each child, the singleton child Tiantian is the "one and only" who matters to his family, and they can't afford the failure of his education in today's fierce competition. They are not alone in battling against such anxieties. As Tiantian's father said, this situation was not confined to people like them who received elite education and got established in middle-class life in Shanghai; rather, most parents in China today had such elite consciousness/aspirations (*jingying yishi*). The popular term *jingying yishi*, used by Tiantian's father, refers to both parents' consciousness of their own elite educational-social background or parents' high educational aspirations pro-jected on to their children. For example, Tiantian's father often took the young boy to Fudan University, a top university in Shanghai and his *alma mater*, with the hope that someday the son would get in this or a better university and build a bright future. Aspirations like this hold true also for parents without such an elite educational background. For example, in her ethnographic book on singleton youths in China, Vanessa Fong (2004) describes the high educational aspirations shared by parents and students across various socio-economic, educational, and professional backgrounds. According to her, singleton teenagers in Dalian, a city in northeastern China, were trying to make a road to the first-world amid the third-world realities, and they "fear that too many people are trying to squeeze onto a road that is not widening fast enough" (Fong 2004: 182). In the book *Governing Educational Desire: Culture, Politics and Schooling in China*, Andrew Kipnis (2011) analyzes why high levels of educational desire have arisen in a county in Shandong province, where most students come from rural families. He demonstrates that such strong parental ambition and educational desire were not entirely the product of China's one-child policy. Instead, they are deeply rooted in China's historical dynamics, where culture, politics, and education intersected to form "the Imperial governing complex" (Kipnis 2011: 90).

Tiantian's mother emphasized the other part of the equation. On the one hand, parents have extraordinary educational aspirations on the only child's future success. On the other hand, there is tremendous pressure toward moral education because early childhood is critical for a child's moral upbringing and because people believe the society at large is undergoing a moral crisis. As she said, "It is now our one and only chance to influence my son when he is very young." She believed that parenting in early childhood was crucial to shaping the child's character, personality, and ways of thinking and doing. She was, however, not sure whether her own or others' parenting would turn out to be successful, and such uncertainty was greatly amplified at a time when the dominant social trends went against the child's healthy psychological development. As she hinted, good parenting was critical for battling against the negative social environment and shaping a mentally healthy child.

Parents believe that, in addition to the child's own future, cultivating morality among young children matters also for the future of the Chinese society and nation. According to this logic, a "bad society" undermines the moral education of its members, while at the same time a "bad education" exacerbates the societal moral crisis. It sounds like a chicken-and-egg situation and no one can answer which comes first. In the moral realm, individual agency—even of the youngest ones—and societal forces impact each other in complex feedback chains, and education mediates between the two. My friend Jianxia, who had taught in various preschools for ten years before she became a stay-at-home mother and homeschooling teacher, made such incisive comments on the relations among education, morality, and the society:

> The purpose of education, I think, is that I hope my children and students will grow up as self-reliant people who can enjoy their own life but are also responsible for others and the society. Why are there so many problems in our society today? Why are we surrounded by poisonous infant formula and food? That's because we lack the moral senses, especially the concern and sense of responsibility for others. We only care about ourselves, and other people's misery or deaths have nothing to do with us. I can pollute this place as long as I make money. I can send my children abroad, and I don't care if others are breathing polluted air.
>
> Look at the reality of education. The most important thing for parents now is to instill among children these ideas: that you need to do well in academics, you need to make money in the future and live a successful life and fulfill your filial piety. See, that's obnoxiously selfish! It's all about your own interests as parents. Then we (parents) go compete against others and harm others. In order to get into a certain position, we do things unscrupulously.

We bribe the officials in order to squeeze our children into a better school, which means at the same time you push the other child who deserves that position out of the game. This is an extremely unjust society. Think about how our children grow up, starting from preschool—oh no, even earlier than that, from when we are pregnant. We do everything we can to get a better doctor (for child delivery) or a bed in the better maternity ward, even through unjust means.[2]

Jianxia was worried about the vicious circle between selfish individuals and unjust society, mediated by bad parenting/education. The tension she described is multifaceted: First, education aims for producing individuals and citizens who care not only about themselves but also about others and the larger society. In the course of fierce competition for all kinds of resources starting from childbirth, however, socializers themselves become selfish and have no consideration for other people's interests. Second, one cannot expect such extremely selfish education to produce "good" children/future members of the society. Third, even the seemingly legitimate educational purposes, such as to make money and become successful, are essentially selfish and unjust if one believes that the ultimate mission for education is to cultivate good human beings. Her comments echo the classical philosophical question of the "moral limits of markets" (Sandel 2010) in the sense that certain domains of humanity that we tend to treasure, such as basic rights to human life and education, are threatened by the encroaching, inhumane market logic. Such complaints are quite common in Chinese public discourse in general, and in the local context of Shanghai, too.

No doubt, problems such as bribery in education and hospitals or unsafe food cannot be entirely reduced to declining personal and interpersonal moral standards. My informants, however, frequently mentioned these problems and tied them to morality and education. The tendency to link morality—framed as personal virtue, education as self-cultivation, and the bigger social order—as a coupled whole is a well-engrained Chinese mentality (Bakken 2000).

I couldn't help but wonder, what is really at stake for these parents and socializers? The anthropological concept of "moral experience" helps me to think in depth about this question. This concept refers to "what is locally at stake": "What matters most in the mundane and extraordinary transpersonal details that bind and define us through relationships, work, and the close politics of a particular place is the overwhelmingly pragmatic orientation of men and women everywhere" (Kleinman 1999: 70). As people act based on what really matters to them upon the specific temporal-local contingencies, there is "a deep mixture of often contradictory emotions and values whose untidy uniqueness defines the existential core of the individual" (Kleinman 2006: 10). Focusing on contemporary China, Kleinman and his colleagues (Kleinman et al. 2011) went on to inquire about the making and remaking of the moral person during China's profound social transformations. Their central argument is that the new subjectivity arising in the midst of rapid social transformations is the "divided self" (Kleinman 2011: 5), a self that is divided by different standards and goals that conflict with one another, such as self-interest versus ethical conduct. One important piece is missing in this picture, however, and that is the dreams and struggles of Chinese parents and socializers when it comes to what really matters for them and their whole lives: the making of the new moral person—their "only hope"—in this increasingly competitive society. As anthropologists of Chinese education have noticed, Chinese parental aspiration for children's educational and career ambitions and success is construed as a moral project, and the moral nature of such a project is intertwined with "the long history in China of parents finding existential meaning in the success of their children" (Kipnis 2009: 215). Along these lines, I will unravel the moral quandaries that Biyu Preschool parents are concerned with, between their educational aspirations and their educational anxieties, in the particular environment of Shanghai.

Building the Moral Foundation in Early Childhood

Cultivating morality in early childhood is a significant theme in historical traditions of Chinese ethics, education, and learning. In today's China, building a good moral foundation from a young age is emphasized in educational discourse, policies, and practice. The importance of moral education in early childhood is also a shared belief among Biyu Preschool teachers and parents. I will demonstrate these points following.

Early Childhood and Moral Cultivation: Historical Traditions and Contemporary Beliefs

It is a deeply entrenched tradition that moral education in early childhood is viewed as crucial to the cultivation of a full-fledged moral personhood, as the contemporary neo-Confucian philosopher Tu Wei-Ming summarizes, "Despite divergent approaches to the actual process of moral and spiritual self-development, Confucianism, Taoism, and Buddhism all share this fundamental belief: Although existentially human beings are not what they ought to be, they can be perfected through self-cultivation" (Tu 1985: 25).

Imprints of this tradition that place an important emphasis on self-cultivation in early childhood are still visible in contemporary education policies (Cheng 2000) and state discourses. For example, since the Chinese government's official Program for Improving Civic Morality (Chinese Community Party 2001) emphasized moral education as an important battleground, the Chinese Ministry of Education announced its Chinese "Little Citizens" Moral Cultivation Plan. This official announcement intended to provide clear guidelines for moral education among three- to eighteen-year-old Chinese children and youths (Ministry of Education of the People's Republic of China 2002). It blended Confucian traditions with socialism and postsocialism values, emphasizing a variety of qualities such as filial piety, care for family, respect for others, cooperation, altruism, frugality, patriotism, politeness, honesty, trustworthy, care for collective property, protecting the environment, diligence and independence, and creativity.

Moreover, a focus on moral education in early childhood figures into parenting goals (Wu 1996) and teaching philosophies (Jin Li 2012). For example, intellectual ideas concern the characteristics of "the Chinese learner"—who excels in academic performance but is more docile and passive in learning—have evolved in recent decades as Chinese educational, historical, and sociocultural contexts undergo rapid changes (Watkins and Biggs 2001; Chan and Rao 2009). But deep continuities regarding the purpose of learning are still observed. Studies about "the Chinese learner" indicate that the belief in perfecting oneself morally/socially as the primary purpose of learning is still prevalent in today's China, and cultural differences in beliefs of learning emerge in early childhood, that is, Chinese children as young as age four talk more about self-improving morally (becoming a good child) than American counterparts (Li 2010: 60).

Early Childhood and Moral Cultivation: Ethnographic Evidence

The idea of "cultivating morality" as an important task in early childhood, drawing on historical traditions and continuing to shape contemporary values, is also shared among the parents of Biyu Preschool. In the beginning phase of my fieldwork, I administered the child-rearing questionnaire with ninety-two families at Biyu Preschool (77 percent of all the families at the time). The questionnaire has twenty questions (some with sub-questions) clustered in three sections, including family socio-economic information, reproduction values, and children's social moral development. The section on children's social moral development consisted of ten questions probing into caregivers' evaluations and attitudes about children's morality in general, the roles of parents, school, and other people, intergenerational similarities and differences in child-rearing values, as well as the desirable and nondesirable moral traits of children. One question was: "What do you think is/are the most important mission(s) of preschool education?" It had seven possible responses:

A. Transmitting basic knowledge
B. Enlightening interest in learning
C. Molding moral character
D. Teaching rules in social life
E. Fostering interpersonal interactions
F. Training daily-life habits
G. Cultivating artistic quality (*suzhi*)[3]

This question allows parents to choose more than one answer, and it is followed by a "why" question to elicit parents' free responses as to why they thought a particular mission was important. Out of the eighty-five families who responded to this question, fifty [59 percent] parents chose E (fostering interpersonal interactions), thirty-nine [46 percent] chose C (molding moral character), thirty-three [39 percent] chose B (enlightening the interests in learning), twenty-nine [34 percent] chose F (training daily-life habits), twenty-six [31 percent] chose A (transmitting basic knowledge), twenty-three [28 percent] chose D (teaching rules in social life,), and five [6 percent] chose G (cultivating artistic quality). Taken together, social moral development (fostering interpersonal interactions and molding moral character) is the most salient theme in parents' responses.

Cultivating morality in the Chinese tradition essentially means to learn to "be human" (Tu 1985) or "act/become human" (*zuo ren*). This is an all-encompassing concept that denotes the nearly endless *process* of coming to understand what it means to be human, how to navigate various kinds of social relationships and contexts, and how to behave in ways that are humane in a culturally specific sense. A large part of this is about ordinary ethics that involve both tacit understandings in the micro-processes of everyday life and explicit ethical reflection, judgment, and discussion (Stafford 2013a).

Some parents also wrote in the questionnaire the reasons why they thought social and moral development was the most important thing in preschool education, and here are a few sample quotes.

Singleton children lack the kind of environment for peer interactions.

Preschool is the first stage in the child's life when one is in a social group. It provides the first platform for children to learn to interact with their peers.

"Group consciousness" (*qunti yishi*) is first built here (in the preschool stage).

Moral cultivation is to teach children how to "act human" (*zuo ren*), which persists throughout one's lifetime.

Only on the basis of good moral character can one expect the child to develop healthily in the future.

The concept of moral character (*dao de pin zhi*), as is used in the questionnaire, usually refers to a set of personal moral attributes that an individual develops through education and experience and molds into his or her personality; these attributes include honesty, humility, kindness, and so forth. For these parents, however, the idea of building the moral foundation is much broader, more inclusive, and more fluid than the construct of moral character. It addresses the fundamental question of how one should live his or her life in a world structured and defined by social relationships. In the Chinese framework that emphasizes the inherent connections between morality and education/learning, this fundamental question is not approached "from the perspective of the individual as a biological entity or as a rights-bearing individual as may be the case in the West"; instead, it is based upon the central tenet that "all humans survive, develop, and flourish in social relationships" (Jin Li 2012: 45). Thus it is not surprising that learning to get along with others/cultivating social "intelligence," as evidenced in the over-majority option of "fostering interpersonal interactions," becomes a core part of what these parents think moral education should emphasize.

In addition to the Chinese notion that mastering how to relate to other people in society is at the core of what it means to be moral, this emphasis on cultivating social interaction skills and capacities in parental responses to my child-rearing questionnaire reflects two trends in contemporary China. One is the rising concern that children born under the one-child policy lack social intelligence because they live as the center of their own universe. The other is the increasing awareness that what matters to children's future success is not only academic performance but also the capacity to navigate the social world and get along with others, which becomes more and more evident as one leaves school and enters the "real world." One also sees the emerging emphasis on children's social moral development in the popular advice literature on parenting and child development from a sole focus on academic intelligence (Kuan 2015; Champagne 1992), to the increasing attention to children's moral development. A lot of parents at Biyu Preschool mentioned to me that they had read books by both Chinese and foreign authors on dealing with children's emotional world and peer interaction problems because these are really important issues they had to deal with on a daily basis.

Teachers also put a great emphasis on morality at the preschool stage. Compared to learning knowledge, teachers thought it was more important to nurture a young child's heart and help the child to build appropriate moral standards and habits. One teacher told me: "If I were a parent, I wouldn't concern myself about how much knowledge my child learns at preschool. Rather, I would find out whether my child's teacher is nice, upright, and nurturing because the teacher's own moral character determines what he or she can bring to my child."

Teacher Tang, who was also a mother of a five-year-old boy (he went to a public preschool), pointed out that her educational approaches and beliefs were consistent across classroom and home:

Take my own son as an example. The school assigns a lot of homework in language, math, et cetera. My mother also urges him to do homework every day. But I never taught him on these subjects. I only taught him principles of how to "act human" (*zuo ren*). For instance, if he does bad things, like dirty talk against his grandma, I will point it out and scold him: "You don't respect elders, which violates moral bottom line. That's why you need to be punished. You can't watch cartoons or play video games. If you correct this mistake, I will forgive you." I won't punish him for not finishing some homework. That's how I educate my son.

Another teacher shared with me her educational ideal and goal:

Human beings will be assimilated to the society as they grow up. Some good habits and moral characteristics will gradually lose or be abandoned. So you cannot get better, but only get worse and worse, eroded by the adult environment. That's why I want to build in young children a stronger moral foundation in the beginning. Then even if they get assimilated to the society, the directions they are in will still be better than those who have no good moral foundation. For instance, if one day, you are waiting for the bus with your child, and your child comes to ask you "Mother, why don't you stay in the line?" you will then feel really embarrassed—face sweeping the ground (*yan mian sao di*).

According to Teacher Fanglin, building a solid moral foundation is pivotal to early childhood education. Her comments also point out two forces that influence moral development, one from the immediate, intimate environment having more weight when the child is still young, and the other from the broader social environment that gains increasing impetus as the child gradually grows up. In her own case, she as a teacher represents the positive force, whereas the society represents the negative force. But in real life, it becomes much more complex with regard to who influences moral development at a young age and how these influences are instantiated.

Who Influences Moral Development, and How?

In addition to probing into the importance of moral development in socializers' eyes, I also examined how parents evaluated the forces that impacted moral development. Because of the broad scope of what "moral development" means to Chinese parents, I lumped together the answers to two separate questions in the questionnaire: "Which do you think is most important for the development of young children's interpersonal interactions?" and "Which do you think is most important for the development of young children's moral character?" The two questions had the same answer options:

A. Families
B. Teachers
C. Peer groups
D. Broader social environment
E. Equal (Same across all four categories)

The percentages of each individual category were quite similar across the two questions, with A (families) voted for by the largest percentage of parents, followed by D (equal/the same across the four categories). Lumped together, this survey shows that, among the various environmental factors, 49 percent of parents thought families were the most important in shaping children's moral development, 23 percent thought the four factors weighed equally, 12 percent

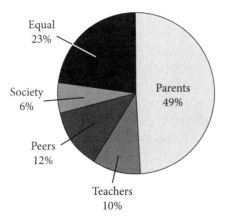

Figure 1.1 Child-Rearing Questionnaire: The Most Important Factor
That Influences Moral Development in Early Childhood

thought peer groups are the most important, 10 percent chose teachers, and 6 percent chose the broader social environment as the most important. See Figure 1.1.

This suggests that parenting is considered crucial to the early development of morality, much more so than the other factors, which corresponds to Tiantian's mother's comment: "our one and only chance to influence him." At the same time, for a considerable number of parents, it is hard to decide which factor weighed more in early moral development. This means many of them also perceive the importance of other factors, even the vague entity "the broader social environment," which is out of parents' control.

According to local people, how do parents/caregivers and other social agents, including the "society" as a totalizing force, influence moral development? One cannot talk about Chinese moral socialization without invoking the notion of learning through imitating models, the crux of Chinese educational and moral beliefs. Much has been said about how the Chinese learn through modeling. Philosophers observe: "In the Confucian tradition, beliefs about how to transform the mind and thereby perfect man's character were intimately linked to assumptions about how people learn. It was assumed that people learn primarily through the imitation of models" (Munro 2000: 135–36). Social theorists have even argued that China is an "exemplary society" from imperial times to our contemporary time (Bakken 2000). Anthropologist Andrew Kipnis examines its linguistic dimensions and generalized from studying knowledge to cultivating morality: "The word 'study' (*xue*), for example, often means to imitate a model in a process of internalization—mental or bodily memorization. Just as one "studies" writing by tracing model characters, so does one "study" how to be a person (*zuo ren*) by imitating the behaviors and dispositions of one's teacher" (Kipnis 2012b: 736). Teresa Kuan traced this mentality to its roots in "a theory of learning that presumes humans learn best when presented with positive models to emulate and negative models to compare oneself to" (Kuan 2008: 114).

None of these scholars have taken a close look at the dark side of "learning through modeling" in China, however; that is, negative models can not only be compared as something to avoid, they can also be imitated, especially by young children who haven't yet built a solid moral foundation. Surprisingly, compared to "positive modeling," such "negative modeling" is a more salient interpretive framework of certain behaviors among children, according to Biyu Preschool teachers.

The stories about Nannan and Junjun, two three-year-old boys in the nursery class who were neighbors in the same building (Nannan was big and naughty; Junjun was small and nice), as Teacher Fanglin told me, illustrated how people interpreted the links between bad parenting and children's bad behaviors:

> Nannan's parents hit Nannan a lot at home and that was how Nannan learned to hit others. One day, Junjun's grandmother who lived with Junjun's family just came out from their apartment. Nannan suddenly lifted a stone-like hard object and threw it onto her legs. Nannan's mother was right there, but she didn't say anything. It was really painful for Junjun's grandma, but because Nannan was not her own grandson, she didn't say anything. It was unbelievable that Nannan's mother didn't say a word—no apology to Junjun's grandma or punishment to Nannan. Another time, it was even worse! Nannan hit Junjun for no reason. Nannan's mother came out. She immediately hugged Nannan, asking: "Are you OK? Were you hurt?" She didn't even take a look at Junjun, who was innocently hurt by her son.

This story provides an example of how teachers evaluate bad parenting and interpret children's bad behaviors as a direct result of such parenting. Moreover, teachers also tend to make inferences about bad parenting merely from children's own behavior, instead of direct observations of parent-child interactions. The story of the spoiled Sayi is such an example. Sayi lives with her parents and maternal grandparents, and her maternal grandma is the one who takes care of her most of the time. Teacher Fanglin said:

> She is an example from whom one can see the shadow of bad parenting. For instance, during free-play sessions, if she needs some toy, she always asks others for it. If she doesn't get it, she will complain: "Why are you so stingy?" I would think, it must be that her grandma had encountered the same situation (asking for someone else' properties) and said the same thing to others. Otherwise where did she learn it? Also, I've seen it when her grandma was with her. One morning in our dining room, her grandma sat beside to her and watched her having breakfast. Several other children were eating at the same table. Sayi didn't like tomatoes, so grandma immediately picked out the tomatoes for her and threw them in the middle of the table. I was so shocked. How could she have no concern for other children who were eating at the same table in that moment? Why didn't she just pick the tomatoes out and put them next to Sayi's own bowl? From this small detail, I got a sense of how selfish her grandma is.

Note that teachers often used the discourse of quality (*suzhi*) to evaluate good/bad parenting or parents. Many studies have examined the discourse and practices of quality, in the Chinese movement of education for quality (*suzhi jiaoyu*), particularly on the relationships between Chinese governmentality and educational practices (Anagnost 2004; Fong 2007a; Kipnis 2006, 2007; Kuan 2008; Woronov 2009). The way Biyu teachers use this term to describe and evaluate parents is imprinted with the signature of quality (*suzhi*) discourse. For example, bad quality (*suzhi cha*) often refers to uncivil (*bu wenming*) behaviors such as being impolite, spitting, littering, and so on. Such comments on civility often have moral overtones, and when it comes to issues in educating children, "quality" sometimes has an explicit linkage to individual moral character. In the previous examples, Nannan's mother and Sayi's grandma are also considered as having bad quality (*suzhi cha*), but in terms of violating commonsense moral codes, rather than violating civil rules.

The Shanghai Milieu: Moral Ecology
in China's Educational Frontier

Shanghai is a microcosm of China in its hectic rise to global power. Actually, it *is* the frontier of China's globalization and modernization, and Chinese people's dreams and struggles are intensified in this city, with booming career opportunities and soaring living costs. Also, in terms of morality and China, Shanghai is definitely an important case to explore. One can find plenty of discussion about the extreme materialism in the city of Shanghai on the Internet and in people's daily conversations. "Bedeviled city" (*mo du*), the nickname of Shanghai, symbolizes both the abundant material temptations and the severe social problems that have arisen in the course of Shanghai's rise as a global economic hub. Moreover, for Chinese people, "Each region and city is associated with a character type" (Osburg 2013: 17). The regional character of Shanghai manifests itself in the ways people think and talk about their social and familial lives and explain certain behaviors and patterns in morality and education. I will tell stories about my own and my informants' moral experience in Shanghai to provide a backdrop for the aspirations for and anxieties about cultivating morality.

Imagine you are Chinese, and you are in Shanghai, just getting into a taxi. What do you think the taxi driver would ask you about, except the address of your destination? During the year I was staying in Shanghai, I had numerous experiences talking with taxi drivers. I was impressed by the fact that almost every driver brought up these three questions: First, did you borrow (the equivalent of "rent" in Shanghainese dialect) an apartment or do you own it? Second, where (which province) do you come from? Third, did you get to marry a Shanghainese man? As a woman originally from an inland province who did not own a property in Shanghai or marry a Shanghainese man, it was not a pleasant experience to confront such questions.

As an anthropologist, however, such conversations opened up windows for me to sneak into the local moral ecology in the Shanghai milieu and to get more intimate understandings of the "moral experience" (what is at stake locally) from a native's point of view. As I lived there and talked to people, I came to understand why these questions stood out and why they seemed so natural to native Shanghai residents. I was not alone in encountering such Shanghai dramas. The parents and teachers of Biyu Preschool experienced all kinds of Shanghai dramas, too, with the general impression that in Shanghai, human beings are evaluated primarily by market capital. These concerns are manifested in specific forms of categorization, such as housing condition (a direct index of your wealth and status) and geographic origin (a direct index of how metropolitan [Shanghai] versus rural [non-Shanghai] you are and an indirect index of your "cultural capital" [Bourdieu 2008].)

The perception of and concern about such a unitary evaluative standard, so-called "money fetishism," was popular in Shanghai and even throughout

China. Based on his research on sexual culture in Shanghai more than a decade ago, James Farrer has already noted that the pervasive motivation of seeking wealth has been "highlighted as a source of moral crisis" (Farrer 2002: 17) during Shanghai's "opening up" in the postsocialist era. Such "market logic," once unleashed, adopted by and applied to everyone in every dimension of life, caused great fear and discontent among the general public. Unlike Farrer, who focused primarily on young adults and sexual culture, my study looks at social comments about education and children. In my fieldwork, on these topics, a salient theme was how people thought that, in their own as well as their children's life, the extreme competition, comparison, and materialism, along with discrimination against those who are disadvantaged, might affect children's education and development.

Shanghai is one of the leading educational cities in China, famous for its top test scores in worldwide competition: Shanghai's public secondary schools topped the world charts in the PISA (Program for International Student Assessment) test, which measures the ability of fifteen-year-olds in sixty-five countries to apply what they have learned in math, science, and reading in both 2009 (Dillon 2010) and 2012 (Hannon 2013). Most recently, Western media also claimed to have found out the secret to Shanghai's success in education, including a deep commitment to teacher training, parental involvement, a culture that values education, and so forth (Friedman 2013).

In contrast with the media attention on educational achievements in Shanghai, the costs of such success are less explored. Such costs manifest themselves in material and nonmaterial forms, including the tremendous competition, comparison, and stress among parents, teachers, and children, starting from preschool or even earlier, encapsulated in the slogan "winning at the starting line" (*ying zai qi pao xian shang*). A recent demographic study in Shanghai provides a sketch of escalating parental expectations for children, the overwhelming pressure on parents to provide better resources for children, and extremely fierce competition among children (Nie and Wyman 2005). I will demonstrate in detail how such competition and stress in education at its starting point is perceived in the local community of Biyu Preschool. I will also describe the huge concerns around the concomitant materialism and discrimination in education. In light of the stories told by parents and teachers at Biyu Preschool, one gets a glimpse at the moral ecology of preschool education in Shanghai. This ecology has a national reach on the one hand and a distinct Shanghainese tone on the other hand.

Material Investments in Children's Education

In my child-rearing questionnaire, I investigated Biyu Preschool parents' SES information and investment in education, through five questions. The first question was "Into what range does your annual household income fall?" with five categories. Because of the sensitivity and privacy issues of releasing income information, some parents chose not to answer this question. Seventy-seven out of ninety-two parents did give an estimate of their family income, as summarized below (Table 1.1).

Note that although the majority of these families have their own parents residing in their apartments or houses for childcare, the annual household income refers to only income from the parents themselves. According to the official statistics, Shanghai had the highest average annual income, RMB 40,188 in China in 2012 (Li 2013). Suppose in all the families of my sample, both parents earn income (which was not true because a considerable number of families had a stay-at-home mother), these families' financial status is still above the average in Shanghai (RMB 40,188 × 2 = RMB 80,376, falling under category A). Especially, the median range (RMB 200,000 – RMB 400,000), which had the largest percentage; this is two to five times of the average annual household income of double-wage-earner families. Considering the non-anonymous nature of this questionnaire survey and the plausible trend that these parents were conservative in disclosure of their actual income information, it is reasonable to infer that the real income levels of Biyu families are somewhat higher than what were reported. Hence by income standard, my sample is a middle-class or even upper-middle-class community in Shanghai.

Another question investigated parents' perception of the ratio of education investment to their family income, and the results are as follows (Table 1.2).

Table 1.1 Child-Rearing Questionnaire: Biyu Preschool Parents' Annual Household Income

Annual household income (RMB)	Number of households	Percentage
A. 50,000–100,000	4	5%
B. 100,000–200,000	22	29%
C. 200,000–400,000	26	34%
D. 400,000–600,000	15	19%
E. Above 600,000	10	13%

Table 1.2 Child-Rearing Questionnaire: Biyu Preschool Parents'
Monthly Educational Expenses

Educational investment/ family income ratio	Number of households	Percentage
A. Above 40%	3	3.7%
B. 20% to 40%	27	33.3%
C. 10% to 20%	29	35.8%
D. 5% to 10%	15	18.5%
E. Below 5%	7	8.64%

In addition, parents were asked to rank order different categories of expenditure:

A. Food
B. Clothing
C. Health care
D. Children's education
E. Housing
F. Transportation
G. Entertainment (leisure, tourism, etc.)

Children's education was ranked very high. It was only second to housing in the *highest*-expenditure category (housing: 47 percent, children's education: 33 percent), and the biggest one in the *second-highest*-expenditure category (37 percent).

I also asked parents to give an estimate of monthly educational expenses broken down into these sub-categories: preschool tuition, educational materials (books, toys, etc.), and "interest classes" (*xingquban*). "Interest classes" (*xingquban*) is a colloquial term that refers to various extracurricular classes that young children are enrolled in, including academic classes such as math, English, language, and various arts classes such as piano, painting, calligraphy, and dancing. Table 1.3 lists the average estimates of each sub-category and the total. I should add that, just as these families' self-estimated annual income varies along a range (see Table 1.1), their self-estimated monthly educational expenses also vary: RMB 1,500–RMB 3,000 in preschool tuition (due to various discount policies of Biyu Preschool according to age, year, *guanxi*, etc.), RMB 50–RMB 2,000 in educational materials, and RMB 0–RMB 2,500 in "interest classes." One can see the level of inequality and diversity among this middle-class community.

Table 1.3 Child-Rearing Questionnaire: Biyu Preschool Parents'
Monthly Educational Expenses

Monthly educational expenses	Average amount (RMB)	Median amount (RMB)	Average percentage
Preschool tuition	2,411	2,500	72%
Educational materials	424	300	13%
Interest classes	709	500	21%
Total	3,347	3,200	N/A

Although there is no accurate way to compare the figures across these different tables, one can still see whether parents' estimates of their annual household income, ratio of educational expenses to annual income, and monthly educational expenses match well. For example, the median annual income range (RMB 200,000 to RMB 400, 000) divided by twelve (months) equals the range of RMB 16,667 to RMB 33,334, which is the median monthly income range. This median monthly income range multiplied by the median ratio range of education investment/family income (10 percent to 20 percent) equals RMB 1667 to RMB 3333, which is the calculated median range of monthly educational expenses. The median amount of monthly educational expenses estimated by parents themselves (RMB 3,200) falls into the higher end of the calculated median range (RMB 1,667 to RMB 3333). This suggests that parents' own estimation of these different parameters match *roughly* well.

The final question in this survey section was: "Do you think child-rearing costs in contemporary Chinese society are too high or not?" Of the eighty-seven parents who completed the question, seventy-eight (90 percent) answered yes. This reveals that, regardless of variation in family social economic status and differences in educational investment strategies, Biyu Preschool parents did perceive the pressure of material investment in children's early education.

Competition, Comparison, and Stress

On July 26, 2012, toward the end of my observations at Biyu, I witnessed this reaction from Yichen, a six-year-old boy from Class 4A, during his last days at Biyu; in a month he would go to a primary school in another district of Shanghai. Yichen was looking through the window. The playground was under renovation, and the children's favorite spot—the big slide—was being taken apart. Yichen complained in a quiet yet frustrated tone: "Go tear the slide up! Have us study and study forever! We will go angry and die!" At that moment, I was so shocked by the anger and grief of this boy, who was already so burdened by school pressure at this young age.

Concomitant with the economic pressure of educational investment among middle-class families in Shanghai, parents, teachers, and children all experienced enormous psychological stress due to the fierce competition and never-ending comparison of children's educational outcomes.

As Andrew Kipnis found in Shandong province's elementary to senior high education, the educational services targeting young children in Shanghai include two broad categories (Kipnis 2012a). First, there are extra-school classes aiming to help with core exam subjects such as math, language, English, and so on, provided by individual tutors or private educational agencies; the other category includes extra-curricular classes in music, dance, art, calligraphy, and sports, which anthropologist Teresa Kuan calls "specialty education" (Kuan 2008). In Shanghai, these two categories are lumped together under this general category of "interest classes" (*xingquban*). In sharp contrast to situations in rural areas, such educational services in Shanghai are available for even the youngest children (age one or earlier), and in greater variety and higher quality. These are called "early education classes" (*zaojiaoban*), and big cities like Shanghai are the primary markets for such education at such an early age, attracting international brands (i.e., Gymboree), followed by more and more domestic enterprises. Actually, a considerable percentage of children had prior experiences in such classes before coming to Biyu's nursery or preschool classes. As children grew, parents became even more eager to send their children to various "interest classes," and they talked among themselves in order to discover what classes other children were in and where such classes were. Biyu Preschool offered extra classes of private tutorship both in and outside of regular school time, such as piano, painting, "Little Show Hostess Class" (*xiao zhuchiren ban*),[4] and dancing. Parents also sought classes taught at professional centers outside the school during evenings or weekends, such as "EF (Education First)" (*yingfu jiaoyu*) for English training.

There was pervasive comparison among parents, not limited to academic performance *per se*. Parents were very keen on getting to know what "interest classes" other children were taking and very concerned about whether their children could match up with other children on "interest class" training, including those in nonacademic subjects. Those who didn't pay as much attention to "interest classes" would get really anxious about their children's future. For example, Siya was a smart and carefree girl in Class 3B. Her parents didn't impose on her extra-curricular training like some other parents did, but her mother expressed her concern to me: "My husband and I seem really 'back-ward' and outdated in education. A while ago when a lot of her classmates were sent to piano or other 'interest classes,' I was concerned about it. Keyu's mother was way ahead of me in planning for her daughter's future.[5] She already knew which elementary, junior high, and high school Keyu should go to. She sent her to learn *Guzheng* (a traditional Chinese music instrument) quite a while ago. Whenever I saw her, she reminded me about the importance of getting these extra skills. She told me I should choose traditional Chinese instruments because traditional Chinese instrument training would bring bonus points to the child during the elementary-to-junior-high examination. I was dumb-founded: I didn't know about this at all! I asked my husband: 'Should we send Siya to these classes, too? Otherwise, I will be so embarrassed when other parents talked about these things with me.'"

Parents and teachers think that educational competition and expectations in Shanghai are exceptionally high compared to most other places in China. Yichen was about five years old when he moved with his parents from Nan-chang, a provincial capital in eastern China, to Shanghai, during summer 2011. His father worked for a big company and his mother stayed at home. They rent an apartment in a nearby neighborhood. During my interview with Yichen's mother, she described to me the contrast between life in Nanchang and Shang-hai, both for parents and the child, and shared with me her deep anxieties: "Honestly, I don't like living in Shanghai. The main reason is life here is just too stressful, and people all focus solely on money and housing. Back in Nanchang, you can see people going out for a walk in the evening, with a relatively peaceful countenance (*mianrong bijiao anjing*). It's not like Shanghai, where life is hectic and everyone wears a long face (*ku zhe ge lian*). It's just too stressful!" She also complained specifically about the "interest classes": "It's unbelievable what the kids have to go through here. Almost every preschool child has to go to several 'interest classes' (*xingquban*) and get several certificates, other than a regular schooling. I regretted immediately after we moved here: I should have forced my son to learn English better back in Nanchang! He had learned English for several years—the preschool he went to in Nanchang was a bilingual school with good English classes. But the standards here are much higher! Now children at K-level master English skills that are officially granted for Grade 3 level."

Such a contrast was also mentioned by a number of other parents and teach-ers, who had working experience outside Shanghai. For example, one teacher of class 3B, Xiaoling, had worked in a similar preschool at Shenzhen, a big city in South China neighboring Hong Kong. She told me: "The atmosphere here in Shanghai preschools is really extreme, [such] that every parent is comparing themselves to others and forcing the child to attend all kinds of 'interest classes' (*xingquban*)." Teacher Fanglin previously worked in a high-end preschool at Shenyang, the largest city in northeast China, prior to joining Biyu Preschool in 2010. She also noticed that "interest classes" were not as popular in Shenyang as they were in Shanghai, even though parents she encountered in Shenyang were all upper middle class. Another teacher, Meifang, used to teach vocal music in junior high schools in Qingdao, a coastal city in Shandong province. She just moved to Shanghai a year ago with her husband and son. Her son went to a public preschool nearby and wasn't prepared for this much emphasis and workload in academic subjects. Although she felt shocked and uncomfortable with the overwhelming educational burden on her son, she chose to conform to the Shanghai norms. She enrolled her son in eight different classes outside regular school time, including math, English, Chinese language, and piano. Reports like this from people who had lived in other major cities in China hint at how competitive early childhood education in Shanghai is.

Yichen's mother summarized the experience in Shanghai as really "humiliating" because she had to face the reality and worry about her only son Yichen's future. When it came to the elementary school admission experience, Yichen's mother used this saying—"a handful of tears, sour and bitter" (*yi ba xinsuan lei*). Good schools, both public and private, were extremely competitive. For some elite primary schools, the admission ratio is less than 1:100. Right after they came to Shanghai, she and her husband had to find ways for Yichen to get into a good elementary school. The family did not have a Shanghai registered residence (*hukou*), so Yichen did not qualify for public schools. For some private schools Yichen's parents were applying for, a detailed procedure was required before he could become a candidate, including a recommendation letter from his current preschool teacher. Then in the spring of 2012, the final semester of Yichen's kindergarten year in Biyu, his parents took him to quite a number of elementary schools for the first round of screening. Such screening included very formal face-to-face interviews between teachers and parents, and between teachers and the small child. In such an interview, the child had to be placed in a big classroom, alone with teachers whom he or she had never met before. He or she had to answer challenging questions posed by the teachers to test his or her "intelligence" in every possible dimension. Tests like this required not only "intelligent" knowledge and reasoning skills, but also, perhaps more important, the psychological capacity to handle this rigid "examination" as well as good communicative skills. And, it is a one-shot game, so the stakes are high. Parents all complained about this kind of "interview," viewing it as a really inhumane and intimidating experience for young children.

This "K-to-1 transition" (*you xiao xianjie*) poses a tremendous challenge to parents. Quite a number of kindergarten parents (Class 4A and 4B) expressed to me their anxieties about their children's performance in the various examinations and interviews for primary school admission. On the one hand, they were even more focused on children's academic learning, and schedules for their children both in and after school became even more rigid in the last semester at Biyu. On the other hand, they made great efforts to use their existing connections to ensure school admission, and many of them indeed fulfilled that purpose through their *guanxi* networks. For example, Xinbao, a boy in Class 4A, who was below average in academic performance, eventually got admitted by the second most prestigious elementary school in Pudong district. Relieved after months of anxiety and worry, his mother shared this good news with me and told me that it would have been impossible without her friend's help. Xinbao's story points to a general truth about the reality of education in Shanghai, or even the whole nation: to win the competition, you must either have outstanding talents and academic performance already shown at a young age or have strong connections, or ideally both!

Gongli *and* Shili*: Materialism, Pragmatism, and Snobbery*

In the context of severe competition and comparison, a lot of complaints from parents and teachers were circulating about the increasing materialism, pragmatism, and the ensuing discrimination that occurred in multiple dimensions of education, including educational goals, practices, and relationships among teachers, parents, and children. From teachers' perspective, parents were often blamed as pragmatically and materialistically oriented (*gongli*) regarding their children's education. Such a sense of materialism and pragmatism went hand in hand with the successful marketization of educational services that cater to parents' increasing needs to invest in their children amid the severe competition.

The successful marketization of Chinese education is closely related to the production of difference and distinction through standardization in a predominantly hierarchical social system, a theme that previous scholars on Chinese parenting and education have harped on (Kipnis 2012b, 2012c; Kuan 2008). Based on his decades of studies in Shandong province, Andrew Kipnis pointed out that the standardization and normalization processes fed into a particular imaginary in which "the social world is constituted in singular, hierarchical terms" (Kipnis 2012c: 189). Drawing on her fieldwork in Kunming

City, Yunnan province, Teresa Kuan also notes that, in addition to resonating with the popular advice offered by educational and parenting experts, parents' motivations in seeking children's specialty education "also point to a kind of cultural politics of class rarely discussed in popular discourse. In pursuing specialty education for their child, parents are responding to social pressures and demands that serve to effect social stratification" (Kuan 2008: 46). In particular, parents in her studies believed that such specialty education would cultivate good deportment (*qizhi*) and enhance quality of life/pleasure among children. Andrew Kipnis points out, for "interest classes" in rural Shandong that bear no direct relevance to success on the university entrance exams in sciences and humanities, three closely intertwined logics were employed by marketers to motivate parents: that this particular activity, such as dancing or music, laid down a foundation (*jichu*) for children's future educational success; that such an activity can generalize into improvements in other core educational domains; that it can enhance children's hidden potential or latent ability (*qianneng*) (Kipnis, 2012c).

Along this line, Shanghai goes much further than Shandong or Yunnan in terms of the standardization of "interest classes" and the linkage to primary school admission, even in the realm of "specialty education," part of the dramatic encounter that non-Shanghainese parents often marveled at. For instance, Yichen's mother complained to me: "This is ridiculous! All the 'interest classes' aim ultimately to put young children to standardized exams for a certificate at different levels, not only English, but also other subjects such as painting and calligraphy. I never anticipated this." Parents value such educational experiences because these certificates might become bonus points during elementary school entrance examinations. A striking example was, according to one teacher, that the reason many parents sent young children to learn vocal music was because they wanted the children to be prepared to project themselves well in karaoke networking (*yingchou*) with superiors. No wonder a lot of parents and teachers thought such Shanghainese education to be extremely materialistic and pragmatic (*gongli*).

The materialistic and pragmatic educational ethos was also manifest, according to parents and teachers, in snobbery (*shili*) across educational settings. First, the young teachers in this school, most of whom came from other provinces and earned far less than the preschool parents, complained that native Shanghainese parents were disrespectful to teachers compared to parents in other cities, and the teacher-parent relationship, which had a strong moral dimension in traditional Chinese culture, was replaced by a materialistic, transactional one. In the traditional Chinese hierarchical culture, teachers are seen as both educational authorities and people who genuinely care about their students' well-being. This kind of moral and emotional affinity could still be found in some parts of China today: "The appellation 'teacher' (*laoshi*) is, in many ways, like a kin term. Once someone has been your teacher (and you have addressed him or her as such), you must continue to address him or her in this manner for the rest of your life" (Kipnis 2009: 216). The impression Biyu young teachers had about parents' attitude toward them, however, stood in stark contrast to this rosy picture.

Xiaoxiao, the head teacher of Biyu, who had worked in Beijing before, lamented: "Parents here in Shanghai do not show the same kind of respect as parents I knew in Beijing. I can tell it just from the tone of their voice." Meifang, who used to be a junior high school teacher at Qingdao, a coastal city in northeast China, also expressed a similar concern: "Here in Shanghai, parents tend to see us as merely providing service and they are the consumers. I really don't like that. How can they not show any respect to teachers? We educate and take care of their children, not just provide economic service!" Of course, the teachers' complaints against snobbish parents were not limited to those native Shanghainese parents. The complaints were in general targeted at parents who not only had higher social status, but also felt superior to those in a lower position. Teachers found such arrogant attitude intolerable.

One day, I dropped into Meifang's classroom to chat with a parent, Keke's mother. She was a native Shanghainese woman who got a master's degree in Europe and married another native Shanghainese who was now a high-level official in a big state-owned corporation. I politely approached her, introduced myself, and asked her if she would be willing to participate in my interview after school. She asked more about my background and agreed. After she left, I started chatting with Teacher Meifang:

Jing: Are you familiar with Keke's mother? How is she like? I am going to interview her tomorrow, and I need your advice!

Meifang: Well, she should be nice to you. Don't worry. You are a PhD (candidate) in America.

Jing: Interesting. Why did you say that?

Meifang: You know what? She is the kind of snobbish parent who treats people differently according to their social status (*kan ren xia cai die*), "look at the people before ordering dishes." I give you a simple example. If it were me who asked her the same question as you did, she would probably not agree to be interviewed. I am not a PhD, nor am I rich.

Jing: OK. Can you tell me more?

Meifang: You remember the teacher Qingqing, who used to work with me at this classroom, and then left Shanghai with her husband and her three-year-old son? She and her husband both came from the countryside, and her husband's job was not good, and it was hard to support the whole family. Knowing that Keke's father was a high official at corporation X, she went to Keke's mother and asked if Keke's father could arrange for a job for her husband. Keke's mother didn't show any respect to her at all, but blamed Qingqing: "Why did you marry such a useless husband? You should have married yourself to a Shanghainese guy." She then collected some of her son's used clothes and gave them to Qing. Not that it was not good to receive used clothes from others, but the way Keke's mother gave the clothes to her was so disrespectful and even humiliating.

The next day, during my interview with Keke's mother, I wasn't treated as badly as Teacher Qing had been. Her sense of superiority, however, still figured into our conversation. The couple was preparing to immigrate to Canada, and she was a big fan of what she called the "advanced" Western educational beliefs, such as emphasizing children's creativity and independence while downplaying the value of the preschool education her son was receiving at Biyu. Toward the end of the conversation, she asked if my then husband was a native Shanghainese, what he did for a living, and how much he earned. Despite my disappointing answers to those three questions, in her eyes, I was still a well-educated "Western" child studies expert, which to some extent helped ease the conversation.

According to the teachers, parental attitudes toward other people and children definitely shaped how their own children thought about others. The story of Xinwen and her mother provides an apt example. According to Teacher Meifang, Xinwen's mother, a high-level manager in a state-owned enterprise, is a self-assuming woman who always treats teachers as if they are her subordinates. The way she talks with Meifang sounds like Meifang should do whatever she tells her to do. She is also obsessed with comparing her daughter to other children. In particular, she looks down upon their neighbor's child, Ke'er, who is also in the same class with her daughter. The following is a story Meifang told about this parent's contempt for Ke'er and how that translated into her daughter's unpleasant moral character.

> The other day, Xinwen's mother came to me and kept boasting about how excellent Xinwen is in everything. But Xinwen is not a very nice child, and I felt like I have the responsibility to report to her mother about it so as to correct her. After I politely reported to her mother about some of the things Xinwen did at school, her mother seemed upset and even angry. Toward the end of our conversation, she asked: "In any case, my daughter at least is no worse than Ke'er, right?" I was so shocked! How could she ever say that? How could she despise her own neighbor's child? Ke'er was not the smartest child or the prettiest girl, but she was very kind-hearted and sweet, unlike Xinwen, who was arrogant and not friendly. After all, every child is different. You cannot compare them on a single plane. She believes, in her bones, that Ke'er and her family are not worthy to be part of her social circle, despite the fact Xinwen and Ke'er still play together after school and go to the same swimming class during weekends. Even for this swimming class, every time she mentioned it to me, she praised her daughter for learning fast and showed her disdain for Ke'er, complaining that Ke'er was stupid.
>
> That's why, I guess, Xinwen also showed a disdain for Ke'er at school. For example, one day I asked Xinwen and Ke'er to help me lift up a table together. Perhaps because Ke'er was not as agile as Xinwen expected, her arms touched Xinwen by accident. I saw a disdainful and impatient look on Xinwen's face. She was apparently not happy with Ke'er and started to complain about how clumsy Ke'er was. Ke'er looked at me without a clue of what was going on with Xinwen. Poor girl! She was so innocent. My heart ached at that moment.

Comparison and snobbery occur in more than one direction. Parents, including both native and "new" Shanghainese, also had issues with such snobbish attitudes visible in schools. Such discrimination was said to be a pervasive feature in many schools. First and foremost, getting into good schools not only depends on the child's academic performance, but also depends on the child's family background. Good public schools set up a high admission bar for children: first, for those who live in the school district, families have to be the owner of housing property for at least three years. Considering the extraordinarily high housing price in Shanghai, this criterion excludes many families who cannot afford purchasing an apartment. Moreover, among such families, only children who hold a Shanghai "household registration record" (*hukou*) are eligible. So, for instance, even if one owns a property, his or her child still cannot go to public schools if the child's *hukou* belongs elsewhere, not Shanghai (i.e., neither of the parents have a Shanghai *hukou*). What about those children who are not eligible officially but end up in the good public schools? They have to work their way through connections or bribery, otherwise their children have to be really excellent in academics and pass the very competitive admission exams. Even the admission exams that are supposed to reflect fair criteria, are in fact not really fair. Weijian's mother, a native Shanghainese woman working in a local administrative branch (Electricity Bureau) after graduating from a junior college, talked about her experiences and impressions of school admission exams for her daughter.

> We heard that the private elementary school admission required not only interviewing the child, but also interviewing the parents. The interview with parents includes, for instance, three English questions and three Math Olympics[6] questions. The director (interviewer) had met "countless people" (*yue ren wushu*), so he just based his evaluations on the parents' educational and socioeconomic backgrounds. For example: for the same questions, if you answered all three English questions correctly but failed in all three math questions, the director would put you in the short list because you have a PhD in the United States. On the contrary, if I answered all math questions correctly but failed in the English ones, the director would not consider me because I only had a junior college degree.
>
>   We had also taken our daughter to the public preschool interview, after she finished the "nursery class" at Biyu. It was a famous public preschool in our neighborhood. Since it was a public school, it shared the same nature as the place I am working for: public schools live off government money (*chi huang liang*), and they don't need to cater to consumers (parents)' needs because jobs are pretty stable there and they will not be fired because of parents' complaints. The public preschool people, from the school guard (*menwei*) to the director, are all snobs (*shili yan*)! They would throw a big smile to you if you look like a rich person but would disdain you if not.

Secondly, after the child is admitted to a public preschool, parents still need to be solicitous—"look at the colors of their (teachers') face" (*kan ren lianse*). One the one hand, teachers there are said to care less about individual children because they have to attend to more children. On the other hand, because they "live off the government money" (*chi huang liang*) and have a secure job— "iron rice bowl" (*tie fan wan*)—they don't have to care about whether parents are happy. A parent from Class 1A (the youngest cohort) was very critical about public preschools: "Public preschool was never part of my consideration. I cannot accept it, especially the attitude of the teachers and staff. In a word, I don't like 'public service' in general. Staff at the post office, state-owned banks, and other public agencies always had a bad attitude to clients, as if you owed them something or you were begging for their favor. I don't like anything that has to do with the government."

Public preschools are also notorious for bribery. Public preschools, especially prestigious ones, have a much higher student-teacher ratio than private ones, so teachers at public preschools cannot attend to individual children's needs as much as teachers at private schools. It is an open secret that parents have to bribe teachers with the hope that their own children will be treated well. Thus, of course, the more one wants the teacher to care about his or her child, the higher the bribery amount should be. Parents told me that the amount of RMB 2000 per month was a common standard at public schools, in cash, gift card, or jewelry, and competition between parents when it came to bribery was like an arms race. The bribery reached such an extent that teachers did not need any explicit script to elicit gifts from parents, and teachers' maneuvers coordinated perfectly with parents' tactics. Jianxia, who used to work in a public preschool, told me this: "One teacher said to a young girl before she went home from school: 'Your mother's earrings are really beautiful!' The girl repeated this to her mother, and the next day her mother would definitely wrap those earrings and send them as a gift to the teacher!"

In contrast to such accusations against public preschools, the private school Biyu seems a reasonable choice for some parents. First, compared to those public preschools, there is much less bribery at Biyu Preschool, although it is still visible in certain forms.[7] The teacher-student ratio (1:8 on average) is also much better than most public preschools (1:20 or more). Also, despite the complaints among teachers and parents, it is farfetched to conclude that the teacher-parent relationships in Biyu have become *entirely* transactional/materialistic by nature. Perhaps compared to other places in China, things that were *gongli* (materialistic) or *shili* (snobbish) were more visible in Shanghai, as some parents and teachers complained. Note, however, that in the daily flow of Biyu Preschool life, *some* teachers and parents are still building authentic, genuine relationships that nurture the micro-environment where young children spent most of their daytime. These are reasons why many parents choose to send their children to private preschools, although in many cases public preschools provide more "qualified" educational services and staff—

"qualified" in the sense of better curriculum, equipment, and more teachers with government-approved credentials.

In addition to making a choice between public and private school, parents and teachers must balance numerous educational concerns, needs, and habits in concrete situations in the educational environment of Shanghai. According to teachers' and parents' experiences and imaginations, the fierce competition, the overwhelming stress, and the *gongli* and *shili* mentalities constitute the core of the educational culture in Shanghai. This educational culture sets up the backdrop for the dilemmas socializers encounter in moral cultivation.

Disorientation, Dissonance, and Despair: Socializers' Dilemmas in Cultivating Morality

> Nowadays there are numerous parenting advice books, and my daughter bought a lot of such books, hoping to get useful suggestions on child-rearing. Sometimes she completely adopts the Western norms. For example, when my grandson Jinqu fell on the ground, she would just let it go without lifting him up from the ground. But other times she forgot the Western methods, because after all she didn't grow up in a Western environment, and my family was not a Western-style family. Also, even if you received the Western values and have such awareness in child-rearing, it's hard to implement them if other people don't believe in those values. In a word, the general atmosphere is not conducive to children's well-being.

This quote from Jinqu's maternal grandfather, a well-educated native Shanghainese, succinctly points out the quandaries socializers in Shanghai were facing in cultivating morality. Such quandaries manifest themselves at multiple levels.

First, socializers are disoriented, as it is difficult to choose between multiple sets of conflicting values in moral education. For example, when Jinqu fell on the ground, the Chinese way, especially for grandparents, was to protect the child and lift him or her up immediately, whereas the (imagined) Western norm, adopted by some parents of the younger generation, would be not to interfere, so as to cultivate the character of independence.

Second, there is some dissonance because parents' behaviors sometimes belie their words and moral education ideologies often conflict with what children encounter in reality. For example, as Jinqu's grandparent said, even if Jinqu's mother prefers the Western norms ideally, in real life she does not always conform to those norms.

Third, some parents despair of managing to balance cultivating morality and securing future survival in an imagined immoral world. One's choice of socialization strategies is inevitably entangled with what other people's strategies and choices are, or, more accurately, is contingent upon one's estimation about what other people will do. As Jinqu's grandfather lamented, it is hard when your beliefs conflict with those of the majority. Moreover, such quandaries are not necessarily isolated from one another. Rather, they are interwoven together in the daily educational dynamics. Both Jinqu's grandparent and Tiantian's mother (refer to the beginning of this chapter) mentioned the most depressing fact—the society is not wholesome and the general atmosphere is not conducive to children's well-being.

Disorientation (mimang) *between Conflicting Values: The "Imagined Chinese" versus the "Imagined Western" Norms*

Conflicts between different values with varying social orientations emerged as recurrent themes in my own fieldwork. I adopt the definition of value suggested by Vanessa Fong in her work on Chinese singleton teenagers' life: "Values are the simple heuristic terms that people often use when discussing aspects of cultural models that they consider good, important, and worthy of emulation" (Fong 2007a: 89). Whereas Fong focused on the vertical direction of socialization and cultural transmission, moral conflicts between parents and teenagers arising from parent-child communication problems (Fong 2007a), I will highlight the horizontal dimension, that is, the dilemmas socializers *themselves* face in choosing between conflicting values in moral socialization, especially the conflicting values between the "imagined Chinese" versus "the imagined Western."

> Personally, I feel like it's a great dilemma for Chinese mothers like me: on the one hand, you do Chinese nurturing-rearing (*yang zhi*); on the other hand, you want some Western disciplining-rearing (*guan zhi*). How would you gear (*jiegui*) your Chinese way to the Western way? Right? You don't want to give up either way. It's very contradictory. For example, you want to give enough freedom to your child, but you also want to protect her. This is something I read from a book: if you want your child to grow in this specific area, you need to loosen your own involvement there. So if you want her to be brave, you'd better let her "eat some bitterness" (*chi ku*). Theoretically I know this, but it's hard for me to stick to this principle in real life. For instance, if I want her to eat more, I should just let her go hungry if she doesn't want to eat. But I can't. I will try my best to put some food into her mouth.

Siya's mother worked from home part time, but most of her time was devoted to family. She constantly questioned her own child-rearing beliefs and strategies, after comparing them with what the experts said in the books or what other parents suggested because her daughter was very stubborn and she didn't know how to handle this. She was concerned that her daughter was not obedient and she was too lenient with her, but at the same time, she was not very sure whether she should follow others' suggestions for being tough with her young girl. Among the child-rearing "battles" she was caught up in, one thing that concerned her most was feeding. In many Chinese families, children at preschool age are frequently spoon-fed by parents or grandparents. This became a source of anxiety for some Biyu parents, and they constantly struggled with it. Siya's mother was an extreme example who even suffered from depression because of dealing with her daughter's feeding problems. Siya was small in size, and she ate very little during meals. As Siya's mother said, she didn't know whether she should let her daughter "eat some bitterness" by letting her go hungry if she refused to eat or go out of the way to feed her. Although parents knew that children would not starve and they refused to eat mostly because at that time they weren't very hungry, the urge to have children eat more and finish a meal at once instead of snacking intermittently seemed unquenchable. As Siya's mother explained, it was not simply a problem of physical health. Essentially, it was about building the moral character of self-reliance and endurance.

Siya mother's comments illustrate what a typical value conflict in moral socialization looks like for young parents in urban China, primarily between the "old"/Chinese values and the "new"/Western values as these parents imagined. Notably, the so-called Western values were advocated as "scientific" and "modern" in mass media and popular parenting advice literature. Many of these parents had read various kinds of parenting advice books, and a lot of the books featured so-called Western parenting styles and compared these with the problems of Chinese children—stereotypes such as lack of dependence, creativity, and concern for others. The term she used, *to gear*, literally meaning to connect two different tracks together, is a vivid metaphor for integrating the Chinese and the Western socialization values. The kind of conflict that bothered her is similar to what Jinqu's maternal grandparent mentioned: when the Chinese, or the "imagined Chinese" way emphasizes interdependence and protection of the child, especially under the circumstances where the whole extended family took care of one child together, the Western, or the "imagined Western" way highlights independence and autonomy. Ironically, instead of understanding "non-interference" as "non-discipline," such independence and autonomy were seen by Siya's mother as a result of parents' strict discipline (*guan*): training children to rely on themselves through relaxing parental involvement and help. In contrast, in the concrete examples of feeding the child and the child falling on the ground, Chinese child-rearing featured nurturance (*yang*), that is, helping and protecting the child through feeding or lifting him or her up.

I prefer the terms *imagined Chinese* and *imagined Western*, instead of *Chinese* and *Western* because this dichotomy has no fixed meaning or boundaries in itself. It only resides in popular imaginations that are by nature subject to changing contextual factors and fluctuating individual experiences. For example, as Vanessa Fong points out, the value of independence (*zili/ duli*) has its roots in Confucian tradition of self-cultivation and acquired new prominence as part of Chinese discourses of nationalism and citizen-building movements from the nineteenth century that are still in existence now; and parents in Dalian (the city where Fong did her fieldwork) also shared this view that children should go through hardships to cultivate independence, which would then enable them to endure future hardships (Fong 2007a: 93–94). This version of "independence" was actually similar to what Siya's mother saw as desirable "discipline," but she emphasized what she considered to be its "Western-ness" instead.

Actually, the overprotecting "feeding" phenomenon that Siya's mother talked about emerged as a target for parental reflection and educational critique quite recently, as an example of bad parenting, in contrast to the modern, Western, and scientific parenting of no-interference at mealtime. Such reflections and critiques arose with the birth of China's one-child generation and were amplified with the emergence of the "4:2:1" family structure during China's growing economy in the postsocialist era (Wang and Fong 2009). Growing up in the Maoist era, the previous generation's experience actually posed a stark contrast with this "nurturing" picture: when parents had to rear multiple children with limited time and resources, no child would have enjoyed the luxury of being fed by parents at every meal until age five. Back then, parents only prepared food and children had to eat by themselves, and nobody would be chased around by grandparents and fed one spoon after another.

As the contrast between the "Chinese" and the "Western" approach is an imagined dichotomy, parents held varying, and sometimes even contradictory, interpretations of what the Chinese or the Western moral socialization values were. Such incongruence is partly due to parents' self-identification with regard to their own parenting styles. For example, Tiantian's mother complained about corporal punishment and considered it as an example of the strict, authoritarian Chinese parenting: "It's said that in the United States, it's illegal to spank or hit the child, right? The police will come if you do that. Although we don't have such legal regulations in China, I do hope that parents have such consciousness of how terrible corporeal punishment is. Honestly, sometimes after I spanked my son, I felt really regretful and heartbroken. Moreover, I read that 'parents who spank or hit their children are most useless and powerless.' And I felt very shameful."

Whereas Siya's mother thought herself to be too lenient toward her daughter, Tiantian's mother blamed herself for being too strict with her son. Whereas Siya's mother thought of Chinese parenting as "nurturing" without discipline, Tiantian's mother considered Chinese parenting too oppressive. Siya's mother saw her daughter as overindulged, in line with the popular stereotype about Chinese "little emperors," but Tiantian's mother emphasized a different stereotype about Chinese parenting. Both overindulgence and oppressive strictness are part of what parents thought of as bad Chinese parenting approaches.

Feeding and corporeal punishment are typical parenting issues that parents struggle with as they find it hard to reconcile the "bad Chinese way" and the "good Western way" for a variety of concerns about the children's well-being. Tiantian's mother was born in the late 1970s, before the one-child policy was launched. She identifies herself as a "post-seventies," to distinguish herself from the "post-eighties"—the first-generation singleton children like Siya's mother and me. Not only do the "post-eighties" parents like Siya's mother or the "post-seventies" parents like Tiantian's mother feel disoriented as they have to choose between the "imagined Chinese" and the "imagined Western" values—whatever these referred to; grandparents—the older generation—also feel confused about what moral messages to convey to their grandchildren.

Jinqu is a four-year-old boy in Class 2A, raised primarily by his maternal grandparents. Both of his parents were born and raised in Shanghai, and his maternal grandfather is a successful and respected businessman. Jinqu lived with his maternal grandparents from Monday to Friday and stayed with his parents only on weekends. Mr. J, Jinqu's maternal grandfather, shared with me his own stories of going out of his way to help others, even strangers. For example, during a group business trip to Australia, he met a teenage boy who was traveling alone on the same flight to start high school in Australia. At the customs clearance, he was found to have carried an amount of cash that exceeded the maximum allowed according to customs rules. The boy was scared and had no idea what to do. Mr. J saw this and went to negotiate with the customs staff, explaining that it was the boy's parents who prepared this money and they had no idea it would violate customs rules. It took Mr. J more than half an hour to settle this issue, and he almost missed his flight. But eventually Mr. J got on board, together with this teenage boy. Mr. J's colleagues on the same trip were perplexed and could not understand why Mr. J would go out of his way to help a stranger. They told Mr. J: "You should be cautious these days. No one would do anything for someone they don't know because you might run into trou- ble. Only silly people (*shazi*) will help strangers now." Cases in which a good Samaritan got exploited by the one being helped abound in media coverage in China today (Yan 2009), a topic I will discuss in more depth in the next chapter.

Although he was proud of sticking to the "old" moral codes himself, Mr. J was worried about his grandson's development.

> Now we adults always emphasize how to teach children to be defensive and be cautious and vigilant against potential threats and dangers in the society. For example, my wife often asks me: "Grandpa, we should arrange someone we know but Jinqu doesn't know to 'lure' him with candies, so as to find out whether he is careful and vigilant enough against bad people." You see, although our intention is good, what we do might have bad side effects on his moral development. By doing so, we actually expose him to the concept of "fraud." What if he develops the belief that by cheating he can get stuff that he desires? If he goes astray, the consequence will be really terrible. It's all due to the bad moral atmosphere in China. In the developed Western countries, you don't need to teach young children about fraud and stuff like that because there if you leave your stuff in the street, no one will steal it, and doors can be left unlocked (*lu bu shi yi, ye bu bi hu*).[8]

Jinqu's maternal grandparent is facing this dilemma of conflicting values. In his own view, he developed a solid moral foundation from the time he was young, thanks to his mother. He chose not to compromise his own moral standards in situations where those standards seemed to be outdated in a fast- developing society. On the one hand, he wanted to pass this successful moral education onto his grandson and mold him into an upright person. On the other hand, he also thought it necessary to teach his grandson to be cautious against a dangerous and immoral society. According to him, these two beliefs contradicted each other because the latter might have the unintended conse- quence of undermining one's moral character in terms of not trusting others or even cheating others. Such contradiction led him to confusion. Note that he also made the contrast between the "imagined China" and the "imagined West": China is dangerous and immoral, but the West is safe and moral. Actually, he had numerous experiences traveling abroad in the United States, Europe, and Australia, and that's why in our conversation, he often mentioned how things were different in China from the Western countries. Although it was definitely an exaggeration to say there was no fraud or crime in the West, and Jinqu's grandfather knew this for sure, still, this kind of contrast between an imagined immoral China and an imagined moral West is quite popular among parents when they talk about the environment of socialization.

Dissonance between Ideology and Reality

In addition to the explicit conflicts between different values, socializers and children are also caught up in more implicit forms of quandaries that I call "dissonance," especially between what socializers say and what they do or what children see in real life. I use the term *dissonance* because these incongruities usually occur in different contexts or occasions, that is, ideology in educational settings versus reality in non-educational settings. In contrast, the two sides of an internal value conflict, as described previously, often target the same situation or issue, albeit with varying motivations or justifications. In contrast with the value conflicts, in situations of dissonance, socializers are actually clear about what the desirable value is, instead of being anxious about choosing between incompatible values. The dilemmas they face, consciously or unconsciously, are to match reality to ideology and values as illustrated in the following instances.

For example, the tension between fairness and favoritism in how teachers treat children emerged again and again in my fieldwork. On the one hand, teachers know that they should treat the children nicely and lovingly. On the other hand, it is hard to be entirely fair with these children, due to various rational and emotional concerns. Although I didn't observe the kind of overt bribery that was said to happen a lot in public preschools, gift exchanges of varying monetary values between parents and teachers did occur at Biyu, too. Teachers believe that, in general, it is unfair to treat a particular child better just because the child's parent requested it or because they have received some material favor from the parent. For example, at the end of May, Biyu held an annual Children's Day (June 1) party in which each class was supposed to contribute two to three programs of dancing, singing, or other formats. Xinwen's mother, the one who Teacher Meifang complained about due to her self-assuming discrimination against other children, came to Meifang and asked her to include Xinwen in a particular dance. Xinwen was previously not selected because of her unqualified dancing skills, and Meifang rejected her mother's request directly and determinedly.

Teacher Fanglin initially planned to stick to this fair policy with her students, too. All her students were included in a collective dance, standing in a triangle shape. She originally determined the positioning of each child based on merit, that is, whoever danced better got to stand in the front. Two exceptions emerged, however. First, Fanglin decided to put Junjun in the very front of that triangle shape because Junjun's mother was her good friend, and Junjun, a sweet and naive boy had become her favorite child. Second, Lele's parents and grandparents were not happy to see that Lele was assigned a position in the back. Lele's mother gave Fanglin a few expensive cosmetic products bought in Hong Kong. Fanglin actually didn't like Lele's parents or grandparents that much because they were too demanding and selfish as could be seen in how they dealt with other parents and children in some previous incidents. She really liked the gift and didn't reject it, however. As a result, she had to assign Lele a new position in the front row of the dance.

Sometimes socializers themselves are fully aware of the incongruities between what they say or believe in and what they do in real life. As I mentioned before, Shanghai education is always considered too materialistic and pragmatic (*gongli*). On a weekend in June 2012, Jianxia, an experienced preschool teacher who later became a homeschool educator after her own children were born, invited me out to a big plaza where our boys could play together. There were numerous children's stores and early education centers (*zaojiao zhongxin*) in that plaza. We saw a well-known early education center named "Winning at the Starting Line." Both of us burst into laughter together just because the name of this center was so *gongli*, and we thought it very funny. Also, as an insider, Jianxia knew that this center's educational approach matched its *gongli* name very well. It was a big early education enterprise that had thirteen branches in Shanghai, and it claimed to offer competitive classes for young children from birth to age six, including a class named "Baby MBA." Then Jianxia told me this story of her friend's friend who felt embarrassed at the fact that she sent her own child to this early education center:

The other day, my friend M and I brought our children together to this plaza. M ran into a college classmate, D, and asked her: "What are you doing here?" D said: "I brought my child for an early education class." M asked: "Which early education center are you going to?" D answered hesitantly: "I am embarrassed to tell you because the name of this center is too *gongli*." D then quickly left without telling us the exact name of the center. But both M and I knew for sure what she meant. It must be this one, Winning at the Starting Line. I was confused: Why would she even want to take her child to that center if she felt so embarrassed about its pragmatic and materialistic-oriented educational approach? Later on I had a conversation with D and got to know that she was actually struggling a lot with which educational approach to choose. As a well-educated woman, she honestly didn't think the current competitive and pragmatic educational approach was ideal, but she still decided to impose it on her own child as it had been imposed on her: "I myself was educated in this system, so my child has to go through the same thing in this environment. There is no alternative way."

Incidents like this illustrate how teachers and parents had to negotiate specific concerns in various contexts that led them to make a compromise between the ideal and the pragmatic, both intentionally and unintentionally.

Sometimes children themselves got confused between what they thought was "correct" through parents and teachers' daily inculcation and what they saw as "incorrect" in real life. The amusing story of Teacher Meifang's five-year-old son shows how the child as an intentional social agent adds to the complexity of the dissonance between ideology and reality.

My husband was attending a driving school so that he can get a driver's license in Shanghai. The other day the three of us (me, husband, and son) went out, and my husband thought of buying two big packs of cigarettes as a gift for his teacher in the driving school. My son immediately asked: "Isn't it that smoking is harmful to health?" He thought the cigarettes were for father himself, so he said to father: "You can't smoke! My teacher said: 'Smoking is harmful to health'!" Father tried to explain: "No, these cigarettes are not for me. It's a gift for someone else." My son got even more angry: "How can you give cigarettes to others? Aren't you harming others?" His logic was very clear and his comments left his father speechless. Since the gift-giving thing was too complicated to explain to my son,[9] father paused for a while and explained: "I am not harming him. He actually likes smoking." My son was so annoyed and stuck to his own logic: "Even if he likes smoking, you cannot give him cigarettes! You should tell him smoking is harmful!" Sitting beside him, I tapped his shoulder, implying that he should stop talking.

We thought this was over and my son would not bring up this topic again. But two days later, something completely embarrassing happened. At school, my son's teacher was talking to the class about issues related to health. She asked the children if they had witnessed anything bad to health. My son stood up and said: "Teacher, my father just did something really bad. Although he knew that smoking was harmful to health, he still bought two big packs of cigarettes and gave them as a gift to someone else. It's bad because it is harmful to other people's health."

He explained the whole story to the teacher and also told me about it when I picked him up at school that day. I asked him: "What did your teacher say?" He said: "Teacher said: You should criticize your father after you go home. What he did was wrong and he deserves criticism!"

This small incident led me think a lot about how to educate the child. One issue is the popular gift-giving (*song li*) trend among adults. The other is the notion that smoking is harmful to health. He was very confused when the two issues came together. And it was really hard to explain the issues to him because he was too young to understand the complexity. The correct way to solve this problem then, I believe, is not to explain these. Instead, when my son first brought up the notion that smoking was harmful, my husband should have responded in much simpler terms: "OK. Daddy will not smoke anymore." He shouldn't have said: "These cigarettes are not for me. They are for someone else." It was too complicated, and my son was too young to understand it.

Teacher Meifang and I both laughed when talking about this amusing story. The multiple ironies that involve teachers, parents, and children made the story an interesting case to present. The story reveals what Meifang called the "popular gift-giving (*song li*) trend" in the adult world. At school, Teacher Meifang emphasized that she tried to be fair with all her students and she had rejected particular parents' request for favoring their children (such as the incident in which Xinwen's mother wanted Meifang to add Xinwen to the dance performance). Just as she mentioned, however, in real life one faced numerous situations where gift giving was necessary and subtle. For example, when they first moved to Shanghai from the northeastern city Qingdao, they didn't have a Shanghai *hukou* (household registration record), so their son was not qualified to go to the public preschool. How did her son eventually get into the public preschool? She told me that her husband had some connections and gave the director a big red envelope (*hong bao*)[10] of more than RMB 10,000 (equivalent of $2,000 in purchasing power)—a standard amount of gift-giving exchange for a spot in a good public preschool. In this story, that her husband wanted to buy two big packages of cigarettes for his driving-school teacher was not extraordinary at all. It is an open secret, or, to use a popular Chinese term, *hidden rule* (*qian guize*), that one has to give gifts or money to the driving-school teachers from time to time, otherwise one would not get any useful training or pass the exam at all. It's ironic that no one likes bribery if it's not necessary, but no one can escape from it if bribery is necessary.

There is also an ironic incongruity between the ideology that smoking is harmful to health and the reality that cigarettes were a good candidate for gift giving. For young children whose only understanding of cigarettes was the meaning of it being harmful, he couldn't make sense of why father wanted to buy cigarettes in the first place.

These anecdotes illustrate the gap between adults' intentions and knowledge, which are congruent with their own life experiences, and children's intentions and knowledge based on their own limited experiences. In this specific story, Meifang and her husband could not explain to her son in justifiable terms why they needed to give some gifts to the driving-school teacher.[11] Thus, her son remained really puzzled about why father wanted to give "bad" gifts (cigarettes), which might harm other people. In this story, the act of gift giving for future favor, according to adults' framework, becomes one of harming others in children's eyes. When the dissonance between what adults teach/advocate and what they do in real life interweaves into interactions with children, children themselves will sometimes become disoriented. This then requires adults to work on reconciling and reharmonizing the old/"sophisticated" and the young/"naive."

Despair and Cynicism: Cultivating a Moral Person in an Immoral World?

All these cases of disorientation between conflicting values and dissonance between ideology and reality grow out of a fundamental tension between becoming a moral versus a successful person. In any given society, becoming a moral person does not necessarily contradict the prospect of achieving success, nor do the two necessarily align perfectly well. For socializers in urban Shanghai, China, however, the fears loom large. A moral person will not fit into a cruel society, will be exploited by the majority who adopt the immoral strategies, and will eventually become a loser in the future—a cost that is too high for the child and for his or her family. Caught up in this "prisoner's dilemma" situation, many parents become cynical about the value of moral education and even the possibility of moral education, as well as despair for the future of Chinese education and the society.

One day after a parents' meeting at Biyu in October 2011, I ran into the father of Gewu, a six-year-old boy who was seen by all people as abnormal because he started speaking really late, and he was mentally slower and emotionally too sensitive compared to most other children. But after days of observation, I actually found this child adorable because he was kind-hearted and affectionate. I thus greeted Gewu's father and told him: "Your son is a very nice child. He is very kind-hearted." But his father sighed and said with frustration: "But a kind-hearted person cannot survive in today's society!" I was surprised by his reaction. But it turned out that, for many parents, cultivating a virtuous person (such as a kind-hearted one) seemed to be at odds with survival of the fittest in this society. Hence moral education in itself is not a totally rational strategy, if not a completely unnecessary endeavor.

Parents find it hard to reconcile the two visions: cultivation of moral character and survival of the fittest in a dangerous society. The tension emerged frequently in my conversation with parents and teachers, between the childish trait of being "naive and innocent" (*tian zhen*) and "simple and pure" (*dan chun*) and the adult-like trait of being calculating (*suan ji*) and scheming (*xin ji*). Parents and teachers hold the ideal that children should be simple, pure, honest, and innocent because children are supposed to be angel-like little creatures whose original good and mysterious nature has not been tainted by the polluted (*wu zhuo*) society. In their daily interactions with children, they often express their affection for those children who they see as innocent and pure. On the other hand, they fear that such children will be unable to adapt to the complicated and a lot of times treacherous society when they grow up. And, without doubt, all parents hope their children will be promising and full of potential (*you chu xi*),[12] a term that represents parents and teachers' hope for their children being successful in the future. Some young children are mature beyond their age (*zao shu*)—already showing signs of being calculative and even scheming. Paradoxically, most parents and teachers predict that it is precisely these children who will be able to survive and succeed in navigating the ominous society.

Dilemmas like this abound in multiple domains of moral education, and some parents become extremely cynical about the current educational scene. They worry that seemingly virtuous behaviors might be interpreted as being motivated by bad intentions or having evil ramifications, and thus moral education is doomed to be "mission impossible." With such concerns, some parents become desperate that the future of their own children and nation is nothing but gloomy. Maomao's father is a typical example. His marriage was severely disapproved of by his in-laws for the reason that he was not a native Shanghainese and didn't have much money. He eventually got to marry Maomao's mom, and his own mother stayed with them to take care of Maomao. He turned out to be very cynical and even resentful about the official idea of moral education and concluded that it is essentially paradoxical for children to become "good" in an evil society.

> When Maomao was born, we didn't have much money. My in-laws didn't want me to marry their daughter, simply because I didn't have Shanghai *hukou* (household registration identity). Actually, my in-laws aren't native Shanghainese, either. They moved to Shanghai before my wife was born. So my wife is a "new Shanghainese." My in-laws looked down upon me, and even until now they don't acknowledge me as their son-in-law, nor do they see Maomao as their grandson. In addition to the tension between my in-laws and me, my wife didn't get along well with my mother, either, during her pregnancy. My wife had postpartum depression. So it has been very hard on me, trying to reconcile the relationship between my wife and my mother. I had to sacrifice my career to some extent, for my family. I had to spend more time at home, taking care of the child, my mother, my wife, and [doing] housework (My mother is very old, and I don't want her to do too much housework.) For the past three years, I [have been] constantly anxious and couldn't sleep well.

Maomao's father is also pessimistic about society's morals and the prospect of moral education:

> Chinese official ideology is all about moral education. For instance, they advocate that children should learn and recite the "Three Characters Classic" (*san zi jing*). But you see, the society is so immoral. What an irony! The result of such a contrast is that, every family, no matter rich or poor, now lives in a strange condition, and everyone's mind/heart (*xinling*) is distorted. All the parents are busy with making money, and they are not happy. They cannot make their children happy, either. Moral senses can only be cultivated when both children and parents are happy together. But when everyone is so stressed under the pressure of making money, no one cares about morality. Even the most natural and intimate relationships are destroyed. And parents only care about pushing children to study and study and realize their dream of upward mobility (*"li yu tiao long men"*). Under such circumstances, moral education is doomed to fail!

Maomao's father is not the only one who realizes the paradoxical situation of cultivating morality in a world perceived as immoral. But when most other parents choose to reconcile the ideal with the reality through various ironic strategies, as Hans Steinmüller puts it, such as saying one thing but implying something else, or modifying one's beliefs, or teaching some ideals while doing something pragmatic (Steinmüller 2013), this father chose a more radical way. He is the only parent of Biyu Preschool I know so far who became a stay-at-home father and homeschooled Maomao, a very rare arrangement among urban Chinese families. Despite all the hardships he went through because he didn't earn as much money as others expected, he still chose to quit his job, without conforming to the predominant *gongli* social norms. Despite all the difficulties against a wholesome moral development in the educational system and the broader society, he still wanted to raise his son to be as happy and nice as possible, through homeschooling. Perhaps deep inside his heart, hope emerged out of despair and cynicism.

Cultivating Morality in a Changing Moral Landscape

China's rapid social transformations are accompanied with tremendous uncertainties and costs to individual self-cultivation, a foundational theme in Chinese thinking. Although this chapter demonstrates the ever-increasing parental aspirations of China's emerging middle class, it also delves into the growing pains from China's rapid rise, by examining the confusions, struggles, and coping strategies today's parents, educators, and children in China are experiencing. Yunxiang Yan calls for delving into China's changing moral landscape (2011) and coins the term *the striving individual* to characterize Chinese people today who are "driven by the urge to succeed or the fear of failure or the combination of both," and the striving individual is caught up in "the entanglement of different value systems" (Yan 2013:282). The striving individual in a changing Chinese moral landscape can be seen in various domains of contemporary Chinese social life. Child-rearing/education is definitely one important domain to examine because the success and well-being of children—most of whom are the family's "only hope"—are what parents are striving for above all.

Teresa Kuan demonstrates that, for parents in Kunming, southwest China, "There is one central question that informs the work of parenting: in the future, will there be a place for my child in society?" (Kuan 2008: 2). The same applies to parents in my research, and it is played out in even more intense ways in Shanghai. The various dreams and struggles of parents and teachers documented in this chapter, against the dismaying backdrop of the Shanghainese moral ecology, paint a picture of the quandary of cultivating morality among the "little emperors" in a perceived immoral world. Given the basic consensus that cultivating morality in early childhood is an important mission in itself, parents and teachers complain a lot about the competition, stress, materialism, and pragmatism of educational mentalities in Shanghai. Caught up in the fundamental quandary between shaping a moral person and forging a future winner, they have to adopt a variety of strategies to cope with this conundrum. Based on his fieldwork on work, family, and the state in rural China, Hans Steinmüller finds that those who are confronted with tensions between "the expected and the experienced, the categorical and the contingent, the official and the vernacular" often resort to "ironic strategies" (Steinmüller 2013:134). He also distinguishes cynicism from irony, as the former is "more radical and exclusive (and therefore susceptible to rejection), whereas the other is more gentle and inclusive" (Steinmüller 2011: 29). How Shanghainese socializers cope with moral education dilemmas can also be interpreted as ironic strategies that display a large continuum ranging from the more inclusive tactics, such as saying one thing but doing another, to the more exclusive sentiments of cynicism and despair.

This chapter provides an overview of the cultural settings, adult ideologies, and quandaries of moral education and development. Subsequent chapters delve into the children's world, explore how children navigate the social world, and examine how the tensions in moral education impact children's own moral experiences.

2 Feeling into Another's Heart: When Empathy Is Endangered

The Dilemma of "Being Nice"

On May 31, 2012, Biyu Preschool held a party to celebrate the Chinese "Children's Day" (June 1). Every class presented two to three short collective performances (three to five minutes each), while teachers, students, and parents were all sitting there to watch. It was time for Class 1A's boys to proceed onto the stage and present their dance, when something unexpected happened. Hanhan, who was supposed to lead the dance, suddenly burst into tears. Perhaps he was overwhelmed by the crowd of the audience and felt insecure, or he saw his mother and grandmother nearby and wanted their company. Laughter spread through the audience, and Hanhan cried even harder. He stopped walking and stayed at the margin of the stage, instead of finding his spot in the front center. The teacher was busy guiding the other children to find their spots on the stage, and all the other children were focused on themselves, nervously walking on the stage and eagerly looking for their parents in the audience. Nobody came to console Hanhan, except one boy, Junjun. When he found Hanhan was crying, Junjun immediately went over to hold his hand and talk to him. Hanhan cried all the way throughout the three-minute dance at the margin of the stage, and Junjun, while dancing in front of him, glanced back to him once in a while with a compassionate look.

This small incident spurred an online discussion among the teachers and parents. One father posted an entry on his blog about this incident and highlighted Junjun's altruistic action: "It was Junjun's simple action of holding Hanhan's hands that truly surprised me and touched me. What a good boy! Junjun is exceptional! At such a young age, he knows how to help and encourage other children. There is 'Great Love' (*da ai*) in his heart." At the same time, he reflected: "Thinking through what happened today, I suddenly realized my failure and blamed myself: What a bad job I did! Why didn't I teach my own son, Maomao, to do the same as Junjun did today?"

Teacher Fanglin posted a reply: "Indeed, a lot of times children's behaviors have kindled reflections on my own life, work, and even human life. Junjun is always so pure (*chun*), innocent, and lovely, but his kindness never gets a reward. Sometimes I am very concerned about him. Children like Junjun are so pure and have no intention to harm others. What will he face in the future when he grows up? I am worried that he will be taken advantage of by others." Fanglin's comment reflects the deep anxieties among parents and educators about what a nice and kindhearted child might encounter in a society full of danger, threats, and injustice. The depressing prospect of a kindhearted child's failure in an immoral society looms large for these future-oriented parents and teachers. Struggling to work out a feasible plan in order to raise a child well-equipped for a perilous society, they find themselves caught up in an almost self-contradictory situation: On the one hand, qualities such as empathy and compassion are deemed precious by most teachers and parents. For example, Junjun was Teacher Fanglin's beloved student, precisely because he was "pure," "innocent," and "nice," to use Fanglin's own words. The perception is that in today's China, these qualities are lacking, especially empathy—the ability to feel with others, or in Chinese terms, to "feel into another's heart" (*jiang xin bi xin*). On the other hand, parents are conscious of the overwhelming uncertainties and complexities these children will face when they grow up.

The case of Junjun, along with the adults' comments, urged me to think about the development of fundamental human moral qualities such as empathy—the capacity to "feel into another's heart"—in the Chinese context. The centrality of empathy and care in the Chinese view of human morality can be traced back to ancient Confucian philosophy (Slote 2010), and findings from contemporary cognitive sciences suggest that the early Confucians are on the right track (Wong 2015). Recent research proposes that the morality of care is one of the human species' moral "taste buds" (Haidt 2012), adapted for caregiver-child attachment and extended to broader social relationships, and empathy/compassion is the characteristic emotion of care (Mageo 2011). This chapter brings together ancient Confucian thoughts and recent Western scholarship on empathy and builds on the theoretical insights in those two convergent streams of thought to analyze Biyun Preschool's empathy education, situated as it is in the broader discussion on the "moral crisis" in Chinese society. Specifically, this chapter examines the following questions: What happened to China, and why do parents and teachers all bemoan the lack of love and the rising of dangers in contemporary social life? What tensions and contradictions of empathy education emerge, and how are they manifest in pedagogical practices? How do children navigate such tensions and contradictions in the ceaseless flow of educational interactions with parents, teachers, and peers?

From Mencius to Rediscovering Empathy

The "Child-in-the-Well" Story

> Everyone has a heart that cannot bear to see others suffer. The ancient emperors had hearts that couldn't bear to see others suffer; and so had governments that couldn't bear to see others suffer. If you lead a government that can't bear to see others suffer, ruling all beneath Heaven is like turning it in the palm of your hand. Suddenly seeing a baby about to fall into a well, anyone would be heart-stricken with pity: heart-stricken not because they wanted to curry favor with the baby's parents, not because they wanted the praise of neighbors and friends, and not because they hated the baby's cries. This is why I say everyone has a heart that can't bear to see others suffer.
>
> Mencius 2A: 6 (Mencius 1998: 55)

This "Child-in-the-Well" story is a famous example to illustrate Mencius's view that "there is in human nature a proclivity or inclination towards goodness"1 (Allinson 1992: 298). Mencius (fourth century BCE), the "second saint" (*ya sheng*), second only to Confucius in Chinese history, claims that *ce yin zhi xin* (a heart sensitive to others' misery) is the seed of *ren*—a key concept in Confucian ethics, referring specifically to benevolence/love/compassion, or broadly to humanity. The famous neo-Confucian master Wang Yangming interpreted this story in his text *Questions on the Great Learning*: "This is why, when they see a child [about to] fall into a well, they cannot avoid having a sense of alarm and concern for the child. This is because their benevolence forms one body with the child" (Ivanhoe 2009: 161). Wang's theory highlights what remained implicit in Mencius's writings, "forming one body (*yi ti*) with others," that is, the metaphysical oneness with others, and this is what we now call "empathy" (Slote 2010: 304) in Western academic discourse. In this statement, Wang emphasizes that the capacity to "form one body" with others in suffering is universal human nature, that both a great person (*da ren*) and a petty person (*xiao ren*) possess it, and the difference between the two kinds of people is the way they look at things, not the basic capacity (Ivanhoe 2009:161).[2] Along the same line, the folk phrase "feel into another's heart" (*jiang xin bi xin*) indicates a Chinese interpretation of empathy that focuses on understanding the other's situation and feeling into the other's emotional states.

This classical Chinese view of empathy, especially the "Child-in-the-Well" story by Mencius, ingeniously captures the key issues in contemporary scholarship on empathy. Contemporary Western scholars have just begun to go beyond philosophical ruminations and investigate empathy as an empirical topic in psychology (Batson 2009), neuroscience (Singer and Lamm 2009), evolutionary biology and biological anthropology (de Waal 2008; Hrdy 2011), and most recently in cultural anthropology, too (Hollan and Throop 2008).

What Mencius calls "heart stricken" aptly illustrates that emotional response is an important characteristic of empathy. The emotional nature of empathy is highlighted by neuroscientists: "An affective response to the directly perceived, imagined, or inferred feeling state of another being" (Singer and Lamm 2009: 82). "Everyone has a heart" of empathy indicates its natural and universal basis, and evolutionary studies suggest that humans are biologically prepared for emotional connections with fellows.

Empathy, however, is more than automatic emotional responses: it is a complex, flexible process that is situated in intersubjective exchanges. That human beings "can't bear to see others suffer" in the Mencian view points to this dimension of empathy, corroborated by social neuroscience findings suggesting empathic responses are modulated by a variety of social factors (for a review, see Singer and Lamm 2009).

Moreover, the emotional and motivational forces of empathy make it a powerful candidate in explaining why one would help another in need (directed altruism) (de Waal 2008). Mencius's thinking is still relevant here: People are "heart-stricken not because they wanted to curry favor with the baby's parents, not because they wanted the praise of neighbors and friends, and not because they hated the baby's cries." Empathy suggests a genuine concern for others, instead of reducing one's own distress or other strategic concerns for gaining favors or building reputation. A heart of genuine concern for others, however, is only an inclination, and an inclination might not necessarily translate into actual behavior. Francis de Waal (2008) argues that empathy does not automatically lead to unconditional altruism, but also involves rational assessment with regard to social distance/relationships, cooperation history, reputation, and so forth.

In addition, empathy is configured and mediated in specific cultural contexts (Engelen and Röttger-Rössler 2012; Hollan and Throop, 2011), and it is never value-free, but always operates within a specific moral order (Hollan and Throop 2008). In the Chinese cultural traditions, virtue is perfectible, the seed of empathy needs to be nurtured through education, and the virtue of empathy is directly connected to social order. For example, in the beginning of the "Child-in-the-Well" story, Mencius argues that a compassionate heart is crucial for smooth and efficient governance: "We all possess these four seeds,[3] and if we all understand how to nurture them, it will be like fire blazing forth or springs flooding free. Nurtured, they're enough to watch over all within the four seas. Un-nurtured, they aren't enough to serve even our own parents" (Mencius 2A: 6).

These key insights in recent studies on empathy, such as tensions between emotion and cognition, between empathic feelings and altruistic actions, and between basic moral propensity and social cultural order, not only speak to ancient Chinese thinking, but also provide theoretical lenses through which to understand contemporary Chinese dilemmas regarding empathy education and development.

Developmental Roots and Routes

Recent findings in psychology and neuroscience highlight the early ontogeny of empathy and feature child development as an important window through which to examine all of the aforementioned aspects of empathy. First, recent research suggests that preliminary forms of empathy already exist in babies (Saby, Meltzoff, and Marshall 2013; Meltzoff 2002), and empathic responses increase throughout infancy (for a review, see Davidov et al. 2013). Second, affective aspects of empathy develop earlier in ontogeny, while the cognitive elements of empathy, such as control and response inhibition, develop later and weigh in as children grow (Decety and Howard 2013). Third, even young children do not just automatically empathize and intervene indiscriminately; they rely on different contextual cues to help them make sense of what's happening and in turn to make decisions (Hepach et al. 2013b; Vaish et al. 2009).

Moreover, empathy is cultivated through culturally specific educational practices from early in life, and children's developmental experience has profound implications on the intricate relationships between empathy and morality. For example, cross-cultural psychological studies find "culturally specific developmental pathways" to prosocial behavior: in cultures emphasizing autonomy and self-other differentiation, young children's helping behavior is more motivated by empathic concerns; in cultures emphasizing interdependence and obedience, the same helping behavior is more motivated by shared intentional relations (Kärtner, Keller, and Chaudhary 2010; Kärtner and Keller 2012).

In contrast to the psychological literature, the ontogeny of empathy is relatively a new topic in the emerging anthropological literature (for a few studies, see Mageo 2011; Hayashi, Karasawa, and Tobin 2009). This chapter aims to bridge that gap by using the key theoretical tools the psychological literature offers, such as empathy and altruism, and emotion (sensibilities) and cognition (senses), to analyze the ethnographic evidence on empathy education of young children in China.

Basic Humanity in a Callous Society: The Case of "Little Yueyue"

A few months after I started my fieldwork, the heart-breaking story of a toddler girl named "Little Yueyue" shocked the whole nation, posed a stark contrast to the "Child-in-the-Well" story depicted by Mencius, and led Chinese people to lament that even basic humanity is being compromised in contemporary China. Yueyue was a two-year-old girl whose parents owned a small shop in a hardware market in Foshan city, Guangdong province. On October 13, 2011, a rainy afternoon, when Little Yueyue was playing in a narrow street in the hardware market, a running van hit her in the middle of the road, and the driver fled away. The whole incident was captured by a surveillance camera in a shop near the accident spot and later aired by Southern Television Guangdong (TVS). According to the camera, it was 17:25 local time when the van hit Yueyue. Several people passed by, saw the little girl struggling, but didn't do anything to help. Forty seconds after being hit by a van, Yueyue was hit by another small truck. After this, several more people passed by and neglected the dying child. The camera recorded a total of eighteen bystanders who saw Yueyue but didn't do anything. Finally, at 17:31, an old woman found Yueyue, moved her to the curb, and eagerly asked around for help. Half a minute later, Yueyue's mother came, cried out, and sent her to the hospital. Seven days later, little Yueyue died.

During mid-October, the case of "Little Yueyue" was the headline of many Chinese newspapers, the focus of Internet discussion, and even covered in major foreign media. This incident set off nationwide "soul-searching in China" (Wines 2011a), and people were asking themselves: "Has China become a callous society, and why?" My aim here is not to answer this sharp ethical question or to provide a comprehensive, multilayered analysis of the reasons and consequences of this accident. Rather, by analyzing people's reaction to this incident, I hope to provide an example to illuminate why Biyu Preschool parents' and teachers' perceive Chinese society as a dangerous place, a place that negates the practical value of empathy and altruism in real life.

The significance of this case is indicated by its salience in public and social media, as well as the pervasive reactions it activated among Chinese people. We all know that cases such as the Little Yueyue incident are extraordinary and abnormal by nature. Just as Yunxiang Yan (2011) argues, discussing events in which a Good Samaritan was exploited by those he helped, "Even if these cases do not happen very often, the fact that they receive so much media attention in today's information society is indicative of their perceived importance and gives them a much greater impact on the minds and behavior of ordinary people" (p. 11). Actually, just a few days after the Little Yueyue incident, CCTV—China's central government TV agency—reported a contrasting case: a little girl in Nanchang city, Jiangxi province, was caught under a truck, but was then quickly rescued by passersby. This positive news did not change the public's perception of Chinese moral decline, though. Not only did it receive little attention from the public compared to that of the Little Yueyue case, but the only reaction to it was criticism against CCTV for not covering the Little Yueyue incident that everyone was concerned about.[4] In this regard, the Little Yueyue case provides a significant example to better understand Chinese people's perceptions and sentiments over the so-called moral crisis, and in turn to discern the complexities of China's "changing moral landscape" (Yan 2009, 2011).

Notably, the public outcry over this incident centered around the bystanders' indifference toward the dying little girl (Ye and Shen 2011). According to a *New York Times* article, within a week after the incident, tens of millions of people had posted comments through microblogs, and in an online survey conducted by the website ifeng.com—a branch of the Hong Kong–based Phoenix media—"some 170,000 respondents, who voted on their own initiative, judged by a wide margin that the toddler's case was proof that the Chinese people's morals and mutual trust were eroding under the pressures of modern society" (Wines 2011b). The very fact that bystanders' apathy became the target of public opinion, and such apathy, interpreted in a moralizing framework, was seen as a symptom of much broader and fundamental social ills, is worthy of closer analysis.

These bystanders, as recorded in the video, became the targets of search by journalists and ordinary people. According to some journalists' investigation (Huang et al. 2011), some of the bystanders escaped and shunned interviews, and some denied they had ever noticed Yueyue at that time. Among the eighteen people, only one woman spoke out about her thoughts when she saw

Yueyue, as she was taking her own five-year-old daughter back home: "I saw a little girl lying on the ground, crying. So I went to a nearby shop and asked a young man if the girl was his daughter, but he said no. Even he did not dare to move the little girl. How could I?" After being identified, these people were all attacked and condemned on the Internet by microbloggers.

Later on, people attempted to dig out the truth, develop a more comprehensive reading of this incident, and reflect on the dangers and biases of the overwhelming moral condemnation of bystanders. As a result, all kinds of psychological, sociological, legal, and historical arguments emerged, pointing to broader societal issues. For example, in a well-organized television debate by Phoenix TV, scholars and freelancers voiced their diverse opinions.[5] Some used the famous case of Kitty Genovese (Gansberg 1964) to illustrate the classic bystanders effect that occurs in modern urban life, calling attention to the universal psychological mechanisms and cautioning against a moralizing interpretation of Chinese society. Some called for self-reflection on the dark side of human nature: what one would do in the same situation might not be different from those indifferent bystanders. Some questioned the parents who neglected their daughter's safety and pointed out missing holes in the Chinese legal system for child protection. Similar to what Yunxiang Yan disentangles in his analysis of Good Samaritans getting extorted (Yan 2009), various contributing factors were pointed out by commentators, such as media reports that exaggerated negative incidents and spread distrust, problems of the legal system in protecting helpers' rights, social injustice in China in the midst of social change that deprived people of basic means and generated resentment, and structural problems in the transition from a traditional society to a strangers' society.

On the one hand, all these well-reasoned analyses did reflect empathic thinking toward people in situations of ethical decisions. On the other hand, one had to realize that the outrage on the Internet was not simply directed to the eighteen bystanders in the Little Yueyue case, but rather, to the (imagined) dismaying picture of human conditions in Chinese society of which everyone was a part. The negative moralizing tendency, to interpret an incident as a result of immoral intentions (such as the perception that strangers are not trustworthy and that the bystanders intentionally neglected the one in need of help) and to link an individual incident to the broader social problems, seems to have become a common sense, default schema, or "cultural model" (Strauss and Quinn 1997) in contemporary China.

Among all the well-known incidents that mobilized people's sentiments and judgments into a discourse of China's moral decay, such as the food safety crisis (Yan 2012), the Good Samaritans being extorted (Yan 2009), and so forth, the case of Little Yueyue was distinctive. This case revealed, according to many Chinese people, a breakdown of basic humanity, and an example of natural moral inclination being polluted or inhibited in social life. Against the various excuses some people found for inaction in this incident, such as institutional and structural problems, well-known microblogger Ran Xiang commented in a television debate hosted by Phoenix TV: "Do we need the government to tell us what is the right thing to do when we see a two-year-old little girl lying in blood?"[6] The implication is that, whatever the excuse is, inaction in such a tragic situation is a violation of basic humanity. The point of this comment, however, was not to criticize other people's moral standards. Instead, it instigated a wave of self-reflection. As a *Southern Weekly* article (Ye and Shen 2011) summarized: " 'The death of Little Yueyue posed a cruel lesson to the public. People began to think about these questions: 'What would I do, if I were one of the passersby? What if the girl lying on the ground were my own child?' Or 'If I were Little Yueyue, what kind of pain and despair would I suffer?' "

Something unique to the Little Yueyue case was the contrast between eighteen indifferent bystanders and one compassionate woman who rescued Yueyue without hesitation. Chen Xianmei was a fifty-eight-year-old waste collector and the nineteenth passerby in this incident. She soon became a symbol for the light of humanity amid the dark immoralities in China. The heroic old lady Chen was selected as one of the "yearly focus figures" by *Southern Weekly* (*Nanfang Zhoumo*)—China's most renowned liberal newspaper. A feature article told the behind-the-scene story of her (Ye and Shen 2011). When feted by the crowds as a hero, she responded with reluctance: "I just did what a normal human being ought to do." Facing the repeated question "Why did you help Yueyue?" she said: "At that moment I just did it, without thinking. There's nothing more to say about it." On October 21, Yueyue died. Chen couldn't sleep that night, preoccupied by the image of miserable Yueyue lying in blood. She recalled the scenario: "At that time (when I saw Yueyue), I cried out desperately, but nobody cared about it, and someone even told me not to meddle in other's affairs (*duo guan xian shi*)." She couldn't make sense of what happened: "I don't understand: Why didn't they (the other passersby) do something to help this poor little girl? Were they truly too busy to lend a hand?" According to her acquaintants, Chen was well known in her original village for being nice and altruistic. When she was young, she once jumped into a river to save two children. She was always ready to help others in need. The television news of Peng Yu (the Good Samaritan who was extorted by the elderly person he helped) did bother her, and her husband had to explain to her: "That's what happens in the city, not the countryside." Later on she moved to the city, and she again did something that's not "normal" in this era: in 2007, when she saw an elderly man who fell on the street, his legs bleeding, she did not hesitate to assist him, unlike the typical, cautious people who avoid helping others in the name of escaping from potential exploitation.

In an article titled "The Death of Little Yueyue Makes Mencius Speechless" (*xiao yueyue zhi si rang Mengzi wu yu*) (Zhang 2011), a law professor at Peking University commented on this incident with a sarcastic tone: "She (Chen Xianmei) became a contemporary moral exemplar, just because she did something that should be done, according to Mencius, by every human being. I don't know if the 18 passers-by inhibited their impulse to save Yueyue because they were concerned about the risk of being extorted, or they never had the impulse to help. In any case, their inaction denied Mencius' self-evident truth." According to Zhang, people's cynicism went even further: The very reason Chen dared to act in that situation was because she was poor and had nothing to lose and no risk of extortion. Did the inaction of the eighteen passersby result from a lack of compassionate impulse, or was it the triumph of rational calculation over instinctive feelings, as Zhang asked? Can we discern if Chen had done any risk-benefit analysis before rescuing the little girl? This story could have many versions of why the eighteen bystanders didn't act and why Chen acted way the way she did, and no one was able to claim which version was more truthful. But the kind of controversy around this case was precisely the reason why it generated heated discussion across the whole nation.

Public attention given to the Little Yueyue case focused on the contrast between the bystanders' callous inaction and Chen Xianmei's instinctive action, instead of other factors such as the careless parents, the irresponsible drivers, and so forth. This very fact reflects the deep discontent, anxieties, and fear of Chinese people over the imagined or real loss of basic morality—such as empathy and compassion—in contemporary Chinese social life, as interpersonal trust has been endangered amid the rapid social and moral transformations and empathic feelings conflict with self-interest.

Ambivalent Education of Empathy:
The Difficult Path to Altruism

The picture of a callous society, amplified through public discourse around incidents like the Little Yueyue case, is the cultural context for empathy education in China. The topic of empathy education harks back to Mencius again, not only because he highlights the "Child-in-the-Well" scenario. More importantly, he believes that virtue is perfectible, that the seed of empathy needs to be "nurtured" through education, and that the virtue of empathy is directly connected to social order. In the beginning of the "Child-in-the-Well" story, Mencius argues that a compassionate heart is crucial for smooth and efficient governance. Mencius believes every human being possesses these four basic moral senses: *ce yin zhi xin* (a heart of compassion), *xiu wu zhi xin* (a heart of shame and disgust), *li rang zhi xin* (a heart of courtesy and propriety), and *shi fei zhi xin* (a heart of right and wrong). Moreover, he believes that moral education is crucial and that cultivating a full-fledged morality through moral education is crucial for building an ideal society: "We all possess these four seeds, and if we all understand how to nurture them, it will be like fire blazing forth or springs flooding free. Nurtured, they're enough to watch over all within the four seas. Un-nurtured, they aren't enough to serve even our own parents" (Mencius 2A: 6).

This classical Chinese view of empathy education is echoed among my informants, but also encounters great challenges. On the one hand, even two-year-old children at Biyu Preschool learn to memorize the "Three Characters Classic" (*san zi jing*), reciting "people at birth are naturally good" (*ren zhi chu, xing ben shan*). On the other hand, parents and teachers of Biyu Preschool were shocked by the Little Yueyue case and shared their concerns and reflections with me.

A young teacher expressed her desperate pessimism: "I used to believe in our Confucian teachings that human beings are born to be good. But after more and more incidents like the 'Little Yueyue' case, I became skeptical about it. I would not blame those bystanders. Honestly, who knows what one would do in such situations. I now more and more believe that human beings are born to be evil." Although her attitude seems extreme, and in real life she still strives for cultivating goodness among her students, such comments nevertheless reflect her feelings of confusion and disappointment.

These perceptions reflect a key challenge that caregivers and educators face: Should one teach his or her own child to be nice, loving, and empathic toward others in a perceived selfish and callous world? What adds to the anxieties about this callous society is a concern for the consequences of the one-child policy, that single children tend to be self-centered, having no concerns for others. These factors make the education of empathy a very ambiguous, even self-contradictory endeavor: In the milieu of Biyu Preschool, teachers and parents see empathy as the foundation of virtues such as altruism, respect for others, and so on. The cultivation of empathy is considered an urgent task for the self-centered singleton children. Therefore, the educators attempt to make the classroom into a good environment for the development of empathy and use a variety of pedagogical methods to instill among the young children a genuine sense of love and concern for their peers, teachers, and parents. When it comes to situations and problems outside the immediate classroom context, however, the sense of empathy and concern for others is often deemed less important or valuable given the risks of being exploited.

The Nascent Empathy: Interweaving Senses and Sensibilities

In my child-rearing questionnaire, the first question in the section of "Children's Social Moral Development" is about the traditional Chinese view of the original goodness of human nature: "Do you agree with the view that 'People at birth are naturally good'?" The five answers are as follows:

A. Completely agree
B. Pretty much agree
C. Neutral
D. Disagree
E. Completely disagree

A (completely agree) was the most popular answer among the eighty-seven parents who responded to this question [40 percent]. Added together, 64 percent of the parents endorsed this "good-natured" view, choosing A (completely agree) or B (pretty much agree).

Within the Confucian tradition, the quote "people at birth are naturally good" is a well-known saying; it is the first sentence in the "Three Characters Classic" (*san zi jing*), a text taught to young children since late imperial times. Biyu Preschool also uses this text in the youngest grade, the nursery class,

Table 2.1 Child-Rearing Questionnaire: Biyu Preschool Parents'
Beliefs about the Original Goodness of Human Nature

Answers	Number of respondents	Percentage
A. Completely agree	34	40%
B. Pretty much agree	21	24%
C. Neutral	20	23%
D. Disagree	11	13%
E. Completely disagree	1	6%

and teaches little children to recite the sentences on a daily basis. Not only do a majority of parents share this belief that children are born to be good, teachers also believe these young children have some inborn moral capacities and that empathy is a typical one. In this section, I will demonstrate how both "basic empathy" and "complex empathy" are construed in the context of Biyu Preschool and how sensibilities (emotional sensitivity) and senses (cognitive orientations) are interwoven in children's developmental processes.

"Basic Empathy"[7] in the Chinese Context: Tacit Transparency, Emotional Sensitivity, and Vulnerability

One of the teachers used the word *tong* to describe young children's basic capacity to detect, feel, and understand others' emotional states. This word literally means "inter-connected," as two rooms are connected so that one can freely enter one room from the other. When used to describe psychological phenomena, it means that two hearts/minds are so transparent to each other that one does not even need explicit explanations to feel with and into the other one's mental and emotional states. I call it "tacit transparency." This highlights the conception of empathy as beneath the level of human language, as an automatic reaction in a fundamentally existential sense. There are numerous Chinese terms that express this sense of tacit transparency, such as "heart to heart/hearts connected" (*xinling xiang tong*) and "two hearts beat in one unison" (*xin you ling xi*).[8]

Nonetheless, in the eyes of parents and teachers, the nascent and precious empathy of these young children is vulnerable because children born under the one-child policy tend to become self-obsessed. Thirty-year-old Teacher Tang (Class 3B), in a private conversation, attributed the high divorce rates and marriage crises in the current generation partly to the one-child policy.

> Once I had a fight with my husband, a very severe fight, almost leading to a divorce. Then a colleague came to comfort me. She was a little bit older than me and had a younger brother. She said: "Why can't you just give in to your husband? He is a singleton child (*dusheng zinv*)." I protested immediately: "How come?! I *am* a singleton too! I am the center of my own family, and everybody listens to me. Why should I give in to him?" See, as that, we were always head to head (*zhenjian dui maiming*). Growing up as an "only child," I feel that people in our generation are not tuned to feel into and care for other people's emotions and moods. Those with siblings are different, at least the ones that I know of. They are much better than us. They know how to give

in and be resilient. We can't humble ourselves. That's why there are so many marital problems.

At first glance, it might sound far-fetched to link marital conflicts to the lack of empathy—to "feel with and care for others"—in the developmental experiences of the only-child generation. That is not a rare view, however. Teacher Tang believed that people growing up as singleton children were less attuned to empathize with others, but so does Teacher Tang's colleague, herself not an only child. That is why she suggested Teacher Tang give in to her husband who was an only child. There is a widespread perception that the only child generation grows up as self-centered and has problems in most intimate social relationships and interactions.

Against the backdrop of such widespread concerns about singleton children's self-centeredness, empathy is construed as a vulnerable thing and therefore highlighted as a precious trait, worthy of educational efforts. Indeed, teachers employed a variety of pedagogical methods with the purpose of nourishing empathy and a concern for others. For example, Momo joined Biyu Preschool in January 2012, as Class 2A's assistant teacher. I interviewed her in July 2012, after she had taught the class for the whole spring semester and successfully established bonds with all of the children in her class. When I asked her what kind of progress her class (age range: 4–4.5) had made in that semester, she immediately said: "A heart of love (*ai xin*), in terms of becoming more sensitive to their own and others' emotions, and getting more attentive and responsive to others' needs."

According to Momo, such progress grew out of positive feedback processes, as empathy was inherently intersubjective and was best nurtured through reciprocal emotional and altruistic exchanges: First, she treated these children with sincere love and encouraged them to love and care for one another. Then, she said, such love and care was reciprocated and reinforced through prosocial interactions. She reflected on how to guide these children to empathize with and eventually care about others, including the teacher herself and peers:

> I think love is the most important guidance. Little by little, they can feel your love and pass on the love to others. I think the most notable progress my students made during this semester is that several of them grew from being apathetic to being extraordinarily compassionate and kind-hearted. Once in a while I will ask them: "Teacher Momo loves you. Do you love me?" They will say: "Yes." One day I was sick, with a serious throat infection, and my voice was hoarse. In class, they were very loud and messy, to the extent that I was sad and

nearly burst into tears. I said to them: "If you continue to be like this, I may cry." I felt so bad, physically and emotionally. But after that, surprisingly, they behaved themselves well the whole afternoon, without making any noise. I think they sensed that I was not well, and they could feel my pain.

In this episode, Momo suggests that children not only detected her emotional states and intentions, but also vicariously *felt* her emotions. In her daily work, she emphasized the emotional aspect of moral education. This was driven by her belief in the important motivational role of empathy in generating a true concern for others and inspiring behaviors such as comforting and helping. Or in other words, she believed that "feeling *with/into* the other" was conducive to "feeling *for* the other," which ultimately led to altruistic actions. That's why she was very proud of the fact that several children in her class who used to be "apathetic" became "compassionate and kind-hearted."

In addition to an emphasis on the affective elements of empathy, she also believed that even for young children, empathy could be powerful enough to trigger sacrificial actions that address other people's needs by inflicting some costs upon oneself. Empathy usually connotes a genuine sense of concern or care for others, encapsulating the primordial elements or foundations of young children's inborn goodness. She mentioned several examples to illustrate how children were compassionate and willing to sacrifice or make compromises in order to help others in need.

For instance, toy disputes happen in classroom frequently. It's normal that nobody, especially children, is willing to give their own favorite toys to others. But when a child cried really heard because he or she didn't get the toy to play, the other child who got the toy would give the toy to that crying child. It was precisely because he or she found that the crying child was so miserable, and such misery ignited his compassion.

Another example was the book donation event.

Once there was a "book donation" event organized by our school to give books to children living in poverty in Xinjiang, a remote ethnic minority province. I told my students: "There are some children in Xinjiang who are really miserable, and they really need your help. Can you bring some books from home tomorrow to donate to them?" The next morning, most children came to classroom with a lot of books, including their own favorites. I was deeply touched. Previously, they would never share some of these books, such as the *Bright Tiger* (*qiao hu*, a popular children's program) books, with their classmates. But this time was different. When they heard that other children were miserable, they pitied those children, and compassion drove them to share their favorite books.

This is striking because what happened in Class 2A poses a stark contrast with an incident in Class 1A at the same event.[9] Children in Class 2A were willing to give their own favorite books to those children in need, whereas some children in Class 1A stubbornly resisted giving unless being threatened by shaming and social exclusion. Tentatively, such a contrast can be explained in the following ways. First, children in Class 2A were generally one year older than those in Class 1A, therefore more mature than the younger ones, both in the cognitive and affective domains. It perhaps made more sense to the older children to donate books to some unknown children far away. Second, in line with her attempts to improve children's emotional sensitivity and concern for others, on this specific occasion, Teacher Momo emphasized the needs and misery of the Xinjiang children. Teacher Fanglin of Class 1A, on the other hand, didn't explain this in specific terms to her students, probably due to a concern that the students were too young to comprehend what was going on.

Empathy and Genuine Concern for Others

In addition to reinforcing practices to cultivate emotional sensitivity among young children as a way to promote altruistic behaviors, teachers also highlight the distinction between the genuine and nongenuine senses of care/love. At Biyu Preschool, Ke'er, a five-and-half year-old girl in Class 4A, is presented as an exemplar for her classmates. The reason is that she was very kind-hearted and "pure and simple" (*dan chun*), as if her inborn good mind/heart had never been polluted by the environment. Meifang, the head teacher of Class 4A, spoke highly of Ke'er:

> Sometimes when the children are playing and I am preparing for classes, most children are completely immersed in their own worlds. But Ke'er will notice I am working and will come to help me in any way she can. It's not that she does it with a purpose. It's just a natural reflection of her kind-heartedness.
>
> One scenario that I remember vividly happened last year, right before the National Day Holidays. Usually, if parents didn't explicitly tell them to do so, young children would not think of saying some holiday greetings to us teachers. But on that afternoon, when I announced the holiday break to the class, Ke'er, out of my expectation, went to *Ayi* Huang (Class 4A helper) and gave her a big, long hug: "*Ayi*, you have been working so hard (*xin ku le*)! Happy

holidays!" These affectionate words and actions just came out naturally and spontaneously from her, without any sentimental pretention. *Ayi* Huang burst into tears, feeling deeply comforted after days of laborious work.

Young children sometimes behaved in an ostentatious way when showing their concerns for others. Teachers did not like it because such behavior was not motivated by a pure and genuine concern for others. For example, Tongtong was a pretty, smart, and talented girl in Class 4A, like a little star at Biyu Preschool. Although she was often praised as a model for other children because of her excellent academic performance, teachers nonetheless also criticized her, describing her as mature beyond her age (*zao shu*) and "adult-like" (*chengren hua*), as well as pretentious (*zuo zuo*). According to her teacher Yoyo, Tongtong is a *xiao ren jing*, meaning very sophisticated and adept at socializing. For example, when she danced on the stage with her classmates, one could distinguish immediately that the big smile on her face was fake and performative, whereas some other children were genuinely joyful. Tongtong was keen on helping others, especially teachers. She would seize the opportunity to show her concern for teachers, asking: "Are you tired? Do you need a rest?" But her teacher, Yoyo, told me that her caring actions were not, or at least not entirely, motivated by pure empathy, but largely by a strategic concern, that is, to please the authority.

Even though in a lot of Chinese social interactions a simple acknowledgement like "*Xin ku le*" (you've been working too hard) is just a plain formality to express politeness and smooth social relations, teachers believed that when Ke'er said it with a big hug and smile, it meant a genuine concern for others. This poses a dramatic contrast with teachers' impression of Tongtong. This contrast reflects the fact that teachers' impressions were not based on a singular example, but accumulated through numerous interactions with these children. It also reveals that teachers emphasize the underlying intentions, rather than the surface behaviors.

Putting Yourself in Others' Shoes: Becoming a Sensible (Dong Shi) Child

Beyond the basic empathic, emotional responses that are linked to a genuine concern for others' well-being, parents and teachers also emphasize how to extend such "basic empathy" to situations that require more conscious and intentional understanding and imagination. They often connect this basic emotional capacity to "putting oneself in others' shoes" (*huanwei sikao*)—an other-oriented process that integrates emotional and cognitive elements. In their eyes, "putting oneself in others' shoes" is an important foundation for moral education in the sense of cultivating altruism. It is also seen as an effective means to foster social coordination and rule observance, hence parents and teachers need to constantly remind children to put themselves in others' shoes. Learning how to put oneself in others' shoes is an integral part of becoming a sensible (*dong shi*) child, as Siya's stories demonstrate.

> We three (father, mother, and Siya) often play a cards game together. Sometimes Siya lost the game, and she would become really upset and cry: "I don't want to play with you anymore!" I asked her: "What if your father loses the game? Would he cry like you?" She didn't say anything.
>
> Later on she learned *huanwei sikao* [putting oneself in others' shoes]. Once she was playing a card game with several other children. She didn't get the best card and became very sad. I asked her: "Siya, I understand that you are very sad right now because you didn't get that card. But think for a second: if Gege (another child) didn't get the best card, would he also become very sad like you?" Siya said: "Yes, he would definitely be sad!" I followed up: "That's right. So do you think it's better if you take turns and each one gets the best in one round?" She said: "OK. Let's try it." So the next time she seemed much happier. I turned to my husband: "See, our daughter finally becomes sensible (*dong shi*) today!"

In this story, becoming a "sensible" child is a gradual process that requires efforts from caregivers. According to her mother, Siya was a willful child who always focused on herself, but in these small incidents, she was reminded by her mother to take others' perspectives and feelings into consideration. Little by little, she came to understand others' situations and feelings, and to better cooperate and coordinate with others in collective behavior.

Also, parents found that teaching children to "put themselves in others' shoes" is an effective way to correct their wrong behaviors and cultivate mutual respect and understanding—sometimes more effective than mere punishment. Maomao's father used to read various parenting advice books, but he found it hard to apply some of the theories in the books to his son. For example, Maomao used to scream a lot and sometimes got violent. According to some of the books, Maomao should definitely get time-out and be immediately corrected. Father found that time-out didn't work for Maomao and only made him even more hysterical. Instead, what worked much better was a long, warm hug plus asking him to think through the situation and think about how he would feel if Father or Mother kept screaming and even hitting him.

Maomao is a typical "emotionally insecure" child. When my wife was pregnant, she was very depressed due to family conflicts between her parents and me. I think that really had negative impacts on the fetus. Not long after he was born, we sent him to my home province, Xinjiang, and didn't get him back until he was two years old. I found him shy, timid, and easily irritable. I feel sad and guilty about that. Sometimes he was so irritated and he screamed at my wife, threw things onto her, and even hit her. I was so angry. I set him on time-out, spanked him, and tried every possible means to correct him. But he just got even more violent. Later on, I reflected on my own behaviors and decided to change my strategy. I didn't scold him or spank him immediately, but went to hug him and talk to him. I asked: "How would you feel if your mother screams at you, throw things, and hit you? Would you like to be treated that way?" He shook his head. After that incident, his behavior changed a lot. Now I often use this "perspective taking" strategy, which turns out very effective.

Maomao's example illustrates the reciprocal dimension of empathy and "perspective taking," which requires caregivers to intentionally check on their own behaviors and show respect to children. More and more caregivers come to embrace this notion of mutual understanding and respect between parents and children, an important component of care and love.

Encountering the Real World: Helping a Beggar on the Street

Within the school setting, teachers and parents treasure nascent empathy and make efforts to nurture it through reciprocal emotional interactions between children and peers or caregivers, with the aim of cultivating altruism—a genuine concern for others. How about life outside school, a world deemed as dangerous and callous? What is the educators' ideology regarding empathy and altruism in the real world? How do they communicate with children to deal with situations that involve real or imagined risks? The case of Jin Ying (Class: 2A; age: 4.5) and her mother, narrated by Teacher Momo, indicates the complex and perhaps even paradoxical nature of empathy and altruism in the dangerous outside world:

I remember in the *Family-School Communication* book,[10] Jin Ying's mother wrote down this incident. One day, mother and Jin Ying were walking along the street in the neighborhood where they lived. Jin Ying saw an old beggar, when mother was looking around in a nearby shop. Jin Ying ran to mother: "Mommy, there is an old 'grandpa' (*yeye*)[11] begging on the street. He is so miserable! Could you give him some money?" The mother replied with a warning: "Nowadays there are liars and cheats everywhere. This old man is probably a cheat, too. Don't believe him." But then Jin Ying still thought this old man was too miserable, so she tried to negotiate with her mother. She pointed to the empty rice bowl in front of the beggar and said: "Mommy, this old grandpa is so miserable. Look at him! He doesn't have anything to eat. Let's go home and get some rice for him. After all we have a lot left over, and it will be a waste if we don't give it to him." Jin Ying begged her to help this old man. In the end, the mother made a compromise, to give the old beggar a little money. The mother thought it was still necessary to teach the child "good things," such as helping others. I am so proud of Jin Ying because she applied what I taught in class—helping others in need—in real life. Some children might not be aware of it when facing the same situation because they didn't know how to use what they learned in class flexibly.

Teacher Momo mentioned this story to highlight how compassionate and altruistic Jin Ying was, as an example of the fruits of her moral education efforts. In particular, Teacher Momo emphasized that Jin Ying not only internalized the principle of helping others in need, but she could also flexibly extend this principle to real-life situations. There are, however, different layers of meaning to this story. For one thing, it is possible that what motivated Jin Ying to help this old beggar was not only the *abstract principle* she learned in class, but also a strong empathic *emotional urge* ignited by the misery she witnessed. As Momo herself mentioned, emotional sensitivity was bettered developed in these children than it had been in the previous semester, and empathy was a driving force for other-regarding actions. Also, in real life, a tension emerged between what Jin Ying learned in class, that one should help others in need, and the message her mother conveyed, that in real life, those apparently in need are most likely liars. Notably, the negotiation between Jin Ying and her mother reveals young children's creativity and agency, despite the tension between the message of being nice to others and that of being vigilant against risks.

This particular incident illustrates a typical dilemma that Chinese people, especially caregivers, face in daily life, as stories of helping beggars on the street have been highlighted in newspapers, on TV, and in social media. Reports and discussions abound, about the various frauds and tactics of fake beggars. For instance, a healthy beggar would appear in a guise of a severely wounded or disabled person to gain compassion and money, and then the case would be exposed on the Internet. According to some news articles, professional beggars (*zhiye qigai*) make a lot of money and lead a middle-class life, which is why this profession attracts a lot of people. As a news report title indicated, "Fraud Beggars Chill Positive Energy" (Zhang 2013). *Positive energy* (*zheng nengliang*) has become a popular term in China in recent years, referring to positive attitudes and behaviors in social life. In most cases, it's not that easy to detect the behind-the-scenes story and the real intentions of a beggar, such that incidents of helping a beggar expose the risk of altruism. The stated risk sometimes becomes a convenient excuse for people's indifference.

Unlike the Little Yueyue or Good Samaritan cases, however, cases of helping a beggar at most involve a mild risk of losing a tiny amount of money. A new trend of critical reflection has emerged in public discussions, in contrast with the previous dominant discourse. Although the previous discourse focused on condemning the professional beggars' cheating behaviors for their detrimental effects on social trust, the new emerging criticism highlights what is missing in people's inaction toward others' misery in general. For example, two news stories recently attracted public attention. The first one featured a young American man (a student in a Chinese university) who showed genuine concern for an old beggar by chatting with her and buying her potato chips to eat and water to drink. According to the report, this young man had indeed been advised by his Chinese friends not to help beggars who might be liars, but he still believed it was good to show love and concern for others (Wang and Jiang 2012). The other story highlighted the recent decision of the Nanjing government to prohibit begging in the city, and experts criticized this policy (Yu 2013): "Even if 80% of beggars were cheats, don't forget there would still be 20% who were not 'professional beggars,' and begging is their last hope. . . . We need to let those truly in need feel the compassion in our society."

The need to instill a sense of compassion and love in daily social interactions makes moral education a significant topic because children are the future hope. Jin Ying's mother was not alone in confronting the challenge of the child's naive compassion toward a beggar on the street. According to a news report (Fang Li 2012), Liu in Wuhan city witnessed this scene: a child was about to give RMB 5 to a beggar, when he was harshly scolded by his mother: "Idiot! Beggars are cheats!" Liu posted what he witnessed on his *weibo* (Chinese version of Twitter) with a comment: "Is it that the fact of too many cheats in the society made us numb? How would the child see the world when presented with this kind of education?" Liu told a journalist that even if the beggar was a cheat, parents should still praise the child for his kind behavior, otherwise the inborn good-ness of children would be killed in the interests of protecting oneself against frauds. Liu's critique received numerous comments, and opinions were divided.

Connecting this story with Jin Ying's vignette, one cannot help but wonder: What moral messages are mothers conveying to their children? How would children construe these messages and react to them? What are the implications for our future society? One might assume that Jin Ying's mother eventually chose to make a compromise in order to convey "positive energy" to Jin Ying, unlike the other mother who called her son an "idiot." The initial aversion and later hesitation in the reactions of Jin Ying's mother, however, certainly con-veyed something to Jin Ying about what the "real world" is like, and perhaps even about what humanity is like.

Developmental neuroscientists find that as children grow up, it becomes less easy for them to be aroused emotionally at others' distress in a direct sense because of a gradual shift to a more cognitive evaluative process (Decety and Howard 2013). A practical indication follows: it is not impossible that the vigi-lant aversion would become the default, intuitive reaction of Jin Ying or other children in their path to adulthood like what is seen in Jin Ying's mother and other Chinese adults. At that point, will empathy and compassion still be the default gut feeling in such tricky situations? These are questions that deserve attention from caregivers, educators, and scholars concerning the nature of empathy and its role in Chinese socialization and moral transformations.

Developing Empathy in the Chinese Context

Empathy is a core foundation of human morality; however, little is known about how young children develop it in real life. My research adds a develop-mental and educational perspective to the emerging literature in anthropol-ogy on how empathy is configured and mediated in cultural contexts. Also, it provides an ethnographic account of how important tensions identified in the recent scholarship on empathy, such as basic emotion versus complex think-ing, altruistic motivation versus actual behavior, and universal propensity ver-sus specific cultural and moral order, figure into moral education in Shanghai, China. Specifically, this chapter has explored how the fundamental dilemma of "being nice," as indicated by the vignette in the beginning of this chapter, is played out in the particular empathy education practices at Biyu Preschool, situated in a significant cultural frame that features generalized perceptions about a callous society.

The pervasive concern about the lack of love and empathy in Chinese social interactions is an important component of a perceived "moral crisis" in China. I illustrate such generalized perceptions through the case of Little Yueyue, a notorious event that inspired nationwide debates on morality, when I was conducting my fieldwork in China. Specifically, public discussion of the Little Yueyue case highlights how the natural empathic emotions and concerns might be inhibited (or not) by rational calculation of risks and exploitation in situations of heightened emergency.

I find a tension in educational practices at Biyu Preschool, which reflects the salient public concerns about empathy and its risks in real life. On the one hand, empathy as basic humanity is much appreciated and promoted in school setting, as a path to the much-valued virtue of altruism in the context of the pervasive concern about singleton children's self-centeredness. My study shows that children in Biyu Preschool are developing a sense of empathy and concern for others, and teachers deliberately cultivate their emotional sensitivity to others' needs and distress. On the other hand, parents and teachers don't want their children to go too far in this direction, especially when facing unfamiliar situations and people. They fear that empathy and altruism, however valuable in themselves, might endanger the survival and success of these children in the future. Socializers thus send contradictory moral messages to children, which might profoundly shape children's development of empathy.

Such tension reflects a central theme of this book, the fundamental paradox of cultivating a moral child in a perceived immoral society, which manifests itself in different ways, as summarized in Chapter 1. This chapter examines such a paradox in the education of empathy, a basic foundation for morality. The next chapter will explore tensions in another important domain of children's moral experience that has broader implications in Chinese social moral order—learning about ownership and fairness through property distribution and disputes.

3 Negotiating Property Distribution: The Contested Space of Ownership and Fairness

Property Distribution and Moral Cultivation

The Layered Narrative: Contemporary Readings of "Kong Rong Modestly Declines a Pear" ("Kong Rong Rang Li")

Jinqu's grandfather, a prestigious Shanghai businessman who had a good educational background and a lot of experiences traveling abroad, was very keen to discuss with me the similarities and differences between Chinese education and Western education. He introduced me to the contemporary controversy over the classic moral example of "Kong Rong Modestly Declines a Pear" and offered interesting comments on moral education in China.

Kong Rong (153–208 AD) was a twentieth-generation descendant of Confucius (Kong Qiu), of the late Eastern Han Dynasty. The story of "Kong Rong Modestly Declines a Pear" ("*Kong Rong Rang Li*") was encapsulated in the elementary moral education text in late imperial times, the "Three Characters Classic" (*san zi jing*): "Rong, at four, could give away the (bigger) pears. To behave as a younger brother toward elders is one of the first things to know." This specific passage is to instill in young children the core Confucian ethic of *Ti*, respect for one's older brother. The original story goes like this: Kong Rong has several older brothers and a younger brother. One day, Rong's father brought a plate of pears and asked him to distribute them. He distributed all the pears according to age, the older brothers getting the bigger pears. But he himself kept the smallest one. His father was amazed at this, asking: "Why did you give the bigger pears to others and keep the smallest to yourself?" Rong answered decently: "I should respect older brothers and care for the younger brother."

Jinqu's grandfather told me:

Teacher Xu, have you heard of this recent newspaper story? In a first-grade Chinese language and literature exam at an elementary school in Shanghai, there was a question following the essay of "Kong Rong Modestly Declines a Pear": "What would you do if you were Kong Rong?" One student answered: "I won't decline the bigger pear." The teacher marked this answer as wrong. Back home, the father of this student got angry with this and posted the picture of the exam sheet on his *weibo* (a popular Chinese social media, similar to Twitter). It became a popular post, and thousands of people are discussing it.

He went on to comment:

A lot of people think it ridiculous for a teacher to judge this answer as wrong. It's an honest answer. In today's China why would a 7-year-old child even think of giving up the better thing to his brother? Not to mention that they don't have brothers anymore. But now in our education system, such honesty is not approved. Only standardized, ideologically correct answers are allowed. Yes, Kong Rong is an exemplar of the Confucian principle of *qian rang* (modesty and deference). But nowadays people see that as *xu wei* (hypocrisy). You tell your mother that you'd rather give the bigger one to others, and your mother will praise you for being modest and eventually reward you with the bigger one. That is what happens in China now. Chinese children learn to conceal their real feelings and preferences from very early on, merely saying things that will please the adults, as a strategic way to get what they want. Children's inborn nature (*tian xing*) is suppressed and distorted. It's such a pity. You are educated in the United States. You must have heard of the American story "John Fighting for the Bigger Apple." It is a similar story. John has an older and a younger brother. One day, John's mother brought some apples and asked them to compete for the best one in a fair way. John did the best in the competition, and got it proudly. See, that's the cultural difference! Why do we Chinese become hypocrites? Why can't we use fair rules like how the Americans do? For instance, whoever does the best gets the best. That's fair. That's where a fair society comes from.

I was intrigued by this incident and these comments. The whole narrative by Jinqu's grandparent actually has multiple layers of interpretation. The first layer is the original story of "Kong Rong Modestly Declines a Pear" ("*Kong Rong Rang Li*"), documented in ancient texts and preserved and interpreted generation after generation. I recalled learning "Kong Rong Modestly Declines a

Pear," both from teachers and through children's books, as part of learning the Chinese classics. The story illustrates the value of modesty and deference, or in Confucian philosophy, "a heart of courtesy and propriety" (*li rang zhi xin*). As one of the four basic moral seeds in Mencius's theory, "a heart of courtesy and propriety" is seen as the foundation for *li*—a key concept in Confucian thinking that summarizes the guidelines for proper behavior in different types of relationships in a hierarchical social order.

A second layer of meaning lies in the fact that the Kong Rong example appeared as an exam question in an elementary school Chinese language class, and a seven-year-old child gave a "wrong" answer. Using classic texts and stories to convey moral messages is a common practice in Chinese education. The original "Kong Rong" story was used in the Chinese language exam as a classic example for the traditional Confucian virtue of *qian rang* (modesty and deference), and the correct answer was "I would decline the pear." So the teacher marked the answer "I would not decline the pear" as wrong.

A third layer of meaning is the child's own reasoning underlying his answer. It is interesting to note that there was one question before "What would you do if you were Kong Rong?" and that was a two-choice question: "What virtue of Kong Rong is worth learning?" and the answers were "(1) Deference and modesty (*qian gong jing rang*)" and "(2) Diligence (*qinlao*)." This child chose the answer: "(1) Deference and modesty (*qian gong jing rang*)," and the teacher marked it as correct. Obviously, this seven-year-old boy understood the message of the story on the exam sheet because he picked the correct answer. According to his father, for the other question—"What would you do if you were Kong Rong?"—his son wrote, "I won't decline the bigger pear" out of careful reasoning, not out of naughtiness. The father later asked his son why he said he would not do the same as Kong Rong did even though he knew the moral message of that classic story. The boy said: "Because I thought the four-year-old Kong Rong was too young to choose to decline the bigger pear," and he did not want to change his answer based on the teacher's judgment.

A fourth layer is the reaction of this child's father: He was angry, because in this specific context, he didn't think it right for the teacher to judge his son's answer as wrong even though he understood why the "correct answer" should be "I would decline the pear" in standard Chinese moral education framework. He believed that his son should have the right to express his true opinions, instead of conforming to the authority, and he also mentioned that his son was a very nice child at home, not a selfish one. He also thought it was fine for a child in today's society not to give away the bigger pear. He took a photo of his son's exam sheet and posted it onto his *weibo* (Chinese version of Twitter) with a sarcastic comment: "Is this what our current education all about?"[1]

A fifth layer is the reaction of Jinqu's grandparent to this incident. His comments imply two criticisms of current Chinese education in general and moral education in particular: First, Chinese education discourages honesty and genuineness, and instead encourages hypocrisy, even though the original "Kong Rong" story was an example of good moral conduct in traditional times and of courtesy and modesty. Second, closely related to the lack of honesty and promulgation of hypocrisy in moral education, China is becoming an unfair society in terms of the distribution of wealth. He cited the so-called American story of "John Fighting for the Bigger Apple" to compare China with the West in education and social justice—that Western cultures endorse fair rules (earning property through individual merit) whereas hidden rules (*qian guize*), that is, nepotism, pervades Chinese society.

From Modesty/Deference to Hypocrisy: The Genuine Child and the Fair Society

On the very day this incident was posted on *weibo*, the post was forwarded thousands of times and received a large number of comments. Within the next few days, major Chinese newspapers and news websites published stories on this incident. According to an analysis by *Guangming Wang*, the official website of *Guangming Daily*,[2] the majority of Chinese social media users endorsed the father's position and criticized Chinese education for killing young children's genuineness by imposing ideologically correct answers onto the innocent child's authentic mind and individual freedom of choice. The newspaper story also pointed out that these children were facing a dilemma because they had to learn the ideology of "modesty" at school and show deference and obedience to school authorities, but at home they were the center of their worlds and didn't have to practice "modesty" at all, so little by little they learned to lie in order to cope with the dilemma (Duan 2012).

It is interesting to note that the seven-year-old child did understand the moral message of this classic story, but his answer to the question "What would you do if you were Kong Rong?" was based on his knowledge or imagination about what would be natural and authentic for a young child. Following this incident, Sina Shanghai proposed a poll on *weibo*, asking people "What would you choose if you were this elementary school student: Would you say 'Yes' (I will give the bigger pear) or 'No' (I won't give the bigger pear)?" Of the participants, 2,858 respondents chose "No" (56.1 percent), 1,067 respondents chose "Yes" (20.9 percent), and 1,169 respondents chose "I don't know"

(22.9 percent).[3] The seven-year-old boy's knowledge or imagination about younger children's natural and authentic response is similar to what the general public expressed on social media.

Because moral education has long been closely intertwined with social order and governance in China (Bakken 2000), reflections on repressing children's authentic thinking/feelings and producing hypocritical behaviors have inspired discussion on macro-level social phenomena.[4] As people selected a so-called American story of "John Fighting for the Bigger Apple" to compare it with the "Kong Rong" story, issues like social justice, property rights, and political culture have all emerged in public discussion. This discussion has always been framed in cultural comparison and connected back to educational experiences in childhood. For example, an independent Chinese economics scholar compares these two stories and argues that the overwhelming moral lesson of modesty, such as in the "Kong Rong" story, runs the risk of invading individual freedom. According to him, encouraging people to give up their own property and framing it as a good virtue goes against the basic principle of market economy in the modern society where individual property rights should be respected (Jun Li 2012).

I could not find any Western source for the widespread (in China) American story "John Fighting for the Bigger Apple." Whether this story is true or not, its popularity in the Chinese media, however, reflects popular imaginations of the West: Western societies are characterized by the rule of law (*fa zhi*) and are governed by what are thought to be fair institutions, whereas Chinese society is notoriously subject to the rule of man (*ren zhi*) and is sustained through personal connections (*guanxi*). Fairness is among the most important principles in maintaining social order in Western society, whereas Chinese society celebrates favoritism. Regardless of whether such an imaginary provides an accurate portrayal, the existence and wide circulation of these comments tell us something important about today's Chinese mentalities: people are discontented with the current situation in China, seeing it as an unfair/unjust society and a society that suppresses and distorts what ought to be natural and genuine in humans from childhood. This reflects the pervasive concern about fairness/justice in contemporary Chinese society, a key dimension of Chinese social mentality in vernacular discussion (Wang and Yang 2013) and official discourse (Beng 2013) as well. It also speaks to a recurrent theme in this book, how Chinese people link children's moral development to broader social order.

Such a multitude of critical comments on this incident leads me to ask the following questions: What do people think are the natural propensities of children with regard to property and its distribution? How do children negotiate property ownership in their daily social interactions? What are the underlying principles and heuristics they use, explicitly or implicitly, to guide property distribution and resolve property disputes? Are they becoming modest, hypocritical, or fair—in the sense of abiding fairness rules such as the merit principle in the case of "John Fighting for the Bigger Apple"?

This chapter focuses on the children's world of property distribution and exchanges at Biyu Preschool. Because dramas of property distribution and disputes constitute a salient theme in preschool daily life, it is worthwhile to explore the nuanced motivations, tactics, and notions of property ownership and fairness in these children's social interactions. I will start with a detailed account of how they initially distinguish object ownership and gradually develop more complex understandings. I will then present experimental and ethnographic data on children's understanding of fairness, especially the principles of equality and merit, in resource allocation. As rules of ownership and fairness are closely related to, or even interdependent on each other, I analyze how children use these rules to guide property distribution and resolve disputes over property, as well as how teachers participate in these practices. The contrast between teachers' non-intervention to foster children's natural development and their intervention to cultivate certain moral attributes leads me to test the case of Kong Rong among Biyu Preschool children and examine how modesty/deference and hypocrisy are developed and interpreted in the local moral world.

Learning Property Possession: Emergence of Ownership Cognition

The fact that the story of "Kong Rong Modestly Declines a Pear" inspired Chinese parents to reflect on what should be children's "natural" or "authentic" knowledge about property possession speaks to the importance of understanding the emergence of ownership cognition. Ownership is in essence social in that it is not about the relationship between people and things, but between different people with regard to things. A mature notion of the property concept includes three rules: that the owner may possess and use the object, may exclude others from possessing or using it, and may choose to transfer rights to the object to another person (Snare 1972). Although these notions and rules look transparent to an adult, scholars have just begun to explore the perplexing questions regarding children: Where does ownership understanding come from? How do young children learn to understand individual ownership?

Scholars propose that children have a natural propensity to possess, and such a propensity is the foundation of developing a moral sense of ownership, which eventually evolves into a culturally specific normative sense (Rochat 2011). Psychologists have investigated children's development of ownership understandings in laboratory settings, predominantly with American children.[5] Recent findings suggest that at eighteen months children can correctly identify the owners of familiar objects (Fasig 2000); two-year-olds hold the first-possessor bias, in that they believe whoever first gets the object is the owner (Friedman and Neary 2008; Friedman 2008). Later on, children learn to overcome the first-possessor bias and use other cues to attribute ownership, understand ownership transfer, and develop a mature notion of ownership.[6] Three-year-olds can go beyond this and attribute ownership according to who controls permission to use it (Neary, Friedman, and Burnstein 2009).

On the one hand, these findings provide useful conceptual tools for me to analyze my ethnographic data. On the other hand, despite this growing experimental literature, there is so far little cross-cultural research on this topic, nor is there ample ethnographic evidence on how ownership rules emerge in children's daily social interactions. Thus important anthropological questions remain open: in what contexts do young children in China develop ownership understanding, what kind of rules and cues of distinguishing ownership do they pick up, and how is ownership knowledge transmitted, utilized, or even transformed by them? China provides a unique case for examining these questions because of the popular stereotype that Chinese singleton children tend to believe that everything belongs to themselves. Informed by the psychological literature and motivated by these anthropological questions, I will report three findings from my fieldwork on early ownership understandings across different contexts and age groups: The first one is about learning one-to-one labeling between object and person among two-year-olds, the emergence of ownership understanding in Biyu Preschool children's collective life. The second one is about first-possessor bias in three-year-olds' object explorations in the classroom setting. The third one is a specific case on how a young girl gradually grasps and updates ownership rules through social interactions in familial settings.

Learning Object-Person Labeling in a Collective Environment

In the beginning of my fieldwork, I was amazed by how quickly young children, in a new collective environment, learned to associate objects with their names, distinguish different objects, and claim individual ownership accordingly. From the beginning of school life, children are put into an environment that requires them to distinguish individual ownership of a few typical "properties" such as their own photo tags, chairs, cups, and so forth. After entering the classroom, the first thing the child is expected to do, and is intentionally trained to do from the first day of school, is to put a "health" tag in a small pocket that also shows his or her photo; these pockets of all the children's photos and "health" tags are placed together in a wall organizer. According to the teachers, photo tags help children recognize and distinguish their classmates. Moreover, photos are used as distinctive labels to define each child's individual property. On the first day of school, photos are attached to each chair so that every child knows where to sit. Perhaps as a side effect, chair-tagging triggers a significant amount of the property disputes in the classroom—such as when a child sits on a chair with the tag of another child's name, especially among the younger children (two- to four-year-olds). Even as some photos drop off the chairs over time, children can still distinguish different chairs and defend their ownership rights, based on nuanced, nearly invisible signs. As Teacher Mitao of Class 2A (age range: 3.5–4.5) told me:

> For me, every chair looks the same. Once I took two chairs with different colors to the children and asked them: "How are these two chairs different?" They said: "One is green, and one is yellow." Then I took out two green chairs and asked them the same question again. To my surprise, they still found the difference, the shape of a tiny corner of the chair. When they were in nursery class, we first had photos attached to each chair. Then there were chair disputes every day. Now, even though there's no photo, they still know how to distinguish and associate each chair with a specific child.

Awareness of ownership in this case is intentionally cultivated by teachers, via the mediation of specific identification tools (photos), and intensified during daily class activities to the point that children themselves can spontaneously and effortlessly distinguish who owns what and justify their claims.

First-Possessor Bias in the Classroom Setting

In addition to such clear one-to-one labeling between object and person, the first-possessor bias—whoever possesses the item first is the owner—represents another major mechanism through which children distinguish and claim ownership in ambiguous situations, which is in line with findings in the experimental literature. Scholars find it to be a strong bias that persists in children even when they are presented with explicit signs of alternative rules, although it can be attenuated or eliminated through the learning of social scripts (Noles and Keil 2011). One important reason why first-possessor bias is salient in the Biyu Preschool context is that properties in the classroom are mostly owned by the school, not brought by children from home. I document the following typical property dispute scenario between two three-year-olds in Class 1A and how I, as an observer, jumped in to probe their ownership intuitions.

One day during the free-play session in Class 1A, Yueyue and Tiantian were both playing with toys peacefully, while I was watching them quietly. Suddenly, Tiantian came up, trying to forcefully get the toy from Yueyue's hands. Yueyue screamed: "No! I won't give it to you! This is mine!" I asked Yueyue immediately: "Is this toy yours?" Yueyue nodded with assurance: "Yes. It's mine." I probed further, pretending to ask an innocent question: "Did you bring it from your home?" Yueyue answered: "No." I continued to ask: "Then, where does it come from?" Yueyue answered, seeming really confused: "I don't know. . . ." I was amused by the whole drama: Initially, Yueyue intuitively claimed ownership through the first-possessor heuristic. But her confidence was soon challenged when I introduced the idea that whoever brought the toy in was the owner. This example reveals how temporary possession, defined implicitly through first-possessor bias, is contested, defended, and eventually redefined.

Learning Ownership in Family Settings: The Case of Yaoyao

Parents often mention the fact that most of these children were the only children in their families, when they talk about children's ownership understandings and property distribution behaviors. For an only child, everything in their world is theirs by default, and typically there is no one to challenge their claim of ownership. The story of Yaoyao (Class 1A) provides a vivid example of how "little emperors" start out thinking everything is theirs, then acquire the *first-possessor bias* through interacting with nonsingleton children. Also, this newly learned rule triumphed over another ownership rule in another family with two children.

According to her mother, Yaoyao is a typical spoiled child, the real boss at home. The reason that Yaoyao grew so strong-willed is that the couple had the daughter at a late age (late thirties, which is considered a late reproductive age by Chinese standards), and they had been bestowing upon her as much love and tolerance as possible. One of the consequences of such a showering of love, in her mother's words, is that Yaoyao became highly self-centered, such as taking for granted that everything was hers. "Mine, mine!" was perhaps the most frequent of her utterances since she became able to speak at around age one. At that time, she didn't have an *explicit* understanding of ownership rules.

Things started to change when she had a play-date with Ranran, a close neighbor, though. What's interesting is that Ranran is not the only child of her family. She has an older sister, and her mother's parenting style is much stricter than Yaoyao's mother's because Ranran's mother has to take care of two children at once and doesn't have the energy to deal with them in the way Yaoyao's mother treats Yaoyao. In Yaoyao's mother's eyes, Ranran is much less strong-willed than Yaoyao. When Yaoyao came to Ranran's home to play, she encountered the first explicit "ownership" rule in her life: whoever gets the toy first can play with it, which was the home rule set by Ranran's mother. Yaoyao readily accepted this rule, and from then on, first-possessor bias became her own rule of thumb.

Yaoyao's mother said, "She didn't have any rules before, so the first rule she learned was well entrenched in her mind." Then the claim "I got it first!" always went before "It's mine!" This rule became so pervasive in Yaoyao's life that she applied and generalized it to all kinds of contexts. Her mother gave me a humorous example: Once Yaoyao's father was going to the bathroom. Immediately, Yaoyao went to stop him, shouting "I am going to bathroom! I am the first who wants to pee! It's *mine*!" She then went ahead to open the door and successfully occupied the bathroom.

Yaoyao later used this first-possessor bias to the extreme and her stubbornness was reinforced. On one occasion, Yaoyao's mother and father took her to a big toy store, and she got interested in a toy plane. When she was about to grab the toy, another boy who was much taller than her came over and said, "I have been playing with it!" He came straight toward her, pointing to the toy: "I got it first!" Yaoyao wasn't willing to give in at all, shouting, "No. I got it first." She believed she was entitled to play with it because when she saw it, the boy wasn't playing with it. Her mother and father were hiding somewhere so as not to intervene, and it went as her mother had predicted: A fight began. Yaoyao held this toy very tightly in her hands, her face turning red. But the boy was much stronger than her, and he finally grabbed back the toy, after forcefully opening Yaoyao's hands by stretching her fingers loose one after another. But then he thought for a moment and said with frustration: "Forget it (*suan le*)! Consider you are a younger sister." Yaoyao, not acknowledging this as a favor at all, announced loudly: "I *am* the first! Of course, I *should* get it!" Thus, the strong-willed little princess Yaoyao won; she got what she believed she deserved.

The saliency of this first-possessor bias is also manifest in the fact that, for Yaoyao, the rule was resistant to change. Apart from playing with Ranran, Yaoyao also visited another neighbor often, a family with a five-year-old girl named Tongtong and a little baby boy. This family had a different rule when it came to who gets to play with the toy: whoever owns it gets to decide who can play. Perhaps because Tongtong was old enough to clearly understand who owned what, she was determined in enforcing the rule. She tried hard to explain the rule and persuade Yaoyao, but Yaoyao just had one thing in mind: "No. I got it first!" To summarize, Yaoyao, starting from "everything is mine" with no justifications, learned the rule of first-possessor at around age two and this rule then persisted, even as she had gotten to know alternative rules at approximately age three.

Although the case of Yaoyao is just one example of how young children learned ownership through daily negotiations, this case inspires me to think more broadly about the intricate dynamics through which emerging psychological dispositions are shaped in familial, educational, and cultural processes. On the one hand, in line with the experimental evidence from the developmental literature, the first-possessor bias does emerge early on and is relatively stable in development. On the other hand, children's daily life is filled with subtle instances and moments of contesting, reinforcing, or redefining this "rule of thumb." Moreover, it is interesting that Yaoyao's mother attributes Yaoyao's stubborn behaviors in declaring ownership for herself to the fact that Yaoyao is spoiled as the precious only child of her family. This interpretation is common among Chinese parents nowadays, and thus we can see how Chinese cultural beliefs around the connections between the one-child policy and moral cultivation trickle into children's life from early on.

Learning Resource Distribution: Emergence of Fairness (*Gongping*) Understanding

In addition to explicit and implicit notions of ownership, understandings of fairness also provide an important foundation for property practices among young children. Fairness is a key mechanism in human cooperation and morality, especially when it comes to how to distribute resources among different parties (Rawls 1971). Concerns with fairness appear across diverse contexts, from small hunter-gatherer cultures to Western, modern societies (Boehm 2008; Gurven 2004; Henrich 2004), though with considerable cross-cultural differences (Henrich et al. 2010).

In recent decades, the ontogeny of fairness has received heated attention across the social science disciplines. Recent research suggests that a concern for the "principle of equality" (Deutsch 1975), that is, all other things considered goods should be divided equally among recipients, emerges as early as twelve months (Schmidt and Sommerville 2011; Geraci and Surian 2011) and guides children's behaviors, preferences, and even moral judgments in infancy, preschool years, and beyond (Burns and Sommerville 2014; DesChamps, Eason, and Sommerville 2015; LoBue et al. 2009). Although these studies focus on children in Western countries, most recently experimental psychologists have found evidence that two- to three-year-old Chinese children in a northeast Chinese city expect equal distribution to two recipients in a laboratory setting (Liu et al. 2015).

In the meantime, researchers have found that another key principle of fairness, the "principle of merit" (Deutsch, 1975)—rewards should be distributed according to how much one deserves them—also has its origin in early childhood, albeit a little later than the equality principle. Preschool children take into account the merit principle both when distributing resources in a third-party role (Baumard, Mascaro, and Chevallier 2012) and when sharing rewards between self and other partners (Kanngiesser and Warneken 2012).

Understanding Equality and Merit: Experimental Evidence

An open question concerns the development of merit understanding among Chinese preschool children and how they reason in a situation where both merit and equality principles can be applied. As part of a cross-cultural collaborative project, I conducted a field-experiment with four- and five-year-old children at Biyu Preschool (Chevallier et al. 2015).[7] I read each child a story (with pictures) of two girls baking cookies together—one got bored and left in the middle of the project to play and the other girl persisted to the end and made three cookies. I then showed the child three cookies (drawings) and asked the child to distribute these cookies to the two characters as she or he wanted to. Before they started to distribute, I also made sure they understood the story, by asking some manipulation check questions. The first phase was free distribution, and if the child didn't give away all three cookies, then we would come to the next phase, forced distribution, when I asked the child to distribute the remaining cookies. After all three cookies were distributed, I asked the child why he or she made the specific distribution decision.

In the first phase, eighteen children chose an egalitarian distribution, nineteen children favoring the big contributor (the girl who persisted to the end), and five children didn't make a decision. In the second phase, most of these children (thirty-five out of forty-two) used the merit principle by giving more cookies to the big contributor, two-choice binomial test p < .001. In terms of their justifications after the distribution, twenty-nine children mentioned the characters' different levels of contribution to the cookie-baking project, eleven didn't respond, and two mentioned other reasons. These results suggest that the four- and five-year-old children at Biyu Preschool have the capacity to apply the merit principle in resource distribution, but some of them need to overcome the inclination to distribute things equally.[8] I also presented the same story to the younger children (three-year-olds), most of whom had a hard time linking the characters' different levels of contribution to their own decisions of cookie distribution, suggesting these children have not yet learned to apply the merit principle to resource allocation in this specific experimental scenario.

At the Junction between Experiment and Reality: The Case of Xiaobei

Although controlled experiments revealed Biyu Preschool children's developmental trajectory regarding equality versus merit, two important principles that guide fairness reasoning, ethnographic evidence helped me to form a more contextualized understanding of these results. In particular, the following case of Xiaobei, right at the junction between experiment and reality, points to the nuances and complexity of children's fairness reasoning.

> One day I was ready to run a new experiment with Xiaobei, a four-year-old boy in Class 2A. He had been familiar with "playing a game with Teacher Xu" (a native translation for "participating in a field-experiment"), in which I gave candies as rewards and tokens to be distributed to two different targets.[9] According to my experimental design, however, this new game didn't involve any rewards (candies). It was simply reading a story to the child and asking him or her some questions related to that story. After we finished playing the game, Xiaobei asked me, looking very perplexed: "Where are the candies?" I answered innocently: "There is no candy." He followed: "Why did you give me coconut candies last time when we played a game?" I had to explain to him: "Sorry, this is a different game, and no candy this time." Xiaobei didn't believe me, so he gathered a few other children and searched through my bag—the one that hosted all my experimental apparatus where candies usually came from. But he didn't find any candy and was very disappointed.
>
> I felt sorry about that, and at noon I went out to buy some chocolate candies in a grocery store nearby. When I came back, the kids had just awakened from the noon nap, and Xiaobei was very happy to see the pack of chocolate candies. He asked me: "Teacher Xu, who do you want to give the candies to?" I said: "One for each of you." He asked further: "Is it only for our class, or is

it for all the classes?" I said: "Only for your class. But what do you prefer, only for your class or for all the classes at your school?" He said: "For all the classes, of course. Because it is not *gongping* (fair) if the candies were only given to one class." I was surprised at his response and had to explain to him: "I only prepare to give to your class because this time I will only play this new game with your class, not the other classes."

This case gives us a hint as to how sensitive young children are toward fairness in property distribution. Although Xiaobei understood the principle of merit and chose to give more cookies to the character that contributed more to the cookie-baking project, his reactions after the experiment (requesting that everyone at his school deserves a candy) showed a strong endorsement of the equality principle. What can we learn from this case? First, I never considered it unfair to give candies only to a specific class because I gave the candies as rewards to those children who participated in my experiment. But the connection between participating in an experiment and getting a reward was not self-evident to Xiaobei. There is another layer of meaning in Xiaobei's reactions, however, which indicates the complex understandings of merit among Chinese children like him. Instead of simply concluding that Xiaobei had no sense of what merit is, I would rather interpret it this way: Xiaobei thought that *everyone*, including himself of course, was good enough to *deserve* the candies, and that there was no need for any external justifications. This means, in the specific case, the merit principle was recognized, except that there was no differentiation of children who deserved more. The popular complaint among parents like me regarding how young singleton Chinese children think they *deserve* everything is not unfounded! Also, I would infer that children's reasoning about resource distribution depends on various factors, that is, whether the resource is scarce and whether distribution incurs a cost to the distributor. As shown in this example, because Xiaobei had seen that I a*lways* had plenty of candies to give to them during my previous experiments, it was natural for him to believe that I would have enough candies this time, too. In some other situations, children were quite savvy about distributing things strategically to particular individuals instead of equally to all, that is, when sharing their own items (such as food and toys), a theme that will be elaborated in the next chapter. This case suggests that the tension between equality (everyone deserves the same reward) and merit (people deserve different rewards) plays out in different ways as children evaluate fairness in varying contexts of property distribution. Moments such as this in my fieldwork, when a controlled experiment merges into participant observation, reveals the interesting chemistry of mixed-methods research.

Dispute Resolution: Negotiating and Enforcing Distribution Rules

Disputes Resolution Dynamics: Domains, Processes, and Interference

Because dispute resolution is an integral part of children's daily social experience, it is important to examine how they develop the abilities to use and enforce ownership and fairness rules when they negotiate distribution disputes to build order into their social interactions. Disputes occur in a variety of domains that matter to these children in their school lives, ranging from distributing material objects such as toys, books, and other classroom properties, to assigning children to statuses without any real material basis. Although some of these statuses didn't have a material format for children to readily claim ownership over, children did fight, for example, over who should be the "engine" (*huoche tou*) of the "small train" (*xiao huoche*)—class line leader, the head of the queue when the class lined up and marched outside for certain activities. Roles like this have significant social meanings and become symbols of social position and recognition in the classroom context.

Although many of the items and roles these children fight about do not really belong to any of them, they still tend to claim entitlement over these items and entities, using a variety of justifications. For example, sometimes they claim they are the first possessor (user) of an item, and sometimes they argue that they deserve something by merit, especially when this particular thing they seek is not a material object. Across all these different situations, ownership and fairness rules are mixed together, referring to one another. Sometimes children do bring their own toys, books, and snacks to class, which might cause disputes. For such disputes, ownership is easier to define, but different opinions might arise during processes of exchange, the owners' decisions might be questioned and rejected by the non-owners, and fairness rules might be introduced and negotiated to settle the disputes. What follows are several cases of disputes that demonstrate how ownership and fairness rules and claims are strategically negotiated and intricately intertwined.

Case 1: Dispute for "Little Teacher"

Today is rainy and the outdoor "morning exercise" was canceled. Class 3A children were kept in the classroom to rehearse gymnastic movements.

Teacher Pingping appointed two girls, Jiayi and Kailin, as "little teachers" to stand in front of the class and lead the exercise. Jiayi and Kailin were the best dancers in their class and always led the morning exercise of Class 3A. Another girl, Tianyang, was very upset and wanted to join in as a "little teacher." Teacher Pingping didn't agree, and reaffirmed that there could only be two "little teachers." But Tianyang was very stubborn and insisted on standing in the front. A boy wanted to drag her back, but she firmly resisted it.

Jiayi proposed a good idea: "Tianyang, why don't you do 'rock, paper, scissors'? The one who wins gets to be the 'little teacher'!" Both Tianyang and Kailin agreed to this, but Tianyang lost. The other children were laughing loudly: "Tianyang lost!" But Tianyang didn't buy it, and she still stood in the front with no intention of giving in. Several children came to drag her back, and the situation became physical. Tianyang started to cry.

It had become a messy situation by the time Teacher Pingping intervened. She ordered all the children to go back to their chairs and suspended the rehearsal: "We won't do it today. We have to leave it for tomorrow, and Jiayi and Kailin will still be the two 'little teachers.'" She criticized Tianyang for not obeying the rules. All the children condemned her: "Tianyang broke her promise! She is not accountable!" Then they started to gossip among themselves about how Tianyang had not been accountable on other occasions.

Kailin whispered to Jiayi and Jiayi said: "This is a good idea!" Another girl, Junyi, came over and asked: "What were you talking about?" Kailin smiled: "It's a secret!" Junyi went close: "What secret?" Kailin whispered again. Then I went over to ask: "What did you just say? What secret? I heard you talking about Tianyang. What is the 'good idea'?" Jiayi smiled: "Kailin said we should let Tianyang lead the morning exercise tomorrow, and we will just sit on our chairs, look at her, and imitate her." Kailin moved her arms around in a clumsy way, imitating Tianyang, and the girls burst into laughter.

The "little teacher" position was deemed very important to these five-year-olds, in a similar way as the "engine" position was for the younger three-year-olds. In this encounter, the merit principle was applied in the teacher's choice of the two "little teachers," which was also endorsed by the students. There was, however, one girl, Tianyang, who did not follow the teacher's rules and wanted the "little teacher" position for herself. Other children intervened, using different methods, both "brute force" and the standard procedure of "rock, paper, scissors," but Tianyang still did not cooperate. Then the teacher had to intervene and punish the violator through suspending the day's activities. Children even mocked Tianyang and came up with an idea to shame her.

Case 2: Dispute for Toys Owned by Children

When I came into Class 3A, Teacher Xiaoling was leading the class in reciting an ancient poem, and Mingyu was sobbing. I asked Xiaoling what happened, and she had asked the children to explain to me.

Niuniu exclaimed: "He wanted to play with my toy."

Teacher Xiaoling: "Mingyu, please tell Teacher Xu what you did."

Mingyu was silent.

Yiyang, another girl sitting next to Mingyu, said: "Mingyu played with Niuniu's toy this morning, and he wanted to play with it again. Niuniu didn't allow it, and Mingyu cried."

Teacher Xiaoling: "Yiyang, please let Mingyu explain it by himself."

Mingyu mumbled when sobbing.

Yiyang: "He said: 'I only played for a few minutes, and Niuniu got it back.'"

Teacher Xiaoling: "Mingyu, remember the toy belongs to Niuniu, right? Niuniu already exchanged his toy with you this morning. Niuniu, could you bring it again tomorrow and exchange it with Mingyu? Mingyu, you have to ask Niuniu youself. Please go to another room and discuss this between yourselves. When you come out, I don't want to see tears again."

The two boys went to another room, and I followed them, peeking through the door to see what happened between them. There was a long silence, Mingyu was still upset, but Niuniu seemed not to care much about it. Then Niuniu put his hands into Mingyu's pocket, found a golden ball toy, and put his own black ball toy into that pocket. Mingyu rejected this exchange.

Niuniu: "I will bring it again tomorrow and let you play with it the whole day. How does that sound?"

Mingyu was still silent.

Niuniu negotiated: "I'll let you play with it for two days, OK?"

Mingyu agreed.

Then the two boys came out and went back to their chairs.

This is a typical toy dispute among young children, a case in which the toys actually belonged to themselves, not to the school. Teacher Xiaoling chose not to interfere and instead let the children negotiate between themselves. She believed that children should learn to negotiate property disputes by themselves in order to acquire proper rules for playing, as she later explained to me.

Mingyu was unhappy at first because he thought it unfair for him to play with Niuniu's toy for only a little while. But Teacher Xiaoling reminded him this toy *belonged to* Niuniu and he was entitled to end the exchange whenever he wanted to. Teacher Xiaoling made a proposal that Niuniu could bring the toy again to exchange it with Mingyu. But for Mingyu, neither an exchange again at the time nor the next day was satisfactory. Eventually, the two boys came to terms with the proposal of an exchange again for two days. Teacher Xiaoling thought this kind of self-negotiation was natural and conducive, specifically, to children's acquisition of ownership and fairness rules, and of children's social development in general.

Case 3: Dispute for a School Possession

Children in Class 1A were playing with toys on the floor, when all of a sudden Ziyu began to cry. Teacher Fanglin went over and asked Ziyu what happened, and Ziyu said Guoguo, another girl, had taken her toy. Teacher Fanglin criticized Guoguo, and then Guoguo burst into tears, too. Fanglin held these two girls on her laps and asked again what had really happened. Ziyu insisted that she got the toy first.

Fanglin turned to ask Guoguo: "Can you tell me what happened?"

Guoguo was crying nonstop.

Fanglin: "When you were playing on the floor, was it that Ziyu and you got the toy at the same time?"

Guoguo nodded and continued to cry.

Fanglin questioned Ziyu: "Ziyu, did Guoguo really take your toy?"

Ziyu nodded.

Fanglin concluded: "I know you too well! Are you the kind of person who would have your toys taken by others?"

Fanglin then comforted them both and explained to me: "I know these two girls very well. If Guoguo really made a mistake, she would be too stubborn to care about my criticism. But today she cried so hard; she must have thought it unfair and felt grieved. Ziyu, however, was crying to hide the fact that she was the one who made a mistake."

Disputes like this happened a lot during children's free-play time, especially among the younger children who have not yet acquired a comprehensive set of distribution rules yet. These younger children frequently used the default rule of first possessor and claimed that they got the toy first. In this specific case, because the teacher did not see who actually got the toy first, she had to ask the children themselves and evaluate their verbal and nonverbal responses to make a prudent decision. Because Fanglin was very familiar with both children, she concluded that Guoguo was the one who actually got the toy first and was unfairly treated.

Socializers' Dilemma: Is the "Genuine" Child Good, or Not?

Across the cases presented previously, teachers were all involved to a greater or lesser extent. They encouraged children to solve the problem by themselves and emphasized communication among the children themselves. They gave children instructions to remind them of ownership rules. They enacted punishment toward children who caused problems because they did not follow rules. That being said, teachers from different classes told me that they would not want to impose a specific distribution rule onto children unless it became necessary to do so. It might be so, for example, if a verbal dispute escalated to a violent physical one, or if teacher believed that the children were too young to come up with a resolution by themselves. An important rationale behind such a default stance of non-interference is that teachers believed that children should have the capacity to learn to negotiate distribution and exchange, what children came up by themselves should be most natural and authentic, and such naturalness and genuineness should be treasured and nurtured by adults. Following this logic, teachers believe that only minimal structure to encourage children's self-negotiation and a few general guidelines to ensure a positive negotiation are needed to nurture such development. Such a rationale and its implications remind me of the "brighten the bright virtue" belief in neo-Confucian philosophy, as explained in the previous chapter about empathy development.

Despite this idealized picture of nurturing children's natural and genuine capacity to negotiate distribution and exchanges, in practice teachers often encounter dilemmas. As the contemporary cynical readings of the "Kong Rong" story suggest, teaching the virtue of generosity in distribution might end up breeding the seeds of hypocrisy among young children. This is because modest and generous attitudes and decisions might distort children's inborn nature (*tian xing*) to obtain what they really desire and turn that into a nonchildish, inauthentic propensity to please the adults for strategic purposes.

Cultivating Generosity or Breeding Hypocrisy

Case 4: Dispute over Play-Zone Assignment

It was free-play time for Class 3B. Teacher Tang announced: "Let me tell you a secret. Whoever drinks his or her water first gets to choose their play zone first." Children were thrilled and all rushed into the dining room to drink water. Xinbao was the first to drink his cup, and Teacher Tang gave him a few play-zone tickets to choose, two block play-zone tickets and one handcraft play-zone ticket. The block play zone was children's favorite, and the handcraft one the least favorite. Siya came to Xinbao when he was about to give one block tag to his best friend, Sicheng. He quickly gave the ticket to Sicheng. But when he was about to keep the other block ticket for himself, Siya got angry and fought with him. It almost turned into a physical conflict. Teacher Tang came to stop the conflict and asked them to work out a way to distribute the tickets together.

Siya initiated the negotiation: "Xinbao, could you give the block ticket to me?" Xinbao responded: "Let me play for a while first." Siya said: "Let me think for a moment first." Then Teacher Tang asked Siya: "Could you go to the handcraft play zone?" Siya answered: "No. I don't want to go there." Another child came, took the handcraft ticket, and left. Teacher Tang turned to ask Xinbao: "Could you give in and leave the block ticket to Siya?" Xinbao accepted it without a word, and Siya happily went to the block play zone like a winner. Teacher Tang praised Xinbao: "You are a good boy! You give what you want to others. Teacher wants to reward you for your *qian rang* (modesty and generosity). This time I'll add a spot for the block play zone,[10] and now you can go there to play also!" Xinbao was thrilled and went to play with his friends.

According to the rules of play-zone assignment, it is not fair to add a spot for a particular play zone if all children could be assigned to already existing spots, however, Teacher Tang used this extra spot as a reward for Xinbao's thoughtfulness and generosity. Initially, Xinbao was not willing to compromise, because according to Teacher Tang's announcement in the beginning, he was the first to finish drinking his water and deserved to choose whatever he wanted. Nor had he expected that Teacher Tang would reward him with an extra ticket to play blocks. Apparently, Xinbao's behavior in this incident was nothing like Kong Rong's, who intentionally declined the bigger pears and offered legitimate justifications for doing so. But still, Teacher Tang used the same term, *qian rang*, to describe what was commendable in Xinbao's behavior. Although in both the "Kong Rong" story and the Xinbao vignette *qian rang* is used to represent the generous behavior in which one puts other people's needs first in property distribution, there are nuances in the ways this term is used in historical and contemporary contexts. Whereas the classical "Kong Rong" story is intended to cultivate the virtue of *qian gong jing rang* (deference and modesty) in a hierarchical family system, in today's child-rearing contexts, when parents and teachers talk about *qian rang*, the emphasis is on generosity and altruism—that "little emperors" should learn to put others' needs into consideration instead of focusing merely on oneself, not on the hierarchical family order.

Later, however, Teacher Xiaoling, the other teacher in Class 3B, expressed concerns regarding the potential side-effects of rewarding *qian rang*: sometimes children would learn from their past experiences, and the next time they encountered a similar situation, they would propose to compromise first in order to please the teachers and get some potential rewards. This concern about *qian rang* turning into *xu wei* (hypocrisy) is in line with the critiques presented in the beginning of this chapter.

A Test of the "Kong Rong" Story among Biyu Preschool Children

Are children really turning from authentic and innocent beings into hypocrites as the popular imaginations of socializers and the general public indicate? Curious about this question, I tried out a simplified version of the "Kong Rong" story on ten children across all age groups in Biyu Preschool during informal conversations with them. I read to them a vignette similar to the "Kong Rong" story. Before reading it, I always asked whether they knew of the "Kong Rong" story. Most children said they had never heard of it. Those few who said they had heard of it could not describe the plot of the story. Then I proceeded to tell the story: "One day, Mother asks this little boy to distribute three pears (a large one, a medium-size one, and a small one) to his older brother, his younger brother, and himself. The three boys all love pears. If you were this little boy, how would you distribute the three pears? Who are you going to give the biggest pear to? Who gets the medium-size one, and who gets the smallest one? Why?" After they finished the distribution and gave their justifications, I added one question: "Do you want the biggest pear?"

Amusingly, nine out of ten children of all ages didn't give the classic "Kong Rong" answer: keep the smallest pear for oneself. Interestingly, the only one who gave the "Kong Rong" answer was the oldest child, Yichen (6.5 years old). Even when I asked him if he would like the biggest pear after he finished the distribution, he still said no. According to his teacher Meifang, Yichen is a very scheming (*xin ji*) student, particularly good at pleasing authorities. For example, he is a frequent tattler, reporting peers' bad behaviors to teachers in order to get teachers' attention and perhaps even praise. Also, sometimes when he was arguing with classmates with an angry look, he would "change his face" (*bian lian*) the moment he saw a teacher coming, and he would pretend to be smiling with classmates, and then turn his big smile to the teacher. Teacher Meifang is thus concerned as to whether he would become too savvy, without keeping his "genuine" qualities as a child. This concern about Yichen, the only student who gave a classic "Kong Rong" answer, resonates with the cynical comments circulating in Chinese social media today: children are being taught, explicitly and implicitly, to become hypocrites, by pretending to act selflessly or altruistically in order to get approval and reward from the authority.

In contrast, the four- to- six-year-olds preferred to give the medium-size pear to themselves, the biggest one to the older brother, and the smallest one to the younger brothers. When asked again if they would like to eat the biggest pear, their answers were consistent with their previous choices. Interestingly, the three-year-olds were hesitant between choosing the biggest one and the medium-size one for themselves. Some immediately said they would keep the biggest pear for themselves, and others said they would have the medium-size one, in accordance with the order of age. This indicates that three-year-olds are starting to show sensitivity to "social desirability," realizing it might be "wrong" to choose the biggest pear for oneself. But most interestingly, when I then asked the three-year-olds whether they wanted the biggest pear to eat, they all said yes.

This test using the "Kong Rong" story among Biyu Preschool children reveals the following trends: First, most of these children ages three to six knew about distributing according to age. Second, the "Kong Rong" choice of getting the smallest one for himself seems really alien to these preschoolers today (except the 6.5-year-old, Yichen, who most probably made his decision to please me/the authority). Third, the older children tended to conceal the desire for a bigger pear better than the younger ones. In other words, in line with adults' popular imaginations, the younger children seemed indeed more "genuine" and less skilled in using the ideologically correct answer to please authorities, confronted with the temptation of bigger pears. Most probably, it is because the older children had more experiences with making a modest choice that would lead to adults' praise and recognition; they had internalized the ideology of modesty to a greater extent.

On a deeper level, the dilemma adult socializers face is not merely a tension between the virtue of *qian rang* (modesty, deference, and generosity) and the vice of hypocrisy. Rather, it is rooted in contradictory imaginations about children's "genuineness" in relation to "goodness." *Qian rang* is good *if and only if* it is out of one's sincere and pure intention to do good for others, and once the intention is not "genuine," modesty becomes hypocrisy. On the one hand, children's inborn nature (*tian xing*) of genuineness is precious and is the foundation of human virtues, as Chinese child-rearing beliefs have emphasized since traditional times. Protecting children's "genuineness" becomes morally good in itself. On the other hand, with regard to the specific domain of property distribution, a "genuine" child possibly means that the child wants to possess everything he or she desires, which is seen as a symptom of selfishness. In this case, children's "genuineness" becomes a grey area. On this note, the seemingly simple notion of children's "inborn nature," framed always in a positive tone in Chinese child-rearing discourses as a liberating force, is actually a contested moral zone in everyday socialization experience.

Possession, Morality, and the "Genuine" Child

Ownership and fairness cognition are two important building blocks that underpin children's reasoning about property exchange (Rochat et al. 2009: 418) and resource allocation (Olson and Spelke 2008). This chapter has examined how children in Biyu Preschool develop understandings of ownership and fairness through everyday practices related to property possession and distribution, an important domain in their moral experience. Whereas it is a heightened educational concern that "little emperors" will focus too much on themselves and have a hard time realizing that not everything belongs to themselves, my study reveals how children at Biyu Preschool grow to understand ownership in more and more complex ways. A lot of them start out believing and claiming "everything is mine," which is perhaps also true with very young children in other places. But they do develop more realistic understandings as they engage frequently in property distribution and exchange activities with their peers. Departing from "everything is mine," these children soon develop the first-possessor bias and apply it in their daily property distribution and dispute resolution. With regard to fairness rules, my study focuses on the tension between two main principles, equality and merit, across both experimental and naturalistic settings. The entanglement of various ownership and fairness concerns in children's actual property possession and distribution experience indicates the value and necessity of examining everyday experience in order to understand children's cognitive development, agency, and creativity.

Based on a close examination of children's property possession and distribution experiences filtered through the framework of ownership and fairness understandings, I intend to expand analytic attention to the broader public discourses about the implications of early moral education for understanding distributive justice in China. This chapter began with a discussion of the contemporary cynical readings of the classic virtue of modesty exemplified in the story "Kong Rong Modestly Declines a Pear." During the reform and opening-up era, Chinese people became more and more cynical (Steinmüller 2011, 2013) about China's past and the present contrast between ideology and reality. In the realm of child-rearing and education, such cynicism is also grounded in a widely perceived contrast between the "imagined West" and the "imagined China." In these settings, Kong Rong, originally a moral icon for the Confucian virtue of *qian rang*, becomes a scapegoat for hypocrisy. Moreover, these broader understandings about *qian rang* and hypocrisy resonate with Biyu Preschool children's reactions to the classic story: in general, only older preschool children begin to grasp the link between giving up a bigger reward and the virtue of *qian rang*, and they acquire this knowledge mostly as a result of knowing that this interpretation is desired by the educational authority.

All these matters are related to the obsession of socializers and the general public with the cultural ideal of the "genuine" child, an ideal that is fraught with contradictions in a world that is perceived to be unjust. A "genuine" child is one who can express his natural, untainted potentials, despite the distorted educational ideologies in a "polluted" society. For example, the accusation of *qian rang* in possession and distribution as *xu wei* —hypocrisy in the sense that one intends to please the authority and in turn get a better reward through a seemingly altruistic action—reflects a yearning for a truly just world governed by fair rules, although what it means by "fair" is far from settled. The "genuine" child, however, is not necessarily an inherently good child, which signals a deep-seated, fundamental contradiction within adult imaginations about children's moral development. Specifically, in contrast to the obsession with the "genuine" child and its liberating potentials here, the next chapter will reveal a dark dimension of genuineness, socializers' concerns over the selfish only child. It will delve into the tension between the daily ideological inculcation of egalitarian sharing and children's actual practices of selective, strategic sharing. In a word, neither the celebration of the bright side of the child nor the concern over the dark side of the child uncovers the full complexities of children's own agency in navigating the social world, evaluating social actions, and weaving together their own social networks.

4 Sharing Discourse and Practice: The Selfish Child, Generosity, and Reciprocity

The Story of "Evil Kiddo"*

On December 31, 2011, a little boy named Chengcheng celebrated his third birthday with his classmates and teachers during regular class hours. From repeated observation I became familiar with the script of such occasions. The idea was to cultivate the moral quality of altruism in these young children through this sharing practice, as parents and teachers were concerned about these children being too selfish, because most of them are singletons under China's one-child policy. In particular, it was emphasized that one should share equally with the entire class. This birthday party largely followed the standard format. In the morning, Chengcheng's parents brought a big birthday cake to the class, and in the afternoon, the teachers in the class organized a party. First, teachers asked all the children to sit quietly, announced to them it was time to celebrate Chengcheng's birthday, and led the group to sing a "Happy Birthday" song in Chinese and English. The teachers then divided the cake into pieces, gave Chengcheng a big piece, and distributed the rest of the pieces equally to other children. The two teachers and two helpers also got a piece for themselves. As a "good friend" of this class, I had the privilege of getting a piece, too. Everything went as expected. Suddenly, Chengcheng saw Ms. Yuan (school director) through the window. Ms. Yuan passed by without noticing what was going on in the classroom. To everyone's surprise, Chengcheng immediately went up to his teacher and said: "Hey, Ms. Fanglin. Didn't you see Ms. Yuan

*This chapter was adapted from the article *Becoming a Moral Child amidst China's Moral Crisis: Preschool Discourse and Practices of Sharing in Shanghai* (Xu 2014).

(the school director)? Why don't you give her a piece of cake, too? You know you should cotton up to your boss (*tao jinhu*)." The teacher was dumbfounded at this and made a nickname for him: "evil kiddo."[1]

Observing the whole incident, I was surprised by Chengcheng, too. What struck me most, however, was not the "evilness" of Chengcheng's remarks, but the contrast between what teachers and parents try to cultivate and what emerges in children's own practices—much more complex motivations. This kind of contrast between norms and reality,[2] with its occasionally comic incongruities, is what motivates the present chapter. Teachers and parents, committed to teaching an egalitarian norm of sharing and busy conveying that norm through (among other activities) ritualized birthday parties, do not generally expect a three-year-old child to be so scheming (*xin ji*). Networking skills and cynicism are supposed to be a hallmark of adult attitudes. But the tension between the egalitarian norm and the strategic motivation, particularly in the domain of social exchange and sharing, is not confined to such occasional *faux pas*. It reflects a deep concern with moral cultivation in contemporary Chinese social life, in particular, the panic of raising selfish children under the one-child policy at the height of a perceived moral crisis.

An anthropological study on sharing among young children can join a fruitful conversation with developmental psychology and contribute to the study of human morality and cooperation (Tomasello 2009). In recent years, scholars across social science disciplines have paid great attention to children's "sharing" behaviors, not only because sharing is common among young children, but also because the early forms and motivations of sharing can shed light on the foundations of human cooperation (Olson and Spelke 2008), dispositions for fairness (Fehr, Bernhard, and Rockenbach. 2008; Hamann et al. 2011), and the roots of human morality (Baumard, André, and Sperber 2013).

Specifically, the psychological literature reveals early dispositions for cooperation, including motivations to be egalitarian on the one hand and to maintain profitable exchanges on the other hand. Recent experimental studies provide evidence that such dispositions emerge much earlier than assumed in classic theories (Piaget 1997; Kohlberg 1984). Research suggests that fifteen-month-old infants expect things to be distributed equally, and such sensitivity to equality is correlated with their altruistic sharing behavior toward strangers in a laboratory setting (Schmidt and Sommerville 2011). Preschoolers display negative emotions to unequal distributions (LoBue et al. 2009). Other studies, however, suggest that children exert subtle judgment in the choice of who should be the target of sharing. They take into account various factors, such as direct and indirect reciprocity

(Olson and Spelke 2008), friendship (Moore 2009), social affiliation (Over and Carpenter 2009), and whether the context is competitive or not (Shaw, DeScioli, and Olson 2012). These intuitions of infants and young children indicate an early propensity to reserve resources for valued social partners rather than extending them indiscriminately among one's group.

Despite an increasing interest among developmental psychologists in examining the nascent dispositions for cooperation in infancy and early childhood, little research has been done to explore how these different prosocial motivations emerge in children's daily experiences and how the transmission of local cultural values mediate such developmental dynamics through educational processes at school, with the family, and in society more broadly. Although recent experimental works reveal the early dispositions of sharing in infancy and early childhood, the vast ethnographic literature reveals the richness of human cooperation and how it is embedded in diverse cultural forms and dynamic historical contexts (Benson 2011). What about the psycho-cultural processes through which our various sensibilities for cooperation in its earliest forms develop into culturally specific practices? In order to fully understand this and other psycho-cultural processes in human development, ethnographic studies are much needed (Weisner 1997). In this chapter, I combine ethnographic methods with field experiments to gain a more comprehensive understanding of children's world of sharing, and ultimately, to bridge anthropology and psychology in the study of children's sharing behavior.

The Cultivation of Egalitarian Sharing

Sharing is widely encouraged by Chinese educators and parents. It is seen as the first step toward promoting sociality and generosity, given the pervasive fear that singleton children will become or remain too selfish. Teachers and parents strongly emphasize the virtue of sharing (*fen xiang*), and in particular, equality (*ping deng*) in sharing, in order to promote altruism and self-sacrifice—a heritage of collectivistic ethics from the socialist era that paradoxically gained new momentum in educating the one-child generation. The standard teaching in this preschool is that the child should share equally and indiscriminately with all of his or her classmates.

Sharing and Concerns on Selfish "Little Emperors"

Teachers emphasize sharing as an important developmental goal for young children. The conversation between Teacher Linlin (Class 2B, age range: 3.5–4) and me (Jing) illustrates a common belief among the teachers.

Jing: As a teacher, what character/moral quality (*pinzhi*) do you think is most important for children?

Linlin: We have always been cultivating sharing among them because disputes over toys occurred a lot in the classroom.

Jing: Why do you pay so much attention to sharing?

Linlin: Because right now every family has only one child, and (the children) are all very selfish. It is indeed effective to cultivate sharing. For instance, when the boy Huangzi first came to our class, he was completely self-centered. He would grab any toy he wanted, very strong-willed. "I just want this! I won't give it to others!" He would cry harshly to get what he wanted. Now, because we often tell the children in class to share things instead of fighting with others, he has changed. He often brings little things to share with the class and fights less for toys. Now he almost never says things like, "I get to play with this toy!" or "I got it first!" Never.

Teachers and parents coordinate and cooperate together to instill the egalitarian sharing principle in young children. At the beginning of each new semester, teachers meet with parents to discuss specific educational goals. During these meetings, sharing was routinely voiced as a common educational goal in the domain of social skills among various domains including literacy, motor skills, artistic skills, and so on. For example, the head teacher of Class 1B (age range 2–2.5) explained: "Our goal is to educate the children so that they become willing to share with other children, things like snacks and toys." The head teacher of an older class, with an age of range 3.5 to 4, went one step further: "You (parents) can encourage them to buy things in the store and let them choose what they want to share."

Sharing is a common theme in the *Family-School Communication* book, especially in regard to the younger children. This book is a weekly collection of teacher reports and parent feedback on children's activities, progress, and problems, and it plays an important role in facilitating teacher-parent cooperation. Parents are anxious about their children being too self-centered and often ask the teachers to engage children in sharing practices. For example, one mother wrote: "My girl is very stubborn and self-centered, so I would like to ask you to help her, let her feel fully the joy of sharing, and guide her to learn how to care her friends and classmates." This mother tried every means to instill a willingness to share in her daughter. When her daughter was not even three years old, she once took her daughter to a charity party, with the hope that the little girl would get some education regarding altruism there. Her teacher endorsed this mother's approach: "This little girl is not willing to share things, but her mother insists on bringing things to share in class. Because if a child is not generous when he or she is young, this child will not become more generous in the future. To make sure she won't get too stingy when she grows up, her mother emphasizes sharing from early on."

Another example is Nana, a strong-willed three-year-old girl who seldom shares anything with others. Her mother put her concerns in Nana's *Family-School Communication book*: "Nana never allows others to use her stuff. The other day I got a fever and used her thermometer. She was so upset at this; she screamed and insisted on getting her thermometer back. I am wondering if similar things happen at school. How generous is she compared with other children?" The teacher responded: "Such things happen at school, too. Nana is strong-willed, and she seldom allows others to use her stuff. I think you should prepare some little things for her to share with other children at school. It will get better gradually." The mother did take the advice and put some chocolate in Nana's backpack, and she brought it to share with her class a few days later.

Some parents offer suggestions on how to create opportunities for sharing: "I've told my daughter: 'You can take your toys and books to share with your classmates and bring them back to home at the end of the day.' Also, I even mentioned to their teacher: 'If it is possible, you could make a sharing corner in the classroom and ask each child to bring his or her own toys and books, write their own names on them, and put them in the sharing corner so that they can share with everyone else.'"

Undifferentiated Generosity: The Egalitarian Norm

Data from my child-rearing questionnaire show that the value of sharing with other children generally, rather than targeting specific individuals, is strongly shared by the children's parents. In this questionnaire, the children's social moral development section consisted of ten questions probing caregivers' evaluations and attitudes about children's morality in general; the roles of parents, school, and other people; intergenerational similarities and differences in child-rearing values; as well as the desirable and nondesirable moral characteristics of children. There was a question on sharing: "Do you think children should share toys and snacks with others?" Respondents could select from four possible answers:

A. Yes
B. It depends on who the target people are
C. It depends on the specific situation
D. No

Among the eighty-eight families who responded to this question out of the ninety-two families who I sent the questionnaire to, seventy-nine chose A (yes) [90 percent], three chose B (it depends on who the target people are) [3 percent], and six chose C (it depends on the specific situation) [7 percent].

The norm is not just sharing, but sharing equally with *everyone* in the group. Children are encouraged to bring enough pieces of candy to share with all other students. If they forget to do so, the teacher will remind them to bring more the next day. For instance, one day Xiaobei brought ten candies to class, but there were thirteen children; the next day, he brought three more, to make sure each child would get one. Some children do not need to be reminded. For instance, Qiaoqiao, a very intelligent and sensitive girl, always brought exactly enough items to share with all other students, no more, no less.

In addition to the daily routines of bringing snacks and other items in the morning to share with all classmates, teachers enacted various other special programs to promote "egalitarian sharing," such as "Sharing Day" and birthday parties, illustrated in the following vignettes.

Case 1: Sharing Day (Class 1C; age range: 2.5–3)
In the morning, children brought a variety of snacks to class, everyone with a big pack of chocolate, crackers, or candies. In this class, there are six children, two teachers, and one *Ayi* ("auntie," assistant/helper in the classroom). Xiaoshi, the head teacher in this class, is instructing children how to share step by step. Step one: Teacher calls one child, and that child comes up to her. She tells the child to open his own pack and get the snacks out. Step two: Teacher calls another child, and this child comes up to her. She tells the first child to give one piece out of his pack to this second child. Step three: Teacher tells the second child to say "Thank you." Step four: The "giver" child replies "You're welcome," and the "recipient" child goes back to his or her seat with the snack. Teacher then calls another child and repeats steps one through four. This sequence goes on and on until every child distributes [the] candies to the other children.

Note that 1C is the youngest grade, a new class with children who first enrolled during spring 2012. The Sharing Day is a new practice to them. It is set up with the explicit goal of familiarizing the children with the routines of sharing. A sharp contrast is found in another class, of the same grade, 1A (age range: 3–3.5). This class also held a Sharing Day, but in the morning none of the children remembered to bring snacks to share, simply because the head teacher forgot to inform the parents beforehand.

As children get more familiar with the basic routines of sharing, teachers will go one step further, that is, they will have the children distribute equally with all the children, without teachers' assistance. Teachers found it a rewarding practice for children across age groups. For instance, the head teacher in the oldest class (4A; age range: 6–6.5) said to me: "I ask them to distribute the items one by one, all on their own. This way they feel a sense of achievement, very satisfied. It's totally different from me distributing the things on behalf of them."

Case 2: Xinbao's Birthday Party (Class 3B; age-range: 4.5–5)

Today is Xinbao's birthday. He brought a birthday cake to share with classmates. Usually, parents would bring a whole big birthday cake, but this time his was a set of identical small cakes. Several children spontaneously asked: "Why is it such a small cake this time?" The girl sitting across from Xinbao, named Ciccy, added a comment with a look of disdain: "Mine is always a BIG birthday cake!" Xinbao responded reluctantly: "How would I know? It's my mom who bought it, not me!" Ciccy didn't give in; instead, she said in a more provocative way: "When I celebrated my birthday, my mom let *me* choose the cake!" Seeing Xinbao frustrated, I stepped in and told Ciccy: "This small cake is perfect! You see: one for each exactly, and you don't even need to cut it to pieces." Xinbao nodded promptly. Then the teacher said: "There were only ten students who came to class yesterday, so I told Xinbao's mom to prepare ten pieces. But today we have more students than expected, and we don't have enough cakes. Can we redistribute them, so that everyone gets half of a small cake?" Children answered: "Yes"! Meanwhile, the teacher explained to me: "Sharing is good. Xinbao isn't a stingy child. This morning actually his mother prepared enough pieces of cakes to share with twelve students. But when he came to school, he first gave one to Mr. Zhao (the driver of the school bus), and then to Miss Zhang (the nurse who does morning-check when children enter the school building). So Xinbao is quite generous."

This scenario points out the normative and moral dimensions of children and teachers' understandings of sharing. Through previous experiences, children have acquired a sense of normativity about birthday cake sharing, that it should be a whole big cake and everyone should get a piece. Also, teachers emphasize not only the action of sharing, but also the intention of generosity. In this case, Xinbao had a good excuse for not bringing enough to share because he had already given generously to other people he knew at school.

What is implied in the teacher's comments is that Xinbao's mother should not be blamed, either.

Notice that teachers considered Xinbao's sharing behavior with school bus driver Mr. Zhao and school nurse Miss Zhang as a form of generalized altruism that Xinbao was willing to share with whomever he met, even with adult staff who were in a lower social status within the school hierarchy. This made an interesting contrast with the scenario presented at the beginning of this chapter, the one in which Chengcheng proposed to share a piece of cake with the school director who just passed by without noticing the birthday party in the classroom. They considered Chengcheng as scheming (*xin ji*) and Xinbao as pure and genuine (*chun zhen*) because Chengcheng was trying to appeal to superiors but Xinbao was just being generous to people who saw him bringing a cake. Moreover, such a distinctive judgment was not based on occasional incidents, but based on their familiarity with these different children through previous interactions. What followed was that Xinbao's "generous" motivation compensated for inadequate resources to share, whereas Chengcheng's "strategic" move got him a bad reputation and an unfavorable nickname.

Tracking children's sharing behavior helps teachers not only to judge children's generosity, but also to discern their parents' generosity and moral quality in general. Teachers further believe that parents' behaviors directly influence children's generosity. The story of Tiantian's parents is an apt example. One day Tiantian's mom wrote in the *Family-School Communication* book: "One of the things that we are proud of is Tiantian is very willing to share his food with us in the family, although he is not even three years old. We are curious about how he is like at school." Teacher Fanglin laughed at it when she read it because she thought Tiantian's parents were not generous at all as they seldom brought snacks to share with class. She wrote back in a rather sarcastic way: "Tiantian often has said to me: 'Teacher Fanglin, I will bring snacks to share in class tomorrow.' He has said it so many times, but never brought in anything so far, so eventually I told him: 'You lied to me!' " Fanglin told me she didn't like Tiantian's parents: "Once I told children to bring some snacks to class instead of always eating others' snacks (freeloading), and Tiantian repeated this to his parents at home. The next morning, when his maternal grandmother dropped him off, she gave a whole piece of candy (in a small house shape) to me: 'Tiantian only needs a tiny little portion, and the rest of it you can distribute to the other children!' But it's only one piece of candy, and how can you divide it evenly into pieces enough to share with all children?'" Teacher Fanglin did not distribute it. She kept it and later asked Tiantian to take it back. Teacher Fanglin concluded that Tiantian's family was not generous at all.

The case of two stingy mothers also demonstrates that what teachers emphasize is not only the action of sharing, but also the motivation of authentic generosity.

Case 3: Teacher Report "A Tale of Two Stingy Mothers"

Last time, Lulu's mother brought a really small birthday cake and gave each child a really small piece. And, guess what? She packed the remains and took them back home. So stingy! Mingming is Lulu's cousin, and Mingming's mother is also like this. Once she brought a birthday cake for Mingming. It was a big cake, but she only gave each child a tiny little piece and packed the rest of it for home. What surprised me most was, when some children didn't finish their tiny little piece, this mother, such a tall person, sat on the small child chair and started to eat the remains of what the children didn't finish, one by one. It was so impressive! Such behavior must have impacted Mingming to some extent.

Children use the language of sharing very early on. My son, Wandou, enrolled as the youngest child in this school right at the earliest stages of learning the norms of sharing. One day, right after school, Wandou was playing in the playground, when his teacher came to him, gave him a piece of candy, and walked away. He immediately blurted out the slogan "We should share with our little friends!" (*xiao pengyou*). I was stunned. He had just started school life two months ago, at a time when he could not speak a single word. Already this twenty-month-old boy was spontaneously stating the standard doctrine of his school. Despite this impressive command of the discourse, Wandou did not in fact bother to share with the other two children who were playing right next to him. Wandou once exclaimed "(We) should share things with little friends" in the middle of taking his bath, but stopped for a moment to think, and then uttered a firm protest, "I won't share with 'little friends'!" Sharing seemed more like a ubiquitous threat in his daily school experience that he would instantaneously protest even in the absence of being requested to share. He would suddenly say, "I *won't* share my little sports car with others," when he was happily playing on his own.

The incident echoes a number of other instances recorded in my field notes in which children would spontaneously use the standard phraseology of sharing, while being reticent to actually share anything. This raises the question: To what extent and in what sense does the egalitarian sharing propaganda actually result in what parents and teachers both expect, that is, a sense of generalized altruism? Alternatively, are children's understandings of these norms and their grasp of social exchange and reciprocation actually more sophisticated than generally assumed?

The Practices of Strategic Sharing

Although teachers and parents make efforts to instill a sense of generalized altruism through the practice of egalitarian sharing, another aspect of sharing is relevant here, namely the motivation to extend favors. Strategic interests are clear in children's own justifications, but also in the parents' and teachers' own implicit assumptions (in contrast to their explicit beliefs) about egalitarian sharing.

The Hidden Logic behind Egalitarian Sharing

Teachers point out that, instead of being truly generous with others, children are driven by social satisfaction and reputation, in particular getting praise (*biaoyang*) from teachers and respect from peers. As Fanglin states: "Most children, or even most adults, do not want to give to others. But children are so motivated by adults' positive acknowledgment. When you commend him because he shares things with others, he feels so good. Even if in his most inner self he didn't want to give, he would still overcome it and make the move of sharing." Furthermore, the child feels so satisfied when the teacher praises him in front of all his peers, as the grandmother of Yuanyuan said: "You know why she is willing to bring snacks to share with class? She just feels so good when the other kids say 'thank you' upon receiving her gift." From this perspective, the routines of egalitarian sharing are more like a collective performance or ritual, instead of intrinsically altruistic actions.

Indeed, besides the "educational techniques of commending" (Bakken 2000: 174), teachers also use shaming to motivate selfish children to share (Fung 1999). In many cases, the way teachers shame children reveals an implicit belief in reciprocation—you share because what goes around comes around—that is distinct from the norm of undifferentiated generosity. The point is, such teachings were far more effective than instilling a doctrine of egalitarian sharing, especially in children who were not willing to share.

Case 4: Minmin, the Freeloader (Class: 1A; age: 40 months)

Minmin is among the few in class 1A who never brought things to share. Teacher Fanglin told me, when parents of this class organized a play-date event during the weekend, everyone brought something to share, except Minmin.

She happily enjoyed others' gifts but didn't reciprocate at all. Mommy asked her: "Would you give some to your friends? I will buy more for you." She responded: "I will have even more if I don't give any to them but you still buy some for me." She even explicitly asserted her "dissent" opinion in class.

On February 15, when Teacher Fanglin distributed chocolate to each child, one boy said spontaneously: "I want to bring chocolate to share tomorrow!" Minmin commented bluntly: "I will never bring my own chocolate from home to share with you guys." The next day, Teacher Fanglin told me: "This morning, Minmin came in with a lollipop in hand. I joked: 'Hi Minmin, since you ate the chocolate I gave you, today you brought a lollipop to me, right?' To my surprise, she burst into tears immediately: 'This is mine! Mine!' She is way too selfish, and I need to teach her a lesson."

When it was time for sharing, Teacher Fanglin gave each child one piece of cracker (brought by a parent) except those who seldom bring things to share in class. Teacher Fanglin said to Minmin: "I won't give you anything today because you never gave anything to the other children or me." Then Teacher Fanglin praised the children who often brought things to share and rewarded them with extra pieces, with the sole purpose of making Minmin feel even worse. She then turned back to Minmin: "Do you understand now that you were wrong?" Minmin answered: "Yes, I know." Teacher Fanglin went on: "Will you bring snacks from now on to share with class?" Minmin: "Yes, I will." For the next few days, Teacher Fanglin spoke to Minmin's mother about her concern about Minmin's freeloading and encouraged her to prepare some snacks for her daughter to share in class: "It's unfair of her to always receive but never give."

On the morning of February 23, when I came into the classroom, Teacher Fanglin couldn't wait to share with me the "good news": "You know what? Minmin brought chocolate to share today! Two days ago, I asked her: 'What will you bring in tomorrow?' She said: 'Chocolate!' But yesterday she didn't bring chocolate. I asked her why, she said: 'It's not that I forgot it. I put it in my backpack last night, but this morning I forgot to bring my backpack to school, so would you remind my mother this evening?' Today she didn't break her promise. I did call her mom yesterday. According to her mother, Minmin initially worried about it because after she gave to other children, the chocolate would be gone. So her mother reassured her: 'I will buy more for you.' Her mother was very surprised at how I had been able to change Minmin's mind because she had taught Minmin numerous times that one should be generous and ready to share, but that didn't work at all. I told her mother that sharing is a mutual thing, and that's how I got her to share."

Minmin's case presents an interesting contradiction between the child's fear of the cost of sharing and the teacher's expectation of generosity. The effective way to solve this problem is for Minmin to learn the lesson of mutualism: what comes around goes around. Moreover, Minmin's mother assured her that sharing would incur no cost to her; on the contrary, she could gain from it. That is why she changed her strategy from not sharing to sharing.

Case 5: Nana, the Spoiled Brat (Class: 1A; age: 41 months)

This bright little girl is the star of Class 1A and the teachers' favorite. But she is also known for her strong-willed self-centeredness. There was a book donation day, and children were supposed to bring some books to school for donation. The intended recipients were children in China's Xinjiang province, an underdeveloped ethnic minority region. According to Teacher Fanglin, Nana had a really hard time the night before. She didn't want to donate her book to unknown children and protested: "If you force me to do so, I definitely will have a nightmare tonight!" Indeed, she screamed out in the middle of the night: "Don't give my books to others! Don't give my books to others!" So this morning, she didn't bring any books. Teacher Fanglin asked her: "Why didn't you bring books?" Nana cried out: "No, I won't!" Fanglin asked: "Where is your heart of love (*ai xin*)? Since you won't give your books to others, we won't give you any food, OK?" Nana screamed: "No!" Actually, Teacher Fanglin had just talked with Nana's grandmother, and they agreed to give her some punishment in order to correct her selfishness. At 10 am, it was reading time, and every child got a book to read, except Nana. Nana cried to her teacher, but only got a cold reply: "you don't give to others, so you won't get anything." Nana gave in: "Fanglin, please forgive me! I promise, I will never do this again! I will bring my books next time!" Teacher Fanglin did not reply. A while later, the teacher asked the whole class: "Who didn't donate books today?" Some child announced: "Nana!" This poor little girl felt ashamed for the first time since she came to this school because previously s thought to be was the smartest child in class and the teacher's favorite. According to Teacher Fanglin, Nana later on explained to her family why she didn't want to donate books: "I don't know those children in Xinjiang at all. If I have to, I'd rather share with children in Fuzhou (where Nana's grandparents lived) because I know them."

Here we see the tension between the dominant ideology, that one should care about all people including those one does not know, for example, a book donation to poor children, and the particularistic logic: Nana wanted to share only with people she knew. Another layer of this story is that the teacher used a shaming technique, based on children's motivation of getting praise from teachers and peers, as well as their fear of being criticized and excluded. The teacher emphasized reciprocation, although she initially wanted to cultivate a generalized altruism in Nana. What happened later proved that such techniques do have some effects: after this book donation incident, Nana started to bring snacks and stickers from home to share with other children.

Strategic Sharing among Children

To the children, a lot of times, sharing is intended to gain reciprocal favors and cultivate relationships. Indeed, "underground" sharing activities frequently occur in the classroom context, going against teachers' rule of egalitarian sharing.

First, children's own sharing activities seem to involve clear differentiation of whom to share or not to share with, as well as well-calculated distribution of how many to share. For example, Congcong (Class 4A; age: 6) always brought some candies in his pockets and shared secretly with the three children he liked most. Usually, he made careful calculations of how many pieces he planned to give to each of his friends.

Sharing is also a convenient way to expand one's network and gain access to a new social group. For example, when Yichen (Class 4A; age: 6) first came to this school after his family moved to Shanghai, he tried very hard to build connections with his classmates. Yichen's mother told me: "He is willing to pay a cost for it. He would save the snacks and toys I gave him to share with the ones he wanted to be friends with." Yichen eventually built his social circle and became an active member of his new class.

On the other hand, turning down others' favors is a signal of terminating a relationship. Xinxin (Class 3A; age: 6) was a special child whose motor development was delayed slightly. When she was three, she liked Xiaomin very much, and her parents suggested that she bring snacks to Xiaomin in order to build a friendship. At first, this strategy worked, and these two girls became friends. But gradually Xiaomin found Xinxin to be abnormal and nobody played with her. Xiaomin intentionally distanced herself from Xinxin. During the second year of preschool, Xinxin was trying to save this friendship, but the same sharing strategy didn't work, and Xiaomin rejected her favors.

Children keep good track of sharing histories in order to distinguish reliable from unreliable social partners, and they make wise decisions to build their own reputation. For one, children feel indebted to give back favors they received and recognize the importance of reputation in facilitating future interactions. For instance, Mingming, a popular boy in Class 2A (age: 4) who always received small gifts from his classmates, once expressed concern to his mom that he had received too much but gave too little, so his mother encouraged him to reciprocate. Children also hold detailed, affect-laden memories of sharing episodes. Sometimes these are positive occurrences when favors were paid back and relationships were strengthened, but many memories are about transgressions, in which the balance of fairness becomes lopsided or the chain of reciprocation breaks down. In such cases, children not only remember situations of transgressions, they also rely on their detailed memories of sharing histories to evaluate good and bad social partners. The story of Kailin and Junyi, narrated by their teacher, provides an example of how moral evaluations are imbued in incidents of "sharing"—evaluations that are not only enacted by children themselves, but also endorsed, albeit implicitly, by teachers.

Case 6: Teacher Report on Kailin and Junyi,
the Innocent versus the Sneaky (Class 3A)

Kailin is an innocent and naive child (*tian zhen*), and she often shares her toys with friends. At first, she liked Junyi very much, a girl who I think is sneaky and scheming (*xin ji*). She often invited Junyi home and shared all her toys, even her favorite ones, with Junyi. But as time went by, Kailin realized that Junyi was not as generous as she was. Once she complained: "Junyi never shares her favorite toys with me." But this innocent little girl Kailin didn't think about it too much, until something happened, at her birthday party this April.

That day, Kailin brought a beautiful birthday cake with some special decorations on it, including a cute heart shape and some colorful little balloons. I told Kailin to help divide the cake into even pieces, and she could decide who gets these special decorations. She gave the beautiful heart shape to Junyi immediately, without any hesitation. But Junyi was not satisfied and requested the balloons. Kailin replied: "Sorry, I can't. This is my mom's gift for me." I didn't want them to have any conflicts, so I asked Kailin: "Can you give just one balloon to Junyi?" She thought for a while and gave one to Junyi, with some reluctance. After the birthday party, when Kailin got ready to bring the balloons back home, I couldn't find them. Then, when I helped the children put on their clothes, I found the balloons in Junyi's pocket. Apparently, Junyi stole them. Her first reaction when confronted was to make an excuse for herself: "Miss Karen, I took these balloons to give to Kailin." She lied, and it was not the first time she took small items from class and lied to me. Although Kailin didn't say anything, thereafter they were not best friends anymore.

Sometimes, transgression of reciprocal sharing rules would not only result in the termination of a friendship or a dislike for the transgressor, but also ignite children's revengeful emotions and actions. For example, during my interview with Sicheng (Class 3B; age: 5.5), he told me why Tony was the person he liked the least among all his classmates. Sicheng often brought a small box of candies to classroom and asked Teacher Xiaoling to keep it as a reward to give to those children who performed well in class. Tony was not a good friend of Sicheng. Actually, Tony was not a popular boy because he was not good in school performance, and he was often seen as a self-centered child. One day Sicheng found out that Tony had stolen candy from his box. So the next morning, he brought an empty candy box to trick Tony. Sicheng's account evinced his anger: "Tony often steals from my small box of rainbow candies, that's why I hate him!" But when he described how he got revenge, he burst into laughter: "Today I brought an empty box in order to fool him, and he ended up getting nothing!"

Revealing Strategic Motives:
Inquiry through Field Experiment

Shanghai preschoolers, although fluent in the ideology of egalitarian sharing, are often reluctant to follow its imperatives. To many parents, most teachers, and perhaps most outsiders, there would be a simple interpretation to this resistance in terms of "selfishness" or, to be less normative, of self-interest. Children's motivations, however, seem less simple and more interesting, as they are often focused, not on refusing to share at all, but on discriminating with whom to share. What seems to be at stake here is less outright selfishness than a proper understanding of the potential benefits and pitfalls of reciprocation.

To verify this interpretation, one needs to go beyond mere observation and use more controlled instruments. That is why I conducted three field experiment studies with preschoolers, the aim of which was to disentangle a general sense of sharing and equality from concerns relating to reciprocation and cultivating valuable relationships. I called these field experiment studies "sharing games," and I ran these simple protocols with eighty children, ages 2 to 6. The advantage of field experiments in this research is twofold: First, although most classroom sharing occurs in a collective setting, the field experiment creates an opportunity to interview individual children privately in a naturalistic environment (their own classroom) where they feel comfortable. Second, although natural sharing situations vary in many different ways, experimental protocols have the same format so that reliable comparison is possible.

I conducted the first sharing game in October 2011, the second one in December 2012, and the third one in February 2012. The three studies were scattered at different phases of my fieldwork, which served two purposes: First, I wanted to avoid bombarding children with similar games in a concentrated time period, so that the children would be more interested in participating, and they would not remember what exactly they had done in each of the previous games. Second, the spread-out experimental timeline allowed me to closely think through each game, including design, results, and interpretations, so that I could better and more flexibly adjust my experimental ideas and strategies. Third, spacing the three studies at critical time-points of my fieldwork provided an opportunity for my ethnographic inquiry and experimental data collection to inform each other in a reciprocal fashion. For example, when I conducted the first sharing game in October 2011, it was only one month after I started my fieldwork, and things still seemed somewhat chaotic. On the one hand, the fact that I had spent a month or so with Biyu Preschool children to develop a basic familiarity with them allowed me to conduct the experiment with them in a more comfortable and natural way, which was important for ensuring valid experimental data collection. On the other hand, at that time I had not yet become a close member of this school community, and a more concrete and meaningful plan of ethnographic data collection had not been developed. By "playing a game" with many of the children in this preschool, children and I got to know one another much better, and I gained a lot of information about their social life through chatting with them (through the mini-interview at the end of the sharing game). Moreover, the results and experiences of this first systematic sharing game helped me to figure out what particular aspects and themes of children's school life I should focus on in later participant observation and interviews (with both caregivers and children), and it facilitated my ethnographic data collection.

These field experiments were designed to probe four assumptions in sharing behavior: First, as the initiator of prosocial behavior, I should make sure that the target of my behavior knows that it is me who shared with him or her, as anonymous giving allows no direct reciprocation. This is called the non-anonymity assumption. Second, the target should be someone who will stay in my social circle because people who leave it cannot reciprocate. This is called the stable partner assumption. Third, the target of sharing behavior should be a specific person rather than any member of a group because it makes it easier to track reciprocation. This is called the individuality assumption. Fourth, I should be interested in pursuing further interactions with the target of my sharing behaviors, first because I may expect that he or she will be motivated to be generous to me more than other individuals, and second because I may thereby recoup my investment. This is called the future-anticipation assumption.

The basic structure of the sharing games went like this. With the teacher's permission, I asked a child if he or she was willing to play a little game with me. If the child said yes, I then brought him or her from their main activity room to their noon nap room or dining room where no one else was around and asked him or her to complete a shape-tracing task. After the task was completed, I thanked the child, gave him or her two candies, and told him or her the candies were a reward for hard work. Note that this task was intentionally designed to make sure that the two candies would be understood as a reward for the participant's efforts or hard work. This is important for several reasons. "Windfall" rewards might distort children's understandings about this task, and they might not really believe they were entitled to share the candies with target recipients as they wished. Also, rewarding children with candies for their good work in drawing tasks is very common in classroom settings, so this design is ecologically valid and easily understandable for these children.

Next, after the candies were rewarded to the participant, I asked whether he or she wanted to share one candy with another child and waited for his or her response for one minute or so. All the children were willing to share, and most of them chose to share one candy and keep the other one for him- or herself. Then the child had a choice between two possible recipients. One was presented as a new student who would arrive at the school the following day and stay as a classmate, while the other was described as a child who would visit the school only for a day. After the choice for sharing recipient was made, I asked the child: "Why do you want to share with this child?" Then I asked whether he or she wanted to use a signed envelope ("This comes from . . . [name of the participant]") or an anonymous envelope ("This comes from a child in your school") to wrap their gift when it was sent to the recipient. I also asked the child: "Why do you want to use this envelope?" The "why" questions were aimed to elicit children's own justifications, explanations, and thoughts about their choices in the experimental tasks. The underlying rationale is that a commitment to generalized sharing and a strategic motivation would lead to different choices. If the goal is to make everyone equal, a visitor and a student are similar; a signed and an anonymous donation have the same result. If, by contrast, one is motivated to cultivate relationships, then it matters that one's gifts should be signed and that the recipients should be valuable partners in a position for future reciprocation.

This experiment also presented an opportunity for me to chat with children about their social life, in particular their experiences of sharing, friendship, and social exchange. Thus, in the end of the experiment, after children had made all the choices, I did a semi-structured mini-interview with them. For example, I asked them the following questions: "Have you ever shared anything with others, like snacks or toys? Who did you share with?" "Has anyone else shared anything with you, like snacks or toys? Who shared with you?" "Who is your best friend? Why do you like him or her best?" "Who is not your friend? Why don't you like him or her?" From these questions, I proceeded onto freestyle chatting; the mini-interview ranged from five to fifteen minutes.

Sharing Game I: Non-Anonymity and Stable Partner

The purpose of this sharing game was to examine both the anonymity and stable partner assumptions. Participants could share an earned reward either as a signed gift or an anonymous one, and they could send their contribution to either one of two children, a new student who would stay at their school or a child who would just stay for a day. Fifty-two children from Biyun Preschool participated in this game, twenty-six boys and twenty-six girls. Ages ranged from thirty months to seventy months (M = 50, SD = 13). In the final analysis, I grouped the children into two categories, two- and three year-olds and four- and five year-olds, respectively.

The game started with a work task followed by a sharing task. For the first task, E (the experimenter) asked C (the child) to accomplish a drawing task. The child was to draw a circle inside each of six geometric shapes on a sheet of paper. As a reward for success, E then gave two candies to C and showed him or her two trays, labeled "for Mingming" and "for Lele."[3] E then explained: "Mingming and Lele both come to visit the school today. Mingming just comes here to play because his own school is off today, and tomorrow he will not be here again. Lele comes here as a new student in your class and will start school tomorrow." E then checked that C knew who each of the trays was for and repeated the explanations if necessary. The experimenter asked the child two questions: (1) "Would you like to share one candy with one of these kids?" [if yes, then] (2) "Do you want to give a candy to Mingming—he won't come back after today? Do you want to give a candy to Lele—he will be in your class tomorrow?" After the child had made a choice, E asked: (3) "Why do you want/ not want to share with Mingming (or Lele)?" and then helped put the candy in the appropriate tray. Then E showed C two envelopes: "Now we should put the candy in an envelope, so that we can send it to Mingming (or Lele). This envelope says 'A gift from [participant's name].' The other one says 'a gift for you.'" And asked (4) "Which one do we use, the one with your name or the one with no name?" After the child made the choice, E put the candy in the chosen envelope and asked: (5) "Why do you want your name on the envelope?" After they responded, children were then thanked for participation.

Results of this sharing game are summarized in Table 4.1. All children but one chose to share one out of the two candies they had received. Both age groups preferred signed to anonymous giving (Yates $\chi^2 = 14.45$, p = .001 for the younger group; Yates $\chi^2 = 19$, p < .001 for the older group; no effect of age, p = .56). For partner choice (leaving versus staying), the younger group tended to prefer giving to the child who would stay (Yates $\chi^2 = 2.45$, p = .07), while the older group showed no preference (Yates $\chi^2 < 1$, p = .71).

Why is it that the older children showed no clear preferences, whereas the younger ones preferred the child who would stay? To evaluate the motivations behind these choices, I also examined the justifications children gave as to why they chose a certain partner. I classified their justifications into three categories: (1) investment motive, if the child mentioned future interactions as the basis for his or her choice, for example, "I chose Lele because he will stay in my class, and I'll make friends with him, and later on he can bring something to me"; (2) fairness motive if children emphasized the need to reduce inequality, for example, "It's not fair if I choose Lele because Lele will stay here and it's possible for him to get more candies from me in the future, but not Mingming"; and (3) no justification as some children simply said nothing and just repeated their choices. Table 4.2 summarizes these justifications.

These justifications may explain why, as children got older, their preference for the stable partner (the child who will stay) dropped to random. First, some of the older children chose the child who will leave out of a concern for fairness. As the table shows, fairness becomes an important motivation for older children, but not the younger ones. Second, as the data suggest, only the older children become aware that one can actually create a possible future reciprocal

Table 4.1 Children's choices of sharing and anonymity in Sharing Game I

Age group	Share at all?	Gift must be signed	Give to child who will stay	Give to child who will leave
2 and 3	19 / 20	19 / 19	14 / 19	6 / 19
4 and 5	31 / 31	29 / 31	14 / 31	17 / 31

Table 4.2 Children's justifications for their choices in Sharing Game I

Age group	Choose the child who will stay			Choose the child who will leave		
	Invest	Fairness	None	Invest	Fairness	None
2 and 3	11	0	3	0	1	5
4 and 5	9	0	3	4	9	7

relationship by investing in the unstable partner. Some older children mentioned the gift they gave was actually a souvenir so that the child who would leave could remember them and might become friends with them in the future.

Sharing Game II: Individuality of Partner

The second sharing game was intended to address the third assumption that a social investment motivation would lead one to invest in a specific individual rather than any one of a set of individuals. Thirty-six children (fifteen boys) from Biyu Preschool participated in this game, and their age ranged from thirty-four to seventy-four months (M = fifty-six months, SD = thirteen months). For analysis, I again grouped the participants into two categories, three- and four-year-olds, and five- and six-year-olds.

The basic structure of this game was essentially similar to that of the previous game, starting with the same drawing task. But in the sharing task, the participants were showed two trays with labels, and E explained that one tray was for "a child who will join our school and stay here" and the other was for "any of the students who may want a piece of candy." The experimenter then checked that the child had understood and retained the relevant information. The experimenter then proceeded to ask (1) the sharing question, (2) the target question, and (3) the justification question as was done in Sharing Game I.

Results of this sharing game are summarized in Table 4.3. All children decided to share their candies. Neither the younger children nor the older ones had clear preferences between the two targets (for the younger group, Yates $\chi^2 < 1$, p = .80; for the older group, Yates $\chi^2 < 1$, p = .66).

Table 4.3 Children's choices of sharing targets in Sharing Game II

Age group	Share at all?	Share with individual target	Share with collective target
3 and 4	15/15	8	7
5 and 6	21/21	12	9

Table 4.4 Children's justifications for their choices in Sharing Game II

	Choose the child who will stay			Choose the child who will leave		
Age group	Invest	Norms	None	Invest	Norms	None
3 and 4	5	0	3	0	2	5
5 and 6	9	0	3	1	5	3

We also examined the justifications for choices and classified them as: (1) investment; (2) norms; (3) no justification. See Table 4.4. This suggests the interplay of two clearly distinct motivations. Most children who chose to give to an individual justified their decisions by appealing to investment potential, for example, pointing out that this person will be grateful, will want to play with them, and so on. By contrast, those who chose the collective virtually repeat official instructions to "share with everyone" because it is "good to share."

Sharing Game III: Future Anticipation

This sharing game was designed to address the fourth assumption, that one should be interested in pursuing further interactions with the target of his or her sharing behaviors. I asked the child to decide whether he or she would like to play with either of two children, one of whom he or she had previously chosen as a target for generosity. The hypothesis was that, if social investment was a consideration, participants would wish to play with the child he or she had already favored because that child might reciprocate favors. By contrast, a generalized altruism hypothesis would not predict a preference. To make sure that the choice of target and then the choice of partner were not driven by some arbitrary preference for one name or picture, the experimenter strongly influenced the participants in their choice of target for generosity. Specifically, I informed them that one of the targets had never had this particular kind of candy before while the other one had plenty of candies. On the basis of previous pilots, we expected that they would choose to give candy to the needy child. Note that this makes the social investment choice of the target as a future playmate potentially more costly given we described the other choice as a "rich" child with many candies, possibly an attractive playmate. Also, I again asked the children whether they wanted their contribution to be anonymous or signed, to reaffirm the non-anonymity feature of strategic sharing. Fifty children ages three to six from Biyu Preschool participated in this game, twenty-two of them boys. Their ages ranged from thirty-seven months to seventy-nine months ($M =$ fifty-seven months, $SD =$ twelve months). For analysis, I grouped the participants into three categories, three to four-year-olds, four- to five-year-olds, and five- to six-year-olds.

The basic structure of this game was essentially similar to the previous two games, starting with the same drawing task. In the sharing task, however, E presented the two boxes as intended for two distinct children, adding that the first child had never had this type of candy before, whereas the second one already had a lot of candies. E showed C the two boxes and checked that the participant had retained the relevant information. Then E asked questions (1 to 5) as in Sharing Game I. Next, E conducted a distracter task, asking questions about the child's family. What followed was a "friend choice task," at which point E showed the boxes with the names of the children and asked question (6), "Which one would you like to play with?" and (7) "Why?" The last step was a memory check: E asked question (8) "Do you remember which child you shared a candy with?"

Results of this sharing game are summarized in Table 4.5. All children chose to share with other children. A Yates-corrected chi-square analysis on answers to a "signed envelope" shows a significant preference for signed gifts in all age groups: three- to four-year-olds, $\chi^2 = 8.643$, $p < 0.01$; four- to five-year-olds, $\chi^2 = 11.25$, $p < 0.01$; and five- to six-year-olds, $\chi^2 = 10.56$, $p = 0.001$.

With regard to choosing a playmate to share with, Yates-corrected chi-square tests showed a statistically significant preference for the target of previous generous behavior in four- to five-year-olds, $\chi^2 = 18.05$, $p < 0.001$ and five- to six-year-olds, $\chi^2 = 14.063$, $p < 0.001$, but not in three-year-olds.

Note that children's choice of a playmate was probably not a simple effect of perseveration (making the same choice twice), because this would have predicted more such choices in younger children, when we actually observed the opposite. Children's justifications for choosing to play with child A (or B) are classified into four categories: (1) "Investment motive" (sharing creates potential partner), for example, "I want to play with A because I shared candy with A"; (2) "Need motive" (having a need makes the receiving party a potential partner), for example, "I want to play with A because she needs candy";

Table 4.5 Children's choices of sharing and anonymity in Sharing Game III

Age group	Share at all?	Signed giving	Share with Child A	Play with Child A
2 and 3	14 / 14	13 / 14	13 / 14	7 / 14
4 and 5	20 / 20	18 / 20	20 / 20	18 / 20
5 and 6	16 / 16	15 / 16	16 / 16	14 / 16

Table 4.6 Children's justifications for their choices in Sharing Game III

Age group	Investment	Need	Other	None
2 and 3	2	2	2	8
4 and 5	5	7	1	7
5 and 6	4	4	4	4

(3) "Other explanations, for example, "I want to play with A because she is cute"; (4) "Zero justification or simply repeating choice." "Investment" and "need" emerge as the two major categories of motivations, among all justifications; see Table 4.6.

Ethnographic Interpretation of Experimental Evidence

Interesting findings emerged out of these three sharing games, pointing to a broader theoretical discussion. Most of the children across age groups were willing to share with others and used a standard normative language to justify this, for example "because it is good to share," "because one should share," and the like. This reflects the fact that these preschoolers, as mentioned previously, can readily express the norms fostered by parents and teachers. Notably, they had gotten familiar with me (the experimenter) as "Teacher Xu," who did not have the same kind of authority as their real teachers did, especially because I didn't engage in any disciplinary practices with them and I was always the gentle and kind adult in their classrooms. But still, they might see me, an adult, as an authority figure. This fundamentally hierarchical relation between "the experimenter" and "the participant," presumably neglected in standard experimental studies in developmental psychology, is nonetheless an integral part of an anthropological understanding of children's social and moral worlds. These young Chinese children are already sensitive to and capable of normative expressions and incorporate consideration of authority figures and social desirability into simple sharing games. This has important implications for understanding how culture, education, and children's developing minds are intricately connected.

Another point that stands out is the intricate connections between the experimental process and its natural context. For example, some children I tested, especially those younger ones, the moment I asked "Do you want to share these candies with others?" immediately stood up and were ready to leave the room to give the candy to their friend in the classroom. I was amused at such spontaneity and had to explain to them the rules of the game again, that the decision was not about sharing with their real friends, but with hypothetical targets.

These children's choices, however, revealed interesting preferences that deviated from the normative imperatives. First, most children (more than 90 percent across all games) did not want to be anonymous givers. They wanted the recipient to know who was being generous with them. Second, most of the younger children (74 percent) chose to give to a child who would stay in their school rather than to one who would not. Finally, 60 percent of children (especially the older ones) said they expected to become friends with the recipient to whom they had given the candy, suggesting that they did see sharing as a way to cultivate a longer term relationship.

Indeed, with regard to the second point, although the older children did not show a clear preference for choosing the child who would leave versus one who would stay, a closer look at their justifications revealed an interesting picture. The older children who preferred to give a piece of candy to the child who would leave justified this choice in terms of cultivating new relationships and expanding their social networks. For example, quite a few said, "I want to share with someone who will not stay because the gift is like a souvenir and the child will remember me." This contrasts with the results in a recent experimental study with American children (Smith, Blake, and Harris 2013), the first study that systematically examines why young children endorse egalitarian norms of sharing but end up acting in contradiction to those norms. Although that study suggests that it is because the weight children attach to the egalitarian norm increases with age, my study presents a more complex picture. As children get older, instead of increasingly endorsing the egalitarian norm, my field experiments reveal that they become more sophisticated in strategic sharing. Their understandings of potential friendships and connections are more complex than those of younger children, and there is more variability in their reasoning and decisions about whom to give to, which is compatible with my ethnographic evidence.

When the Developing Mind Meets the Evolving Culture: Cooperative Motivations and *Guanxi*

The tension between the educational norms of egalitarian sharing and the children's own strategies, revealed in both ethnographic and experimental evidence, is of course not specific to Shanghai preschools or even to China, even though it takes on a highly specific intensity and moral overtone in the Chinese context. An intriguing question, however, remains: Why is it that despite the ideological bombardment of an egalitarian norm in educational settings, strategic favors pervade children's sharing practices? What does the cultural and educational context have to do with this tension? In this section I try to demonstrate that the early development of different prosocial motivations are highly sensitive to and constantly shaped by the ongoing cultural and educational dynamics.

Cognitive psychologists, evolutionary biologists, and economists have reflected on these contrasting aspects of human cooperation, between *altruistic* and *mutualistic* motivations. The former principle suggests that people are motivated to share, simply because they are concerned about others' welfare and are prepared to incur costs to benefit others (Boyd et al. 2003; Gintis et al. 2003). But there is another possible interpretation of such generous behaviors in terms of a motivation to build mutually advantageous, reciprocal, longer lasting exchange relationships (Baumard et al. 2013; Tomasello et al. 2012).

All this is given a very specific twist in the Shanghai context. No discussion of exchange, trust, reciprocation, and morality in modern China can avoid considering the omnipresent norms, practices, and debates surrounding *guanxi*, a defining feature of Chinese social interactions. Chinese social interactions are pervasively imprinted with the signature of *guanxi*, the practice of reciprocal gifts and favors in establishing personal connections.

The main assumptions of *guanxi* are that one should extend favors whenever possible and cultivate mutual goodwill, that reciprocation is expected, and that connections are useful. Most Chinese people find this motivation to create, calculate, manage, and foster relationships entirely natural and essential to social life. The nuanced social sensibilities encapsulated in the *guanxi* norms include (1) *xinji*, calculation and scheming in planning for and making decisions about sharing; (2) *renqing* (Yan 1996), a sense of moral obligation to maintain the flow of reciprocity; (3) *ganqing* (Kipnis 1997), human sentiments and good feelings that emerge out of and simultaneously drive these practices, and (4) *renxin* (Chang 2010), the pivotal role of the creativity of the human heart as agentive, flexible, and future-oriented (Liang 1984) in the constant transformations of different social relationships. Far from a static cultural essence, *guanxi* is resilient and dynamic, continuously adapting to new social transformations as well as shaping them (Kipnis 1997; Yan 1996; Yang 1994; Yang 2002). The notion of relationships as strategically cultivated and fluid is well expressed in the Chinese term *la guanxi*—"to pull the connection"—making a connection and establishing a relationship.

*Guanx*i is a subject extensively examined in China studies across social science disciplines, but what is new in this chapter is what *guanxi* practices in the adult world might have to do with young children's social interactions.

Children at Biyu Preschool spontaneously adopt strategic attitudes to cooperation. Such strategic attitudes resemble, although in a fairly rudimentary way, the requirements of *guanxi*. They assume that partners are valuable and that generosity creates partnerships, but also that not all partners are equally valuable and that one should expect and monitor reciprocation. Also, children's sharing practices integrate both cognitive calculation and emotional intensity in fluid ways. As noted previously, memories of past exchanges and incidents support moral evaluations of partners' accountability as well as one's own indebtedness, as Ellen Oxfeld found in adult moral life in a rural Chinese community (Oxfeld 2010).

It would be naive to assume that young children are unaffected by *guanxi* practices in the broader social world. In the age of a moral crisis, sharing is intended by caregivers as a way to cultivate a sense of altruism among the spoiled "little emperors" in a perceived immoral era. Their own *guanxi* practices, however, inevitably contribute to the amplification of the moral crisis, in which corruption is an important theme. Such practices are visible to young children in subtle ways. The culture of bribery in the Chinese education system is notorious (Levin 2012). At Biyu Preschool, parents tried every possible way to cultivate a relationship with the teachers, so that their child would be favored or at least not ignored. They sent various gifts to the teachers in private, including expensive performance tickets, gift cards to major shopping malls, or skincare products from Hong Kong or the United States. Parents sometimes invited teachers to have dinner with their family as a way for the child to develop a personal relationship with teachers. Favoritism intruded into the classroom, as teachers felt indebted by some parents' favors and obligated to pay more attention to their children, for example, assigning certain children better seats in the classroom or giving them a leading role in class performances. Parents implicated their children in these negotiations. They prepared small gifts, such as snacks, for their children to bring to teachers, just as they told the child to use sharing as a means to cultivate friendship with some particular children. It is not unusual to see a three-year-old chatting with the teacher secretly and giving her some small snacks to signal a special fondness for the teacher. Nor is it rare to see a teacher giving a particular child some candy as a special favor, unnoticed by other children.

So the feedback chain goes both ways between psychological and cultural processes. On the one hand, some early cooperative predispositions or capacities, identified in the psychological literature, enable young children to recognize certain features and principles of *guanxi* practices they are exposed to;

otherwise these patterns would have been entirely opaque to them. This partly explains why they are not motivated as much by a generalized altruism. On the other hand, *guanxi* practices in the adult world as well as in certain educational contexts reinforce the "particularistic mutualism" logic and motivation among children, and thus children's strategic sharing behaviors proliferate in their social interactions.

It is a typical Chinese way of gift exchange—sending gifts to one's superiors to gain favor in a hierarchical system (Yan 2002). But in this as in the broader context of Chinese social life, one should not be too quick to equate *guanxi* with bribery. In many cases, the parent-teacher relationship is not merely a monetary, transactional one, but can evolve into sincere friendship. For example, Fanglin, the head teacher of Class 2A, became very close with Junjun's mother. Junjun's mother treated Fanglin like a younger sister, and Fanglin would go to Junjun's mother for advice when she had problems in her personal life.

This positive feedback chain of favoritism has unintended consequences, however; that is, children become aware of *guanxi* and the benefits it brings. That is how three-year-old Chengcheng, the main protagonist of the vignette in the beginning of this chapter, could be aware of the need for a preschool teacher to "pull the connection" with her boss.

More amusingly, one can see in the following vignette the gap between a child-version strategic favor and the fully fledged *guanxi* practice in the adult world. This "evil kiddo," although having successfully gained favors from Director Yu, was nonetheless not entirely cognizant about the complexities of the adult hierarchy, such as the status of the helper (*Ayi*). One day, Director Yu gave him some candy, but he was puzzled by the fact that his beloved *Ayi* Zhang (an assistant/helper in his class) didn't get a piece. He took *Ayi* Zhang out of classroom: "Why didn't you ask Director Yu for a candy? I know she is Teacher Fanglin's boss, and that's why Fanglin didn't dare to ask her. But you are different. She is not your boss. I am taking you to see her and get a piece of candy for you." *Ayi* Zhang laughed at him and went away embarrassed. Chengcheng mistakenly believed that *Ayi* Zhang was not in a subordinate position relative to Director Yu and assumed that it was OK to ask for a candy for someone who was not in a subordinate position. He genuinely liked *Ayi* Zhang, but his well-intended, yet naive invitation embarrassed her because it deviated from social interaction norms in the adult world. This scenario illustrates an intriguing moment when the developing mind has partially absorbed, but not fully internalized, the cultural norm of *guanxi*, as this complex cultural norm is more elaborate than the basic cooperative motivations developed in the earliest years of life.

Sharing, Generosity, and the Selfish Child

Promoting sharing behavior constitutes another important cultural theme in Chinese moral education, as parents and teachers believe that this is an effective way to combat only-children's selfishness and foster their generosity. Similar to what is happening in other moral domains such as empathy, ownership, and fairness, however, cultivating generosity through sharing is also imbued with contradictions between ideology and practice, and adults' concern over the selfish child obscures the complexity of children's motivations that underlie sharing behavior.

This chapter examines how the tension between the discourse of egalitarian sharing and the practice of strategic sharing is formed and transformed in daily interactions at Biyu Preschool. Going beyond the simplistic story of the selfish child, this chapter takes a close look at children's world of sharing. It combined ethnographic and experimental methods to delve into the ontogeny of different cooperative motivations and the deeply entrenched *guanxi* norm in China and shows how psychological mechanisms and cultural practice together shape moral development.

Although the beginning vignette reveals the eye-opening fact that a three-year-old already shows strategic sharing motivations resembling *guanxi* in the adult Chinese world, contrary to the egalitarian sharing ideology emphasized by teachers, the scenario at the end of this chapter illustrates a liminal moment in children's moral development when children's nascent cooperative motivations meet local cultural norms to form their own heuristics of social interactions. Heuristics like this, revealed in snapshot-like vignettes and field experiments in preschool life, not only reflect the influences from the adult world, but also indicate children's mysterious creativity and agency. The next chapter, going beyond specific domains of moral development, explores the all-encompassing cultural concept of *guanjiao*, with a focus on the layers of tensions emerging in Chinese child-rearing beliefs and practices today, as well as children's agentive, anti-disciplinary tactics.

5 Disciplining the Little Emperors: Navigating on Shifting Grounds

Re-Examining *Guanjiao*, the Chinese Way of Child-Rearing

At 4:00 p.m., children in Class 1A started to watch a cartoon episode on TV. They sat properly in a row, waiting for the teachers and helpers to help them put their outfits on. I happened to overhear this funny conversation between Teacher Fanglin and a boy named Pengpeng when Fanglin was putting on Pengpeng's coat.

Fanglin: Pengpeng, who bought you this coat, Father or Mother?

Pengpeng: Father.

To everyone's surprise, Pengpeng added immediately: Father spanks me, and Mother puts me in the "little dark room" (*xiao hei wu*).

I came to Pengpeng and started chatting with him.

Jing: Pengpeng, so your father spanks you at home?

Pengpeng: Yes. Father spanks me when I keep playing blocks at night and don't go to bed.

Jing: How does father spank you?

Pengpeng voiced out "pia-pia" to mimic the sound of spanking, lifting one hand to mimic the action.

Jing: And Mother locks you in the "little dark room"?

Pengpeng: Yes. She puts me in the "little dark room" when I refuse to go to bed.

I burst into laughter, and Xiaoya the assistant teacher came to us when she heard our conversation.

Xiaoya asked Pengpeng: "Does your paternal grandma (*nainai*) rescue/save you?"

Pengpeng: Yes!

Jing: How?

Pengpeng spontaneously opened his arms and answered with a smile:
A sweet, sweet hug!

Pengpeng, the only child of his family, lives with his parents and paternal grandparents in an apartment in the nearby neighborhood. Both of his parents are busy at work, and his paternal grandparents, especially his grandmother, are the major caregivers. Two working parents, grandparents taking care of grandchildren and housework, and co-residence of the three-generation family are typical elements of a middle-class family in Shanghai and other cities. This funny anecdote is just one of many episodes related to an omnipresent theme in children's daily life at home and school, that is, *guanjiao*. Both a verb and a noun, *guanjiao* is the primary term my adult informants used in reference to disciplining the child, compared to other terms such as training (*xun lian*), teaching (*jiao dao*), and control (*kong zhi*). This word consists of two characters: *guan*—to govern/look after, and *jiao*—to teach/edify. Taken together, "to govern/look after" and "to teach/edify" constitute two sides of the same coin. Beliefs about *guanjiao* are represented in the Confucian child-rearing classic the "Three Characters Classic" (*san zi jing*), such as "to feed without teaching, is the father's fault" (*yang bu jiao, fu zhi guo*) and "to teach without severity/ strictness, is the teacher's laziness" (*jiao bu yan, shi zhi duo*). These are popular sayings even in today's society. Young children at Biyu Preschool recite these sentences at school because the "Three Character Classic" is the very first "classic text" they learn. When asked about why children need discipline (*guanjiao*), my informants at Biyu Preschool, both parents and teachers, have mentioned this common proverb, "Nothing can be accomplished without norms and standards" (*Wu guiju bu cheng fang yuan*). This proverb literally means "without a ruler or a compass, one cannot draw out a square or a circle." This metaphor highlights the role of *guanjiao* in shaping children's moral character for their future success. This chapter aims to provide an in-depth analysis of *guanjiao* in Biyu Preschool children's school and family life because *guanjiao* is a salient cultural concept in Chinese education and child-rearing, and disciplinary and training practices undergird moral development in the domains/areas examined in previous chapters, such as learning to care for others, to respect and negotiate property rules, and to share with others.

This folk term *guanjiao* is a significant research theme in Chinese socialization and child-rearing literatures across the disciplines of anthropology, psychology, and education. In the classic article "Chinese Patterns of Socialization: A Critical Review" (Ho 1986), psychologist David Y. F. Ho proposes that family socialization in China displays distinct patterns that differ from Western societies, including dependency, obedience, and achievement motivation. The theme of parental control in Chinese child-rearing is developed in ethnographic studies, in which scholars demonstrate the importance of the folk Chinese concept *guan* or *guanjiao*. In a comparative study of preschool education in three cultures (United States, China, and Japan), Tobin and colleagues (1991) point out that although the word *guan* literally means "to govern," it also has a positive connotation—"to care for"—in the Chinese cultural context. Compared to teachers in American and Japanese preschools, *guan* as a distinct Chinese educational approach emphasizes the Chinese teachers' control and regimentation of children (Tobin et al. 1991). A decade later, David Y. H. Wu, an anthropologist who participated in the original "preschools in three cultures" studies, summarized the old and new empirical evidence in Chinese child-rearing and argued that the preoccupation with training children to control impulses prevailed in Chinese preschools and kindergartens, and so the concept of *guan* is still central to understanding the Chinese way of discipline in classrooms (Wu 1996).

In addition to school education, this distinct Chinese approach is also found as a typical characteristic in mother-child interactions in Chinese families. Psychologist Ruth. K. Chao (1994) argues that the dominant, ethnocentric dichotomy in Western child-rearing studies that contrasts "authoritative" and "authoritarian" parenting styles obscures important features of Chinese parenting associated with the distinct cultural notion of training. Based on standard measures that incorporated both traditional notions of authoritative-authoritarian parenting and Chinese child-rearing, she studied European-American mothers and immigrant Chinese mothers of preschool-aged children. Although the Chinese parenting was usually classified as "authoritarian," featuring strong parental control, her study also illustrates the supportive dimension of mother-child relationship connoted by the concept of *guan*. Within the general ideas of "training," she demonstrates that the Chinese "concept of training includes high involvement and a physical closeness that is not part of the authoritarian concept, and it is quite distinctive in the Chinese" (Chao 1994:1117).

In contrast to immigrant Chinese families in the United States, child-rearing in mainland China met a unique challenge in recent decades, that is, the one-child policy. Based on a questionnaire and an interview study of parents in Shanghai and two neighboring villages in the early 1990s, Wu (1996) concludes that parents were still preoccupied with the focus on children's obedience or disobedience, and the traditional Chinese way of discipline still prevailed in China despite newer concerns about the one-child policy eroding traditional values. He proposes to "stress the concept of *guan* as the characteristic feature of Chinese socialization" (p. 13) and connected this essentially Chinese way of socialization to China's "diehard authoritarian, collective, nationalistic political culture" and the "conservative Chinese cultural tradition" (p. 25). Vanessa Fong also examines the issue of disciplining singleton children in her book *Only Hope* (Fong 2004), where the concept of *guan*, both discipline and self-discipline, is used by parents and teachers to explain teenagers' academic success and moral upbringing in urban Dalian (pp. 116, 119).

Expanding on this body of literature, I try to reexamine this concept of *guanjiao* in this chapter by delving into the internal tensions emerging throughout the whole set of discourses and practices of *guanjiao* at Biyu Preschool. While the existing scholarship on Chinese socialization tends to essentialize the unique Chinese notions and patterns of discipline in the theorization of *guanjiao/guan*, it obscures the complexities of child-rearing practices under contemporary Chinese social transformation.

First, there are pervasive and nuanced tensions between different socialization agents within the same family or across family-school contexts as a result of varying habits, values, and power differentials. Although the survey study in the 1990s discovers detailed variations on parenting beliefs and behaviors between urban and rural parents, as well as between families with schooled children and those with nonschooled children (Wu 1996), tensions between different family members and between family and school in *guanjiao* dynamics are left unexplored. In the context of child-rearing, discipline builds up and builds on an asymmetrical power relationship between adults and children, involving sometimes the dyads of the parent/teacher and the child, while other times the more complex, multiparty dynamics of multiple caregivers, the child, and his or her peers. For example, the opening vignette in this chapter reveals the intergenerational tensions among Pengpeng's family regarding how to discipline him. According to the conversation related at the beginning of this chapter, in Pengpeng's eyes Father and Mother were strict, while grandmother was affectionate and less strict. One caveat is that the *little dark room* (*xiao hei wu*) is just an exaggerated term adults use to threaten or frighten very young children (normally younger than age six). Although sometimes children do get punished and left alone in a room for time-out, it's rarely a scary dark room.

Also, the very fact that Pengpeng narrated the "inside stories" to teachers in the classroom context points to the information flow between home and school—that teachers would get to know about children's family life from children themselves. It is actually quite common for teachers to ask children about what happened at home. A lot of times teachers intentionally inquire about children's family life in order to know children's circumstances better and adjust their disciplinary practices at school accordingly, and this kind of family-school dynamics was an essential part of the *guanjiao* processes. On the one hand, parents and grandparents still held similar, general expectations on preschool education, as David Y. H. Wu points out in his 1996 article:

> Chinese authorities and experts have promoted preschools as a solution to spoiling presented by the single-child family. Both authorities and ordinary parents believe that preschools provide single children with the chance to interact with other children and that teachers are best qualified to correct the negligence or errors of single-child parents.

On the other hand, my study reveals much more nuanced discrepancies between teachers and parents on concrete disciplinary beliefs and practices. For example, parents' concerns about school discipline as too rigid and not healthy and teachers' judgment that some parents' disciplinary approaches were not appropriate, either too harsh or too lenient.

Second, the tensions and exchanges between different socialization agents in the family or at school are complicated in the context of raising single children amid China's profound social and moral transformations. For one thing, tensions within the family are heightened in this new age of "4:2:1" families along with the co-residence of three generations. Scholars have coined the term *intergenerational parenting coalition* as a culturally appropriate unit of analysis for understanding child-rearing in contemporary urban China (Goh and Kuczynski 2009; Goh 2013). In such situations, the only child is not only the center of parental and grandparental attention, but also the center around which discrepancies, fissures, and conflicts arise, between mother and father, between the younger generation and the older generation, between in-laws, and even between paternal and maternal grandparents. Also, although the survey and interviews conducted a decade ago by David Wu's team suggested that the concerns over "spoiled only children" reinforced the circulation and implementation of traditional child-rearing values with their emphasis on the importance of obedience, it was also found that in rural areas where traditional values were better preserved, children were doted on by parents more than those in the city. Actually, as Pengpeng's story suggests, his grandparent is more lenient than his parents, which is a pretty common accusation against grandparents today, although supposedly, they are the people who hold more traditional beliefs. This raises the question: What are the "traditional" values? What are the "new" ones? Are they imagined or real? How do the imagined and the real speak to each other and interact? As my analysis in the following sections will demonstrate, today's parents in Shanghai, compared to the early 1990s, are facing new challenges with regard to *guanjiao*, and today's child-rearing goals are much more complex and multifaceted, beyond merely reinforcing the tradition of cultivating an obedient child.

Third, there are internal tensions and struggles within the same socialization agent. As the previous chapters suggest, parents and teachers are caught up in profound quandaries of moral education, between choosing among values at conflict, between reconciling ideologies with reality, and between cultivating a moral child and a successful child—all in an perceived immoral world. The existing literature on *guanjiao* emphasizes its importance both in achieving academic success and developing moral character, however, the potential tension and conflict between the two has seldom been examined, perhaps because the so-called "moral crisis" has not previously been a salient theme in Chinese social life or in education discourses. Also, although *guanjiao* appeared as a consistent and coherent construct in the Chinese socialization literature, what emerged in my fieldwork was a different picture, where even the same individual's *guanjiao* beliefs are not devoid of ambivalences and his or her practices are teeming with ambiguities.

Last but not least, young children's own voices are also underexamined in the literature on *guanjiao*. Ethnographic studies are uniquely positioned to provide a space where children are seen as social actors who play an active role in shaping their own social world (James 2007). The rise of the only child generation in China poses unique challenges to the traditional frameworks about the obedient Chinese child, and ethnographic studies have just started to reveal the agency and power of children themselves in constructing Chinese family and kinship dynamics, but primary school children are so far the youngest age groups in such studies (Goh and Kuczynski 2009). Along these lines, my research reveals that even very young preschool children are not passive subjects of *guanjiao*. Children exert their own agency in the world of *guanjiao*, not only through narrating what happens in their life, as Pengpeng did, but also through various strategies of "anti-discipline," driven by their own understandings and evaluations of adults' *guanjiao* practices. Children themselves are an integral part of *guanjiao*, negotiating between multiple adult socializers and shaping their own developmental trajectories.

This chapter will explore the multifaceted *guanjiao* beliefs and practices in tension in Biyu Preschool children's family and school life. I will first introduce socializers' perceived urgency regarding the necessity of *guanjiao*, as a response to their concerns over undesirable moral character and personality traits of the "little emperors." What follows is an analysis of the variety of *guanjiao* beliefs held by teachers, parents, and grandparents, with a focus on the tensions of balancing between different and conflictual beliefs and how such balancing is enacted in multiplayer socialization dynamics. I will then document actual *guanjiao* practices at home and school, highlighting several important disciplinary techniques as well as children's own anti-disciplinary tactics.

The Perceived Necessity and Urgency of *Guanjiao* with the "Little Emperors"

Because more than 90 percent of the students at Biyu Preschool were single children, anxieties and concerns about psychological problems of the "little emperors" emerged as a recurrent theme in my conversation with caregivers. Such anxieties and concerns resonate with the public discourses on singleton children's psychological development, as scholars have pointed out over the last two decades (for a review, see Settles et al. 2013). In this context, discipline is seen as an urgent necessity, an important means to shape the ideal child. I used a questionnaire survey, in-depth interviews, and participant observation to explore the perceived necessity and urgency to *guanjiao* children at Biyu Preschool.

The Most and Least Desirable Traits: Evidence from My "Child-Rearing Questionnaire"

In my child-rearing questionnaire, a survey I took during the beginning phase of my fieldwork, I included two questions that probed what parents thought were the most and least desirable moral characteristics of their children. One question was: "What are the moral traits that you most want your children to develop?" The answers were:

A. Kindness/caring (*shanliang/aixin*)
B. Obedience (*tinghua*)
C. Sociableness (*shanyu yu ren jiaowang*)
D. Independence (*duli; you zhujian*)
E. Other (e.g., _____)

The other question was: "What are the weaknesses that you most want your children to correct?" The answers were:

A. Selfishness (*zisi*)
B. Disobedience (*bu tinghua*)
C. Unsociableness (*bu shanyu yu ren jiaowang*)
D. Lack of independence (*bu duli; mei zhujian*)
E. Other (e.g., _____)

Parents could select multiple answers so that they didn't have to make a difficult choice when different values weighed similarly in their belief system.

These items were inspired by Vanessa Fong (2007a)'s findings from her longitudinal studies of Chinese singleton teenagers in Dalian City. In this article, Fong developed five constructs of values from the local terms that were most commonly used by parents when they talked about values that children should learn: obedience, caring/sociableness, independence, and excellence. Following Fong, I used similar terms as a heuristic shorthand (Fong 2007a: 89) in my own questionnaire survey. The Chinese term for obedience in the context of raising young children, *tinghua*, literally means "to listen to the words (of authority)," alluding to the value of submission to authority. I used obedience/disobedience as one dichotomous set of values that I believed to be an appropriate candidate, as discussed in Fong's article and the literature on Chinese socialization and discipline.

There are a few differences, however, in the way I chose and used the terms. First, I didn't use excellence (*youxiu*) because the section of my questionnaire that included these two questions were designed to elicit parents' beliefs in children's social and moral development specifically, instead of cognitive development/academic performance. Second, I separated caring from sociableness and integrated caring with kindness to form a distinct construct. In the context of my fieldwork, *caring* refers to one's intrinsic quality/disposition to care for (*guanxin*) and be kind to others, often phrased in local terms as "with a loving heart" (*you aixin*). For example, if a child spontaneously goes to comfort another child who is crying, or if a child spontaneously helps another in need or shares things with others, adults will comment that this child is a person "with a loving heart" (*you aixin*). In contrast, *sociableness* is a very general term for interpersonal interactions, referring to the child's capacities and skills to get along with others, make friends, and navigate the social world with ease and wisdom. As Fong notes, parents in Dalian "were worried that, having missed out on experiencing the reciprocities of sibling relationships, their children would be poorly prepared to deal with the web of social relationships they were supposed to cultivate once they reached adulthood" (Fong 2007a: 92). Parents of Biyu Preschool children have similar concerns about their children's preparedness to cultivate valuable social relationships. Third, although I used the term *independence*, what it refers to in local terms is not entirely the same as the explanation given in Fong's article. In addition to the emphasis on autonomy in the sense that children should learn to *act* on their own instead of being too dependent on caregivers, another dimension of independence refers to the ability to *think* on their own, in other words, to exhibit independent thinking. This independent thinking component points to a potential conflict with the value of obedience, which is something worthy of interest as I am exploring continuity and change in Chinese child-rearing values.

A total of ninety-two families (one parent in each family) responded to these two questions. For question 1 ("What are the moral traits that you most want your children to develop?") 129 answers were collected (see Figure 5.1). The possible responses were:

A. Kindness/caring
B. Obedience
C. Sociableness
D. Independence
E. Other

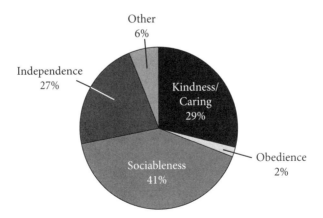

Figure 5.1 Child-Rearing Questionnaire: The Most Desirable Character Trait in Children

Of the responses, fifty-four (41 percent) chose C (sociableness), thirty-eight (29 percent) chose A (kindness/caring), twenty-nine (22 percent) chose D (independence), eight (6 percent) chose E (other [such as courage, be outgoing, etc.]), and only two (2 percent) chose B (obedience).

For question 2 ("What are the weaknesses that you most want your children to correct?"), eighty-eight answers were collected (see Figure 5.2). The possible responses were:

A. Selfishness
B. Disobedience
C. Unsociableness
D. Dependence
E. Other

Of the responses, thirty-one [34 percent] chose C (unsociableness), nineteen [25 percent] chose E (other [such as self-centered, self-willed]), sixteen [17 percent] chose B (disobedience), fifteen [16 percent] chose A (selfishness), and seven [8 percent] chose D (dependence). Several observations from these results are notable.

First, parents highlighted the importance of cultivating interpersonal skills, building social relationships, and navigating the social world; this was shown because sociableness and unsociableness were chosen as the most desired and least desired characteristic. This is especially relevant to concerns about "little emperors" because most children didn't have a sibling environment.

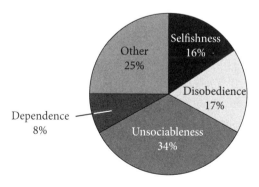

Figure 5.2 Child-Rearing Questionnaire: The Least Desirable Character Trait in Children

Second, kindness/caring was seen as the second important positive trait, whereas selfishness of singleton children was also a common concern for parents, next to unsociableness and disobedience.

Third, contrary to the survey results of parents in urban Shanghai and its neighboring villages more than a decade ago (Wu 1996), obedience was the least chosen among the various positive traits by today's Biyu Preschool parents. On the other hand, disobedience is still a relatively popular concern in terms of undesirable traits. This suggests that although parents don't want their children to be disobedient, they nonetheless don't emphasize obedience as an important goal of socialization and discipline as much as those who responded to Wu's survey two decades earlier.

Fourth, independence was considered an important positive trait to develop, weighing much more than obedience. This indicates, to some extent, a departure from traditional socialization values compatible with a strictly hierarchical society. Also, as the current society is undergoing major social transformations, children and parents are facing a high degree of uncertainty, and independence in terms of making decisions and navigating the social world on one's own becomes increasingly important and valuable. On the other hand, lack of independence was not seen as a severe weakness. Finally, nearly a quarter of answers about the least desirable trait went toward E (other), which led me to further explore what alternative answers parents gave. Among those who did write down a specific trait as an alternative answer, some explained that their children were too self-centered, some highlighted lacking self-control, some pointed out being too vulnerable/cannot accept criticism or setbacks (*buneng chengshou cuozhe*), and others pointed out bad temperament such as getting angry easily. Together with unsociableness, selfishness, disobedience, and lack of independence, these traits were frequently mentioned in my conversations with teachers, parents, and grandparents as problems associated with singleton children that require effective discipline (*guanjiao*) to correct. In what follows, I will elaborate the manifestations or symptoms of such traits (imagined or not) in children's daily life.

Manifestations of Undesirable Traits: Evidence from Interviews and Observation
The Self-Centered "Little Emperors"

> Mr. J. (Jinqu's maternal grandfather): I think my daughter is successful, in terms of academics and career. She is very smart. But how about her personality? I don't think she has developed a good personality. She doesn't care much about

other people. It's such a common weakness of singleton children, that they are *ziwo zhongxin* (self-centered) and *wei wo du zun* (very egoistic).

Jing: Especially those good students who perform well in academics and are the stars of their class all the time?

Mr. J.: Yes. Those "good students" in academic performance do not necessarily turn out as virtuous. Good moral character is cultivated since very young, and it will influence one's whole life.

My conversation with Mr. J., Jinqu's maternal grandparent, revealed a common concern among the older generation about singleton children's self-centeredness. Jinqu's mother was among the first-generation of singletons. After she grew up, Jinqu's grandparent realized this tension between excellent academic performance—ultimately translated into career success—and good personality and moral character. Jinqu's mother graduated from an elite university in Shanghai and married another native Shanghainese man who had experiences studying and working abroad. They two were both busy with work, and Jinqu had been living with his maternal grandparents almost since he was born. Jinqu stayed with his own parents during weekends only, even though his parents lived close to his maternal grandparents. From the story of Jinqu's mother, Jinqu's maternal grandparent was even more worried about Jinqu himself, also a singleton child who received too much attention at home.

These young children are accused of seeing themselves as the centers of the whole universe. For example, at mealtime, the child throws everything he or she doesn't like into their parents or grandparents' bowls. The children are so used to doing this that they naturally extend this habit to classroom settings. Before they are disciplined and internalize the new collective norms for classroom settings, they simply throw food they don't want into other children's bowls. Teachers often see this as a sign of being spoiled and not caring.

The Demanding "Little Emperors"

Singleton children are also seen as too demanding. In Shanghainese dialect, there is a very special term for it, *zuo*, meaning spoiled, demanding. Biyu Preschool parents and teachers use this term a lot when they talk about the children. Teacher Fanglin once commented on the difficulty of teaching Shanghainese children: "Children in Shanghai share one common characteristic, that is, *zuo*. That's why it's a very tough job to take care of them day by day. But on the other hand, you can't blame the children. It's simply because the adults dote on them too much at home."

Sayi, a three-year-old girl in Class 1A, is an extreme case of a demanding (*zuo*) child. For example, when she first came to preschool, she would do almost nothing on her own. If the toy she was playing with fell onto the floor, she would not bother to pick it up by herself; instead, she would shout loud to make the command: "The toy fell!" She simply expected the teachers to pick it up for her. Or if there was anything that annoyed her, she would exclaim: "I am angry!" with her arms crossed, like an arrogant boss. When the teacher ignored her commands and warnings, she would scream hysterically. After a few incidents like this, she went confused and grieved, explaining to her teachers: "At home, whenever I say 'I'm angry,' my maternal grandma will come immediately to me and calm me down." Sayi, the girl always pampered at home, had to learn the hard lesson of dealing with problems on her own and listening to her teachers.

The Disobedient "Little Emperors"

Although obedience is no longer the ultimate criterion of an ideal child, as the questionnaire survey reveals, extreme disobedience, on the other hand, is still seen as a typical problem with singleton children. Disobedience (*bu tinghua*), which literally means "not listening to words," including disrespect to authority and non-observance of rules, is also a common theme that figures into socializers' worries about "little emperors."

The following conversation occurred among three mothers: Xixi's mother, Ming's mother, and me (Wandou's mother). Xixi and Ming lived in the same building; they had been having play-dates since they were one, and their mothers had also become close friends. During our conversation, Xixi's mother complained to me about Ming's mother's child-rearing approach. Ming's mother's lack of authority over her son and her son's disobedience went hand in hand, reinforcing each other. Xixi's mother even linked this phenomenon at one's early years in life to the future outcome in adolescence and adulthood.

> Xixi's mother (talking to Jing [Wandou's mother]): Ming's mother spoils her son too much!
> Ming's mother: I don't think so! I am OK. Sometimes I am very strict.
> J: How do you (Xixi's mother) think?
> Xixi's mother: She definitely does!
> Jing: How?
> Xixi's mother: For example, her son (three-year-old) still needs four meals of milk a day, which is not necessary or healthy at this age. But she simply cannot change it because her son is too strong-willed and she cannot manage him.

Ming's mother: What's more, when he drinks milk, I have to hold him in one arm, and my other hand holds his bottle.

Xixi's mother: Why can't you change your mind? In a family, you should be the authority, and he should listen to you. Not the other way around.

Ming's mother: But he is so stubborn! If I don't do things according to his will, he will simply say, "I won't eat."

Xixi's mother (talking to Jing): I've told her many times! This won't work! If he cries, just let him cry!

Jing: I agree with Xixi's mother. Yes, you cannot always give in to your child.

Xixi's mother: Why are there so many rebellious and unmanageable teenagers now? It is simply because they were not obedient to parents from very early on. Disobedient young children will become trouble-makers when they grow up.

In addition to disrespect for parents' authority, some children are seen as unreasonable and disrespectful regarding rules (*bu jiang li*). Xiao Bei, a four-year-old boy in Class 2A, is such a child, according to his teachers.

> Xiaobei's father has a lot of business trips abroad, and his mother is the one who takes care of him. His mother got pregnant with him at an older age than average (in her late 30s), and she absolutely doted on him too much. Not to mention that his mother is not an assertive woman in any way. She never gets angry with anyone, and her son becomes her boss. No matter what wrong things he does, she will yield to him. At school, however, you explain the rules to him, and he will simply not listen at all. He always thinks he is right in everything. He is so headstrong (*ren xing*) and unreasonable (*bu jiang li*)!

In addition to blaming adults for not asserting authority, parents and teachers also compare the only-children with those who have siblings, always making the link between disobedience and singleton status. That there is no competition between or imitation of siblings make singleton children more self-willed and unwilling to follow rules or parents' commands.

The Vulnerable "Little Emperors"

There is also a widespread concern among socializers about single children's psychological well-being, expressed in phrases like "psychological bearing capacity" (*xinli chengshou nengli*) and "psychological quality" (*xinli suzhi*), referring to the capacity to accept criticism, tolerate failures, and endure hardships. These children are seen as too vulnerable as a result of overprotection at home, where caregivers' high expectations, attention, and praise make them conceited.

Ziyu's mother, a successful high-level manager in a big company, explained to me why she thought cultivating good "psychological quality" was more important than achieving academic and career success. Her worries about her own daughter being too aggressive and thus vulnerable to difficulties were not uncommon.

Jing: What do you think is the most important goal of education?

Ziyu's mother: For me the most important thing is not academic success, but psychological quality. She (my daughter) should learn how to adjust her mood and mentality properly because she is too aggressive, always desiring to be number one, the best. Children like her really need to learn how to better adjust their expectations.

Jing: So many children are like this. They all think they are the best.

Ziyu's mother: Unfortunately, that's just the reality of our whole society. Everyone is competing against one another. The key message of our education is you should win. But as grown-ups, after experiencing the vicissitudes of real life, you will discover, although success in academics and career is important, ultimately your happiness doesn't depend on that. Instead, it depends pretty much on your own psychological capacity to adjust yourself properly.

Tiantian's parents contrasted the experiences of this younger generation to the previous generations who had gone through really tough situations, and analyzed why young children today are so vulnerable.

The capacity to adjust one's own psyche is indeed a crucial thing. Looking back to our experiences, I would say that people in my generation were actually good at it, perhaps because parents in the old days could not give so much attention to kids, so we got to learn how to deal with problems in real life by ourselves, and we went through the process of adjusting the self and improving the self. But children today receive too much attention, which makes them hardly prepared for difficult situations in life.

You know what? I have always been thinking about this hypothetical situation: if the cultural revolution were to take place today, how many young people could survive? I mean there were many people who endured the cultural revolution and survived, right? If my son wouldn't commit suicide after things like the cultural revolution, it definitely means my education of cultivating psychological quality is a success.

Tiantian's mother brought up the topic of the cultural revolution to compare psychological quality across different generations, which reveals socializers' deep-seated anxieties and uncertainties about the spoiled young children's
psychological vulnerability. Tiantian's mother was born in the late 70s, before
the one-child policy was launched. She was well educated and had read a lot of
parenting advice books, both foreign and Chinese. Enthusiastic about psychological and educational aspects of child development, she was very deliberate in
thinking about the short-term and long-term impacts of different child-rearing
approaches.

> I felt bad (about corporal punishment) not because I was concerned about
> his physical health, but actually because I worried about whether corporal
> punishment would harm his heart—have detrimental effects on his psycho-
> logical well-being. You see, other children in China now are all indulged with
> excessive love (*chong ai*), but ours was very strictly disciplined since he was
> young. I'm afraid he will be too timid and overcautious (*wei shou wei wei*) in
> the future, whereas everyone else is open and confident. I don't know if there's
> a correlation between these two. When we were young, we were all spanked
> by parents before. But the social environment is different now. When we were
> spanked, we didn't care about it at all, nor did we feel shameful or hurt. We
> would go out to play with other kids immediately as if nothing had happened.
> We could heal (the psychological wound) by ourselves. But how about young
> children nowadays? They are indulged with so much love and they always
> need your attention. How can they ever heal themselves (*zi yu*)?

A lot of parents share a similar concern: Singleton children tend to have
a really big ego. One of the typical symptoms is that they are psychologically
vulnerable and do not know how to handle adverse situations and manage
negative emotions. Moreover, Tiantian mother's consideration of psychological vulnerability is primarily based on the concern about its long-term conse-
quence for children's future well-being in a challenging environment.

Against the backdrop of these perceived problems of singleton children's
personality, the psychologically healthy child seems to become an increasingly
important goal of child-rearing, compared to the obedient and filial child in
the previous literature on Chinese socialization. For example, Rui's mother is
seen as an exemplar of the successful mother because her daughter is excellent
not only in academic performance, but also in her good personality and well-
rounded development. Rui's mother told me: "I don't think good exam score
and ranking is the most important criterion to evaluate a child. To me, the

ideal child is not necessarily an obedient one, because we adults are not always correct, and obedience sometimes kills a child's creativity. So the ideal child is one of creativity and one that cares for others and respects others—in a word, one with a healthy personality." To sum up, it is a central mission of socializers to mold the "little emperors" into ideal children through cultivating the desirable personality traits and trimming away the undesirable traits.[1] *Guanjiao*, the means to achieve such an end, becomes crucial in socialization.

The Search for the Golden Mean: Balancing between Varying Beliefs in *Guanjiao*

Socializers at Biyu Preschool are searching for the "golden mean"—*zhong yong zhi dao* in Confucius's terms—amid a complex reality, because they have to balance between all sorts of beliefs in *guanjiao*, beliefs that sometimes conflict with one another or don't fit into the changing landscape of child-rearing in contemporary urban China.

*"Pen-Rearing" (*Juan Yang*) versus "Cage-Free-Rearing" (*San Yang/Fang Yang*)*

Terminology in animal breeding, such as the contrast between "pen-rearing" (*juan yang*) and "cage-free-rearing" (*san yang/fang yang*) has become a popular Chinese vernacular concept in child-rearing, as socializers are seeking out a realistic balance between independency/creativity and conformity in children's psychological development. This analogy features the contrast between two general child-rearing styles, "pen-rearing" (*juan yang*) and "cage-free-rearing" (*san yang/fang yang*). Although the former emphasizes the importance of setting up detailed structures and boundaries in children's daily life and protecting them from the dangers of the outside world, the latter embraces the value of giving children enough freedom to explore on their own, exposing them to the outside world, and encouraging them to become independent children.

It is hard for parents to choose between these two approaches. When children are under heightened attention and pressure in a society lacking a sense of security, as stories in the previous chapters reveal, the pen-rearing (*juan yang*) approach, which emphasizes setting up constraints and protection, seems to most parents an inevitable choice in today's urban China, and it is true that this is the dominant child-rearing model in urban China. On the other hand, such pen-rearing (*juan yang*) runs the danger of being too oppressive and compromising children's creativity and autonomy. In contrast, cage-free-rearing (*san yang*) nonetheless bears the potential of nurturing children's independence and autonomy. The comparison between the real China and the "imagined West" often figures into parents' evaluation and comparison of these two approaches.

> In Western countries, school learning is an open space, and children are granted enough freedom to do whatever they want to. Here in China, our environment is terrible—food is poisonous, air is polluted—everything is dangerous, whereas in the West they have much more control and monitoring over their living environment. That's why we are under so much tension and stress, and we all want our children to get the best. Thus we strive to control our children's life in every possible way. That's why our children are so rebellious—they are too stressed at school. For example, in the morning, Biyu Preschool requires all the children to wash their hands, using the cold-water faucet outside the school building. Maomao will follow this rule, no matter how cold it is outside. But after coming home, he would protest: "Father, I won't wash my hands!" even though it's warm and he can use warm water. Why? Because their own desires and preferences were suppressed at school, so they need an outlet to release their feelings.

Maomao's father isn't alone in his concern that children's natural propensities (*tian xing*) are suppressed in the school environment because there are too many rules and restrictions. For example, Biyu Preschool celebrated the 2012 Children's Day with a big party in which each class presented singing and dancing performances. Teacher Fanglin in Class 1A took this event very seriously and composed a "collective dance" for the whole class and had her students rehearse this dance almost every day for a whole month. These three-year-olds gradually remembered all the movements and structures of this dance in a very rigid way, and they did a terrific job at the party. But after watching their performance, Tiantian's mother shared with me her concerns:

> I really don't think it's necessary for children to go through such a stiff process of repeated rehearsals every day. They are children, not athletes. I would like to see them doing things naturally and spontaneously, and I think that might be more beautiful than an impeccable collective dance where every child had to move in the exact ways their teacher told them to do. It's like a robot show. This kind of training might be detrimental to their development, say, killing their creativity.

Some parents try to balance and compensate the rigidity of "pen-rearing" by allowing children to relax and release their energies after school, for instance, in outdoor activities and free-play time. Yuanyuan's mother is such an example:

When I grew up in the countryside, there was plenty of stuff to play with, free of charge. Unlike now in the city, everything for kids to play costs money. Moreover, kids don't know how to play because they have already been "formatted," and their creativity was restricted by rules at school and home. For example, some kids today don't even know what to do if thrown into a sand field. That's why sometimes when Yuanyuan brought a toy and asked me to guide her, I would encourage her to explore the toy on her own. The moment I come to guide her, my own perspectives and thoughts would influence her. At school, she is inevitably restricted by all sorts of rules, so whenever away from school, I try my best to let her feel relaxed and released. I am a proponent of "cage-free-rearing." I always encourage her to play outdoor, enjoy nature, and also go to hang out with other children. That's why she is outgoing and not shy.

Yuanyuan's mother, in her mid-thirties, was born in Shanghai but grew up in the countryside in one of the inland provinces with her parents and didn't come back to Shanghai until college age. Comparing her own childhood experiences in inland China in the 70s to her daughter's current experience in cosmopolitan Shanghai, she was worried that the current child-rearing and educational environment was not conducive to the cultivation of children's creativity. In addition, based on her knowledge and imaginings about the foreign way of "cage-free-rearing," she was disheartened by the dominant urban Chinese child-rearing approach because it was strangling young children's self-confidence and independence.

Look at how foreigners raise children! Foreign parents adopt a hands-off approach, and they just encourage their children to play on their own and become independent (*zili*). I think that's the right way. In China, when going to the park, we need four to five adults just to accompany one child. I like to take my daughter to play in a child center near Century Park. There are a lot of families from Taiwan and Singapore. Once I took her there and we saw a very high slide at nearly a vertical angle. The local children were all scared to climb up and slide down. But the Taiwanese and Singaporean children were not scared at all!

Why is there such a difference? I believe it's because "he who has no prior knowledge knows no fear" (*wuzhi zhe wuwei*). Those "cage-free" children have fewer constraints imposed upon them, and they therefore fear nothing. But our children have been under too much attention since they were born, and bounded by too many expectations and rules. So they naturally know what to fear, and they can get a sense of parents' judgment and preferences from parents' looks and not-explicitly-expressed attitudes. They have a sense of such matters from very early on, and I believe this results from the whole society's imposition. So our children easily feel unconfident and scared. Their psychological well-being is compromised and challenged.

Interestingly, the so-called foreigners in Yuanyuan's mother's story were Taiwanese and Singaporean who supposedly belong to the "Chinese" cultural lineage in a broad sense. She didn't specify what the different attitude in child-rearing derives from, but one can infer, from this episode as well as from her narrative of her own childhood experiences, that the particular sociocultural transformations in mainland China were the background of both narratives, and the unique one-child policy is an important piece of this puzzle. In addition, during my interview with her, she also asked me about American ways of child-rearing and whether public discourse and imagination about the Western child-rearing approach matched what I had witnessed in my years in the United States. From her perspective, the current environment of child-rearing in China was not a desirable one, compared to both the imagined Western environment and the alternative Chinese cultural contexts exemplified in other places such as in Taiwan and in other eras such as during socialist times. Child-rearing in contemporary urban Shanghai-China is always evaluated in reference to and comparison with other, albeit imagined, cultural contexts. Rather than something enacted in their own lived experiences, the otherness of these alternative cultural communities and its realness emerged in their imaginations or their nostalgia.

Authoritarian Discipline versus Democratic Discipline

> Shenshen: I don't like Teacher Linlin. I like Teacher Cherry.
> Jing: Why don't you like Teacher Linlin?
> Shenshen: Because she is too angry.
> Jing: Teacher Cherry is also angry sometimes.
> Shenshen: But Teacher Cherry's anger is very light (mild).
> Jing: How is it like when Teacher Linlin is angry?
> Shenshen: She shouts at us.

I was not surprised when Shenshen, a little boy in Class 2B, told me "Teacher Cherry's anger is very light" and Teacher Linlin shouted at them. Teacher Linlin was known for her strictness and the orderliness of her class, and Teacher Cherry, the assistant teacher of Shenshen's class, was more like a big sister to these children, instead of an authority figure. But still, the secret between Shenshen and me—that he liked Teacher Cherry better than Teacher Linlin—suggested that young children were actually very sensitive to the disciplinary approaches of their caregivers. Socializers in urban Shanghai are struggling to negotiate a middle way between the authoritarian and democratic discipline. Such negotiations point to the tension between enacting authority over children and showing respect to them.

Teacher Linlin is a proponent of authoritarian discipline, and her students in general dare not disobey her commands. When I asked her about tips for successfully managing the twenty-six children in her class, she explained to me:

> Actually, there's no special strategy or shortcut. I think you just need to be strict with them and have them listen to you, obey you, and correct any wrong behavior at once, without any exception. Nowadays many people say we need to respect children, but my experience tells me that you have to find out a limit of such respect. The bottom line is you are the authority.

But some teachers preferred a more democratic approach in socialization. For example, Teacher Xiaoling in Class 3B said:

> I like the democratic atmosphere in a classroom or in a family. For instance, Tianhe's parents show respect to Tianhe's opinions in a lot of ways, and they will share things with him and have him participate in the decision-making process. I think this is a good parenting approach.

Note that Teacher Xiaoling, although a very gentle and kind "sister" to her students, didn't give in to children's requests unconditionally. She would talk to children patiently to set up boundaries instead of forcefully imposing rules without prior communication with children.

Besides teachers, parents also have varied opinions, choosing between the more authoritarian and the more democratic approach in disciplinary practices. Siya's mother told me this story:

> Once Teacher Tang asked the class: "What do you want to do when you grow up?" Siya answered: "I want to become a good mother!" After school, when I heard this conversation from her teacher, I asked Siya: "Why do you want to become a good mother?" I thought she would say something like "a good mother can take care of her baby." But she said: "Because a good mother can govern/discipline (*guan*) children!" I felt so ashamed at her answer. After that, I paid attention not to reinforce the authoritarian aspect of mothering.

Rui's mother, the exemplar mother of Biyu Preschool, didn't like the authoritarian approach, either. She shared with me what she thought was most important in parenting, that is, to respect the child as an independent person with her own psychological individuality, so parents should not impose their own will and preferences on the child, but instead should try to build up mutual respect between the child and the adults. As I observed, more and more young, well-educated parents came to embrace the democratic approach to discipline, which emphasized mutual respect and communication. This trend in urban middle-class families suggests a departure from the kind of *guanjiao* practices documented in the previous literature that featured authority and obedience.

"Tiger Mother" versus "Good Mother": The Way toward Excellence

When I returned to fieldwork in 2011, two child-rearing books were popular in Shanghai. One was *My Mothering Experience in the United States* (*Wo Zai Meiguo Zuo Mama*) (Chua 2011), the Chinese version of the popular, controversial book *Battle Hymn of the Tiger Mother*, written by Amy Chua, a law professor at Yale University who successfully trained two daughters to academic excellence. Another one was *A Good Mother Is Better than a Good Teacher* (*Hao Mama Shengguo Hao Laoshi*) (Yin 2009), written by a mother who worked as a high school Chinese teacher in China. She had a master's degree in education and her daughter got into Tsinghua University (the top school in China) at the age of sixteen. While Amy Chua promoted her tough approach as quintessentially Chinese parenting, the Chinese title of her book highlighted the Western flavor of it: "mothering in the United States." While American critics blamed Amy Chua's Chinese parenting for its various flaws, the Chinese readership didn't think Amy Chua's approach was representative of Chinese parenting. Indeed, the much milder "good mother" approach of a Chinese mother in the Chinese social context was much better received in China.

During my fieldwork, the contrast between the "tiger mother" and the "good mother" frequently figured into conversations with Biyu Preschool mothers, like this one with Tiantian's mother.

I read the whole "tiger mother" book within a day, and I also read the "good mother" book. These two books present two totally different conceptions. I really hate this "tiger mother." She has two children, and she forced one to learn piano and the other one to learn violin, using corporal punishment. She would say: "If you don't practice it, I will burn all your toys!" She copied her own father's approach. When she was young, even if she got the number two score in her class, only next to number one, her father would go to her school to scold her: "Shame on you!" I really cannot agree with this "tiger mother."

But look at the Chinese mother in the other book. She is definitely more lenient toward her daughter and gave her daughter much more freedom to do things on her own. It's not that she set up no boundaries for her daughter. Her daughter is definitely well disciplined. What is distinct about this "good mother" is that she respects the natural dispositions/inborn nature (*tian xing*) of children and channels these dispositions in a good way that aligns with natural laws (*ziran guilv*). For example, she allows her daughter to play videogames because she believes it's children's natural curiosity to explore these things and you cannot keep your child from being exposed to videogames for her whole life. For the first two days, her daughter was too immersed in videogames and didn't have time to finish homework or *erhu* (a traditional Chinese instrument) practice. Then she asked her daughter: "Maybe from today on, you can try finishing homework and *erhu* first, before watching TV and playing games." Her daughter realized the problem of indulging in these other things, and she learned to set up and balance priorities.

Her daughter turned out really excellent—she went to Tsinghua without studying bitterly hard! Also, her daughter is excellent not only in academic performance. She gets along with others very well and is a nice and popular girl, willing to help others. She not only focused on academics, but also got to explore other interesting things in her life, such as videogames, TV, and martial arts fiction. She was also a leader (class president, *ban zhang*), but she quit the job when she didn't enjoy it anymore. You get the sense that she really enjoys her life, instead of doing things bitterly. She is a successful case of well-rounded development.

Most importantly, in that "tiger mother" book, I couldn't find any descriptions on her daughters' inner world—their own feelings and perspectives. But this "good mother" really attends to her daughter's psychological well-being from early on.

As Tiantian's mother summarized, the "tiger mother" case and the "good mother" case provide two different ways to train children for excellence. Which way is better? Different people might have different takes on this, as the "tiger mother" book has ignited controversies both in the United States (Maslin 2011) and in China (Sohu News 2011). Qiqi, a piano teacher at Biyu Preschool, appreciated the "tiger mother" approach because as she believed, it instilled the characteristic of perseverance in a child from a young age, which was crucial for future success. Her father was like a "tiger father," forcing her to practice piano for nearly two hours every day for more than ten years, using physical punishment. At first she hated this, but later on as piano practice became a naturalized habit/routine for her and she played piano better and better, she learned to appreciate her father's efforts. Now as she taught piano to young children, she was worried because a lot of parents were reluctant to force children to practice it for an hour a day, and she thought this was not conducive to the development of perseverance.

Most parents I talked to, however, preferred the "good mother" approach and found the "tiger mother" bizarre. They understood that perseverance was important for children in achieving excellence, but they disliked the way perseverance was trained by the "tiger mother," accusing her of harming children's psychological well-being. On the other hand, as Tiantian's mother described, the "good mother" is not a mother who sets up no boundaries. Instead, she is the one who helps her child to set up boundaries on his or her own, utilizing children's natural dispositions and the natural laws of human development, not against the basic limits of children's psychological development. In implementing her approach, a particularly important goal is to train children's perseverance in sticking to principles. For example, children will naturally want to eat when they are hungry. But these days, Chinese parents are very concerned about children not eating enough; they chase the child around trying to feed him, and mealtime becomes a tough battleground. What this "good mother" did when her daughter was young, however, was different: If her daughter rejected food to eat, she would just let her go. She would not chase her daughter around trying to feed her, but would wait patiently until her daughter came to her to ask for food. Mealtime turned out to be an easy task. This simple example illustrates the disciplinary strategies in the "good mother" approach.

As the "good mother" explains, parents should discover children's interests and potentials, and create an environment to nurture those interests and realize those potentials, instead of imposing parents' own interests onto children. She found that her daughter loved reading, so she created ways to satisfy her daughter's interest in reading, and through reading her daughter got to see beautiful things in this world and did not waste too much time on other things. Another example is a well-known story spread on the Internet of a child who wants to be the one applauding for others, instead of receiving applause as the best student.

We parents often emphasize too much on academic performance and ignore other aspects such as the ability to get along with others or care about others. There is a writer who talked about his parenting stories and became famous in social media. His son is not good at academics, and they try every possible means to motivate him, but he just doesn't like studying. Whenever he is forced too hard, he falls ill. Then they decided not to torture their son. Although his exam scores were not high at all, he became the most popular student in class, beyond teachers' expectations. Once his teacher asked the whole class about their favorite classmate, and all the children chose this boy because he is a really kindhearted child, always ready to help others. His son told him: "All the people want to become the best and win others' applause, but there has to be someone who applauds, right? I want to be that clapping-hand person to cheer up others."

These stories bring to light how well-educated parents critically receive popular parenting advice and consciously compare these varied threads of knowledge with their own parenting practices. Such a knowledge circulation, evaluation, and application process is situated within the broader transition toward attending to children's inner subjectivity in Chinese education, a new trend emerging in the rising Chinese middle class (Kuan 2011, 2012). Increasing psychological stress on children in a competitive educational environment and an uncertain society is a crucial concern for parents. Caught up in extreme pressure and competition for academic excellence, more and more urban middle-class Chinese parents have begun to embrace the belief of cultivating sociable, caring, and psychologically healthy children.

Negotiation among Multiple Caregivers: The Search for Harmony

Just as the episode at the beginning of this chapter reveals, the "little emperors" are usually taken care of on a daily basis by multiple adults both at home (parents, grandparents, and nannies) and at school (teachers and helpers). When different caregivers have varying statuses and roles within child-rearing settings and have to balance the various value contradictions described previously, negotiation among these different caregivers becomes an integral part of *guanjiao* practice amid real-world contingencies. Such negotiation typically takes place between mother-in-law and daughter-in-law, between mother and daughter, between husband and wife, as well as between paternal and maternal grandparents. The search for a harmonious family life unfolds in such tense negotiations.

I asked this question in my child-rearing questionnaire: "To what extent are your child-rearing beliefs different from those of your parents?" I gave parents five choices:

A. "Different like heaven-to-earth" (*tian rang zhi bie*)
B. Greatly different
C. Different
D. Slightly different
E. Not different at all

Among the eighty-eight parents who answered this question, 58 percent of them chose C (different), 24 percent chose B (greatly different), 11 percent chose D (slightly different), and 3 percent chose the other two extreme options, respectively. So the majority of parents did think that intergenerational differences existed and were not trivial.

Grandparents are often stereotyped as spoiling the child, and when it comes to intergenerational differences in child-rearing beliefs, parents complain about grandparents a lot. One thing I found out is that, if I was having any problem eliciting opinions from a parent, typically the mother, all I had to do was to ask what she thought of her mother-in-law's child-rearing approach. All mothers readily had a lot to say on this subject, mostly complaints against the mother-in-law.

A lot of times the conflicts result from the intergenerational differences in child-rearing values, and the mother often blamed her mother-in-law's beliefs as old-fashioned and unscientific. But there is another kind of tension underlying the apparent value conflicts, that is, the tension of fighting for the power to be the gatekeeper and principal caregiver of children. Chinese mothers-in-law often take for granted that the grandchildren were an inheritance/possession of the paternal lineage, a belief continuing from traditional times (Yan 2003). That is why sometimes even seemingly trivial issues in child-rearing can lead to conflicts between daughter-in-law and-mother-in-law.

For example, Kaikai's parents are both native Shanghainese, and they lived in the same city with Kaikai's grandparents. The comments from Kaikai's mother, a well-educated stay-at-home wife, aptly illustrate how daughters-in-law think.

> It's such a deeply entrenched (*gen shen di gu*) Chinese mentality that the grandson belongs to their (in-laws') household/lineage. But of course he is first and foremost *my son*! Different people of course have different child-rearing beliefs. I really think my approach is scientific and my mother-in-law's is not. For example, during the previous holidays, our big family went to Hainan (a tourism site) together. One evening we went to a buffet, and my mother-in-law got a full plate of bananas and mangos for Kaikai: "Do you want it? Do you want it?" We had not started eating any main food or dishes yet, and I told

her: "He will 'get inflamed' (*shang huo*) from these 'hot fruits.' He cannot eat it now."[2] Am I right? He didn't even start to eat any rice yet, and he had eaten a banana earlier that day; how could he fill his stomach with another banana? Mango is an extremely "hot" fruit, not to mention we were then in the tropical area, so he would easily get inflamed. But my in-law ignored what I said. She went straight to Kaikai and gave him the plate. Young children love sweet fruit, so how could he even reject the fruit plate? And my in-law protested against me: "Look. Not that *I* wanted to give it to him. It's *he* who wanted to eat the fruits!" I was so angry at this: so you should give whatever the child wants? That's not good for him! Then I confronted her: I said "Don't give it to him," then "Don't give it to him!" She was not happy with what I said at that moment, but my husband didn't see it. He was far away from us.

Such conflict sometimes causes marital problems between husband and wife, so the daughter-in-law has to adapt various strategies to maintain the basic harmony in the household.

Kaikai's mother revealed one tenet: do not complain about your mother-in-law in front of your husband. As in the aforementioned episode, her husband was not involved when the two parties had this dispute with each other. According to her, that's "a lesson I learned with blood and tears" (*xuelei de jiaoxun*):

She (mother-in-law) is not your own mother! You can say whatever you want to your mother, but not to her. Also, never complain about her in front of your husband! If you really cannot tolerate it, you can complain to your girlfriends. But never to husband! That's his mother, and men all have a special affinity for their mothers. Even if your husband thinks you are right and she is wrong, he will still be unhappy. So I have to tolerate it and restrain myself from complaining to him. When I was young, whenever I complained about his mother to him, he would be angry. Then I learned to tolerate it. This is a blood-and-tears lesson!

Another solution, especially popular in native Shanghainese families, is not to live together with paternal in-laws; it's more common for the young couple to live alone or with the maternal in-laws. In today's Chinese discourse on gender and marriage, "native Shanghainese men" (*Shanghai nanren*) is a stereotyped category: native Shanghainese men are less dominant or masculine than Chinese men in other regions (i.e., Beijing and other northern parts of China); they do more housework and cooking than their wives at home, even if they earn more money than their wives outside, and they treat their wives more gently than husbands in other parts of China. On the contrary, native Shanghainese women are believed to be more dominant and powerful at home. People often joke that native Shanghainese men "have no status" (*mei diwei*) at home (Lan 2010). This stereotype stands in stark contrast with the image of the Chinese men as the boss of the household in traditional patriarchal families in a hierarchical society (Baker 1979; Freedman 1966; Hsu 1971). A famous Taiwanese writer, Long Yingtai, wrote a Chinese article featuring "native Shanghainese men" during the 1990s (Long 1997) and described some scenarios she encountered in socialist Chinese literature and real life in the post-socialist era about various native Shanghainese men who were diligently doing housework and trying hard to please their wives. As a writer and cultural scholar who had married a German husband and lived on various continents before, Long compared Shanghainese husbands with Chinese husbands in traditional eras and in other places, as well as men in countries such as Germany, Sweden, the United States, and other Western countries. She argues that, with respect to all these alternative contexts, Shanghainese husbands are a rare anomaly in gender relationships:

> I am a woman from Taiwan who has lived in America and Europe for twenty years. I've traveled from Russia to South Africa and from Israel to the Philippines. I thought nothing in the world would really surprise me, until I got to know Shanghainese men. . . . "Men educated in the socialist system are really liberated," I said to myself. . . . Although I did my homework on mainland China's gender equality after the socialist movements, I didn't anticipate that Shanghainese men were such a unique group and scarce species in the whole world.

In the complex transformations of Chinese gender images, the marriage relationship, and family power dynamics (Yan 2003), the Shanghainese household in the dawn of the twenty-first century is an interesting case. In line with the fact that the native Shanghainese family features a dominant wife and a submissive husband, the wife's own mother/the husband's mother-in-law (*zhangmuniang*) enjoys a high status in the extended family and often becomes the main caregiver of the grandchildren. Interestingly, native Shanghainese daughters-in-law, such as Kaikai's mother, often look down upon the traditional Chinese way of living with the extended family and prefer the Western style of not living together with the older generation. At the same time, most of them choose to invite their own parents to live together and take care of the children and only reject their in-laws as Kaikai's mother did:

My son is raised by my mother, and thus does not have really intimate attachment to his paternal grandparents. Whenever my in-laws complained about it, I laughed to myself: "Of course, he is not attached to you. He is *my* son, and he doesn't need to be intimate with you." Before my son was born, my in-laws actually wanted to come live with us. Fortunately, my husband didn't listen to them. I warned him beforehand: "Think for yourself! If your mother and me didn't get along, especially when we have different opinions in child-rearing, with whom would I argue, your mother or you? You. Then our marriage will be done." He understood the situation and made the wise decision.

Although not living with paternal in-laws mitigates daughter-in-law/ mother-in-law conflicts, things are not smooth, either, when the mother and the maternal grandmother take care of the child together—a common co-residence pattern in native Shanghainese families. The mother often blames her own mother for spoiling the child with unscientific child-rearing methods, and mealtime is a typical battlefield in this regard. For example, Tiantian's parents are both native Shanghainese, and Tiantian's maternal grandparents have lived with them since he was born, whereas Tiantian's paternal grandparents, who also lived in Shanghai, were allowed to see Tiantian only once a week. Because he was a relatively short boy, Tiantian's eating habits were a big concern of his parents, and they had tried every possible method to train him to eat faster and more. The following comments from Tiantian's mother illustrate this:

> I admire the "good mother" in that popular parenting advice book and wanted to use the same approach: if the child doesn't finish his meal within thirty minutes, then remove his food without scolding him, until he feels hungry and asks for food. But Grandma screwed up our plan every time because she would jump to feed Tiantian when she saw Tiantian's plate was about to be removed. I couldn't implement my disciplinary techniques with him because my mother was there. But I couldn't say: 'Mother, just leave us!' We need her. Just do the math: Which costs more, my mother's presence or her absence? To be realistic, if my mother gets angry and leaves us because of my son's eating habit, we would have nothing to feed us (Grandma did all the cooking, because the young couple didn't have the time to cook)!

Disagreement over such issues existed not only between mother and grandmother, but also between husband and wife. For example, although Tiantian's mother preferred the "good mother" approach—a softer discipline, Tiantian's father was nonetheless a fan of the tougher approach. When I interviewed them together, Tiantian's father talked about the "eagle father" parenting that had become famous in Chinese social media and ignited controversies. The "eagle father" was a successful businessman in Nanjing City, and he believed that young children should be disciplined in an extremely tough way as young eagles were trained: an eagle mother would throw a young eagle off a cliff so that the young one would learn how to fly. He trained his son in an extremely tough way from an early age, such as forcing him to do near-naked exercise on snowy days, in order to cultivate extraordinary perseverance, and now his five-year-old son does show an extraordinary intelligence test score as well as physical skills such as piloting an ultralight aircraft (Fears 2013). Although Tiantian's father wanted to train Tiantian to become an exceptional man, using tougher disciplinary techniques, Tiantian's mother was worried:

> I feel like most Chinese fathers want their boys to become "somebody" and they have higher expectations than mothers. But when the sons grow up, they are not close to their fathers who were strict and tough to them. There isn't a close bonding between them. I don't like this pattern. You see, most Chinese men are closer to their mothers than fathers, which I don't like.

People like Tiantian's parents are actually very responsible caregivers, otherwise they wouldn't be so concerned about these issues. However, some of the younger parents who themselves grew up as spoiled only-children are much less involved and dominant in child-rearing than were their own parents. In such cases, conflicts tend to emerge not between the younger and the older generation, but between the paternal and maternal grandparents, especially when the two families live close to each other. Gao Sayi, the most demanding girl in Class 1A, is being raised in such an environment. I remember my short conversation with her when she was playing blocks in the classroom:

> Jing: Hello Sayi. Can you tell me who plays with you at home?
> Sayi: My maternal grandmother.
> Jing: What does your father do at home usually?
> Sayi: Dad watches the computer (surfing the Internet).
> Jing: How about your mother?
> Sayi: Mother watches TV.

Sayi's parents are young, in their early twenties, and their families are wealthy. Although her parents are not originally from Shanghai, after they came to work here, her grandparents bought several apartments in this same neighborhood and moved here. So now Sayi's maternal grandparents live with

Sayi and her parents in the same apartment, and her paternal grandparents live just upstairs. The young couple doesn't have to do anything at home, and they don't pay much attention to Sayi's education, either. Sayi's maternal grandmother is the dominant one in child-rearing in their family, and she is also the major caregiver. Sayi once told Teacher Fanglin that her grandmother was more like a real mother, and she wanted to call her "Mother." But her maternal grandmother spoils her so much that even her paternal grandfather, who is normally not strict with her at all, became worried about her. The two had disagreements over several issues. For example, Sayi's maternal grandmother did not want her to go to preschool, and it was her paternal grandfather who insisted on sending her to school, to have a peer environment and to learn things. Once, in the morning, the six of them (two parents and four grandparents) sent her to school together, and it was spectacular! I noticed that her paternal grandfather was not happy with her maternal grandmother, perhaps because the two disagreed on whether to send her to school or not.

To people outside China, the scene of six adults accompanying one child to school might seem odd and the tension between the two sets of grandparents might seem farfetched. This has, nonetheless, become an increasingly common phenomenon in today's China, when more and more only-children enter reproductive age and have their own parents live together or within close proximity. My son, Wandou, actually was the center of the "4:2:1" structure in our family. As my own parents and my then in-laws lived in the same city, whenever we took Wandou back to my city, it became an issue how much time to allocate to each side. Also, I had to make efforts to avoid potential conflicts between the two sets of grandparents as to how to discipline the child. I have also heard stories about my own friends whose child had to spend three-and-a-half days equally in each of the two sets of grandparents' homes every week, and also cases of couples who got divorced because the two sides fought for greater power over and more bonding with the beloved young child. The so-called Chinese *guanjiao*, far from being a monolithic concept, is a battleground teeming with familial tensions arising from value conflicts and power struggles among multiple players.

"Battle of Wits and Courage" (*Dou Zhi Dou Yong*): *Guanjiao* Dynamics at School and Home

I often heard this phrase "battle of wits and courage" (*dou zhi dou yong*) from parents and teachers when talking about disciplining children, a phrase that I also use when talking with my own friends about how to deal with our children.

This phrase vividly points out the characteristics of disciplinary practices—that *guanjiao* is dynamic, challenging, and full of tension. Amid a variety of *guanjiao* techniques in child-rearing, this section highlights a few important ones in which presocialist and socialist legacies mingle together with new, Western child-rearing trends.

Shaming: "Struggle Session" (Pi Dou Hui)

Because shame is an important concept in Chinese socialization (Fung 1999), it is not very surprising that shaming is used in Chinese classrooms and home settings. How teachers use shaming to motivate young children to engage in good/moral behaviors such as sharing has been demonstrated in previous chapters. What I want to emphasize here is that at Biyu Preschool shaming is not only used to directly instill moral values like altruism. It is used pervasively in all sorts of occasions to correct children's behaviors that do not meet teachers' expectations.

For example, when Class 1A was learning a new song, some children cooperated with the teacher and focused on singing, whereas other children were not paying attention to singing or were making strange noises. At that time, Teacher Fanglin started the following conversation:

> Fanglin: Weiwei's voice is beautiful. But Yangyang's voice is not. I don't like his voice. Do you like it?
>
> Children shook their heads and responded together: No. We don't like it.
>
> Pengpeng added: Pengpeng doesn't like it, either!

Note that the point of shaming in this episode is subtle and implicit: The underlying intention of Teacher Fanglin was to tell children that they should sing in a normal way instead of making strange noises and that they should listen to her instructions. But she didn't explicit say "Yangyang, you should not make such noise." Instead, she invited all the other children to side with her and join in the negative evaluation of Yangyang's voice. The young children, with no doubt, echoed to their teacher's preference—and this episode was not merely about expressing one's preference; it was more about shaming Yangyang under a collective gaze. After this conversation, Yangyang felt ashamed and didn't make such noise again.

When I was observing episodes like this, what popped into my mind was the practice of a public "struggle session" (*pi dou hui*) (Thurston 1980) during the cultural revolution and other campaigns in the socialist era. The struggle session, which in Chinese literally means "a meeting for criticism and fight," was a form of public humiliation used by the Communist Party during the socialist era. In such sessions, "the masses" (*qunzhong*) were mobilized to verbally and physically abuse bad people such as political rivals and class enemies. In a lot of cases, those who joined the humiliation were fellow villagers, colleagues, friends, and even families of the target people being humiliated. Although shaming in the classroom didn't involve physical violence or abuse, teachers' techniques of mobilizing other children and inciting a collective gaze of judgment, disdain, and condemnation were indeed effective.

Ostracism: "Cutting Oneself Off from the People" (Zi Jue Yu Renmin)

The power of such a judgmental collective gaze manifests itself not just in shaming scenarios, but also in ostracism. Besides letting all the children know and judge that someone's behavior was bad, ostracism goes one step further by excluding (or threatening to exclude) this particular bad child from the community/collective unit. Scenarios of ostracism are reminiscent of the popular socialist slogan to criticize class enemies, "cutting oneself off from the people" (*zi jue yu renmin*), as ostracism in classroom settings and ostracism in the socialist political life both utilize human beings' inherent yearning for social belongingness and fear for social exclusion.

Sometimes teachers threaten the bad child that they will send him or her to another class, which works especially well for younger children. Class 1A and Class 1B are the only two classrooms in the first floor and children belong to one cohort. Teachers of these two classes often warn children that they would have to leave their own classrooms and go to the other one if they did not behave well. Sometimes teachers sent to time-out the bad child and had the child stand outside the classroom in the hallway. Also, sometimes the bad child would be punished by being made to stay in the classroom while all the other children left for activities in another classroom or on the playground. At those moments, the boundaries between the included and the excluded, marked physically by the classroom door, are sharply perceived both by the child being punished and by the others who are watching this *guanjiao* scenario. In many cases, young children would burst into tears, screaming harshly, ashamed and scared, as in this example.

One morning, Junjun made a mistake in class, because when Teacher Fanglin commanded the class to line up for going to the English class, he didn't pay attention to it and was still playing with his small chair when everybody else had already stood in a line at the classroom door. Teacher Fanglin was angry with him because she was always concerned that Junjun, her favorite boy, was too naive and inattentive in terms of being unaware of what's going on around him. Because Junjun's mother, Teacher Fanglin's close friend, had asked her to discipline Junjun as much as she could, Fanglin felt obliged to use whatever strict method she could, so long as Junjun's bad behaviors and dispositions could be corrected.

Teacher Fanglin called on Junjun's name: "Junjun, You can't go with the class this time! Stay at your seat!" Upon hearing this command, Junjun, who wore a carefree smile one moment ago, suddenly burst into tears: "No! I don't want to stay here! I want to go to the English class! I want to join the 'small train' (*xiao huoche*, children's term for their queue/class line)!" Teacher Fanglin didn't give in: "No! You have to stay here!" The assistant teacher, Xiaoya, and the helper, Auntie Zhang, led the other children to leave the classroom and go upstairs for their English class, and Teacher Fanglin stayed with Junjun in the classroom. Watching the "small train" moving—his beloved classmates walking in a line—Junjun cried even harder.

What strikes me most in this scenario is the fact that Junjun, who previously was not a fan of English class and sometimes didn't want to go there, suddenly became so scared and disappointed when getting to know that he could not join his peers for their English class. This case illustrates the power of ostracism in disciplining young children.

Self-Criticism (Ziwo Piping)

Self-criticism (*ziwo piping*), in which the subject criticized himself or herself in public, was a widely-used disciplinary technique by the Communist Party to control and transform people's minds and thinking (Kleinman and Kleinman 1994). Whether teachers consciously knew the disciplinary technique of self-criticism as a legacy from the socialist era or not, this technique was successfully used in Biyu Preschool, especially toward the older children (five- to six- year-olds). Apparently less harsh than shaming or ostracism, it is nonetheless an effective means to correcting children's mistakes.

During collective gymnastics (*zao cao*, morning exercise) today, some children in Class 4B were not very focused, and they didn't follow the teacher's instructions on the physical movements, and instead were chatting with other children. Teacher Yoyo was not happy, and she ordered the whole class to stay on the playground while all the other classes were dismissed back to their classroom. She asked the class to sit in a circle, under the burning sunshine.

Yoyo: "Is there anyone who thinks he or she didn't do a good job today?"

Nobody answered in the beginning. After a minute of silence, Teacher Yoyo continued to probe: "Those who can criticize themselves are really good and courageous children. Only after you realize your problems can you make progress." Then a couple of children raised their hands and confessed that they didn't pay enough attention to the teacher's instructions and didn't finish the physical movements. Teacher Yoyo praised these children and allowed them to go back to classroom.

Teacher Yoyo raised her voice and asked again: "Is there anyone who thinks he or she has already done perfectly well and has no problem at all? It's alright to think so." She looked around at the rest of the children, but nobody said a word.

Then Tongtong protested: "Let's go back to classroom! The sun is burning!"

Teacher Yoyo was angry: "I am more burned than you are. I am facing the sunshine and you are not! Why don't you stand out to criticize yourself and acknowledge your mistakes? Aren't you sympathetic with me at all, seeing me burned like this?"

Tongtong remained silent, as did the other children.

Teacher Yoyo summarized: "Whatever you do, you should concentrate on it and do well. When you eat, focus on eating. When you do the morning exercise, focus on the morning exercise." Then she asked these children to go back.

In this episode, self-criticism was used to encourage children to confess their mistakes and remind them of the merit of concentration and devotion, an attribute emphasized by teachers and parents as integral to academic success.

"Little Class Head" (Xiao Banzhang): *Agent of Power*

In addition to evoking self-criticism, another effective and efficient way for teachers to get compliance is to grant power to some particular children by designating them the title of "little class head" (*xiao banzhang*) and letting these head children monitor their classmates. It is a popular technique among all age groups to cultivate leadership skills and confidence among these head children, while at the same time exerting power efficiently.

When Yaxi was chatting lightheartedly with children sitting next to her, Teacher Meifang called her name: "Yaxi is our 'little class head' today. Little

Class Head, start your work now!" Yaxi lifted her head in joy, immediately ended her chatting, stood up with a really serious look, and stared around the whole class like a real authority.

Although the duties of the "little class head" were tedious, Yaxi enjoyed this job very much and immersed herself in disciplining her peers. She monitored each child's behavior carefully and sent out commands and orders from time to time: "Zirui, Look at your feet! Keep them under your chair!" "Xinwen, Put your hands down!" Children had to get her approval for things like going potty, standing up, walking around, and so forth. At lunchtime, Yaxi came to me with a proud smile: "Teacher Xu, I am a 'little class head' today!"

Children love to serve as the "little class head" because it brings them honor from authority and prestige among their peers. As children get a taste of power, however, unintended consequences might result, such as tattling, a thorny issue in preschool classrooms. Sometimes those who are not a little class head on that particular day still nag teachers, reporting every detail of other children's transgressions and bad behaviors, or even directly criticizing and rudely correcting these children. For example, Chengcheng, a three-year-old boy dubbed as the "evil kiddo" by his teachers, is one student who tattles a lot. Although Teacher Fanglin never named him as the head student, he likes to please Fanglin through tattling. He would report to Fanglin tiny little things such as A didn't drink his water in the cup, B didn't sit properly, or C said something bad about D. Instead of being pleased by Chengcheng's loyalty and vigilance, Teacher Fanglin was so annoyed because she thought it was bad for Chengcheng to try to build a good image for himself by revealing what was bad about other children.

Corporal Punishment: To Spank or Not to Spank?

Corporal punishment, which used to be an important part of the traditional Chinese disciplinary complex, is being challenged as a child-rearing practice in the postsocialist era. Although Pengpeng in the beginning vignette of this chapter reports that his father spanked him a lot at home, corporal punishment is not a common *guanjiao* technique applied to Biyu Preschool children, or at least its use stirs controversies among parents and teachers. For example, Rui's mother had the following comments:

> We adults tend to think that when children don't behave well, you need to spank them or scold them. But let's ask ourselves: Are you trying to discipline the child or just to release your own anger? Unfortunately, often times it is the latter, which is really bad. When children are young, they are not as strong as

us, and they cannot rebel or protest. This leads to two possible consequences: In some cases, the child will become too dependent and timid because he follows whatever adults tell him to do. In other cases, the child might remember the humiliating experiences well and will rebel against adults when he or she grows up. Perhaps those parents who like to hit children used to be treated by their own parents the same way when they were young, therefore they don't know how to educate their own children.

Rui's mother is seen as the exemplar mother of Biyu Preschool, admired by a lot of teachers and parents because Rui, the product of good parenting, is excellent both in personality and in academics. For Rui's mother, corporal punishment is not part of her disciplinary philosophy and she always respects her daughter and communicates with her.

Parents feel ambivalent about corporal punishment partly because they criticize themselves as not doing a good job to control and regulate their anger and impatience, in line with what Teresa Kuan found about Chinese parents' emphasis on "emotion work" (Kuan 2011). Other times it is not because of regret, but because of uncertainty: they are not sure whether corporal punishment is a necessary and good approach to child-rearing. For example, Weijian's mother said:

> I am very strict with my daughter, and sometimes I hit her. But every time after I hit her, I regretted so much: My daughter is already a very good child, and she has to observe a lot of rules already. Why do I need to impose even more rules on her? So sometimes I told my daughter: "Mom really doesn't want to hit you. If for some reasons I really couldn't control myself, you should do something to keep me from hitting you. For example, you can cry and beg for my forgiveness, and I might stop hitting you."

Weijian's mother is also a successful mother in the community, although according to herself, she is "very strict" with Weijian. She feels like sometimes children do need to be spanked, but she often feels regretful after hitting her child.

Another reason parents caution about corporal punishment is they worry children will imitate such violent behavior. Parents believe that children are not born to hit others, but they learn it as they see others doing it, especially parents. Teachers tend to judge whether parents hit children at home from whether children hit others at school, and those parents who often hit children at home are judged as being of "low quality" (*suzhi cha*).

At Biyu Preschool, teachers never hit children, and even if some of them think corporal punishment is good for children sometimes, they never implement it, mainly due to concerns about physical abuse. On the other hand, it is often said that in some other preschools, especially public schools, corporal punishment is not that rare, and some children are indeed heavily abused verbally or physically. Recent years have witnessed increasing attention and concentrated media exposure of child abuse cases, which have stirred harsh criticisms and controversies in public discourse and caused panic among parents over children's safety at schools.

For example, in late 2012, a young preschool teacher, Yan Yanhong, became a target of public resentment because she posted on her own blog several pictures of abusing her students. Scenarios such as lifting a child up by holding him by his ears, putting a child into the trash can, and so forth became her means of entertainment. Those who browsed her blog were shocked and revealed the photos to parents, which eventually led to legal suits against her. Waves of condemnation poured out on the Internet, accusing not only this preschool teacher for being intolerably cruel but also the broader society for being extremely immoral. Chai Jing, a famous TV hostess and public intellectual, dug deeper into Yan Yanhong's personal life and revealed the complexity of this case: the "child abuse" behavior was the culmination of various life contingencies of a poor working-class girl trying to live a better, to some extent, faked life in an increasingly unequal society (Chai 2013). As Biyu teachers later told me, although doubtlessly it was extremely inhumane to physically abuse children, this incident actually reflected the magnitude of stress that these poorly paid, overworked preschool teachers were burdened with as they were stuck in big cities in a fast-changing society in which the hope for a better life dimmed and no outlets for negative sentiments existed.

Children's Anti-Guanjiao Tactics

As the phrase "battle of wits and courage" (*dou zhi dou yong*) suggests, *guanjiao* dynamics always involve children's agency in their own actions, words, and thoughts. In addition to direct strategies such as blunt disobedience and stubborn protest, often seen as negative characteristics associated with "little emperors," children actually employ a variety of subtle strategies that turn *guanjiao* dynamics in new directions. I call these "anti-*guanjiao* tactics" and illustrate them through the following examples.

Children are very good at pleasing authority, in a variety of forms at home and school, to terminate the embarrassment of being disciplined and to prevent potential punishment.

> Haoran always wears high-quality sweaters with fine textures and unique styles, and every morning his mother puts him in a different sweater. *Ayi* Zhou (Class 3A helper) likes researching these children's sweater styles and textures so that she can learn these and knit together beautiful sweaters for her own grandson. Haoran's sweaters are always *Ayi* Zhou's favorites. Yesterday, Haoran didn't behave well during lunchtime, and *Ayi* Zhou was very angry with him, scolding him for bad table manners and disobedience to her words. You know what Haoran said? He immediately smiled to *Ayi* Zhou: "Dear *Ayi*, Don't be angry with me! I'll wear the sweater with your favorite style tomorrow!" *Ayi* Zhou felt funny and embarrassed, and stopped scolding him. Today, Haoran indeed wore to school *Ayi* Zhou's favorite sweater! What a clever boy! I would never expect a four-year-old to be so sophisticated in pleasing adults.

In addition to pleasing, another common strategy is to pass judgment on the parents because parents normally don't want to be seen as bad mothers or fathers, especially by their own children. Sometimes children stick to the criterion that parents should love them—and in such cases, of course, love is defined in the children's own terms. For example, Siya's mother always worried that her daughter was not well disciplined because she was not only very stubborn, but also full of wits to defeat her parents' *guanjiao* tactics and make them feel powerless.

> The other day Siya went home grumping: "Our homework is too much!" After writing out a half of the homework, she didn't want to finish the other half. I tried my best to encourage her to finish the rest of her homework, but she wouldn't listen to one word of mine. In the end, she blamed me seriously: "You are really not a good mother!" I was confused, and asked her: "Why did you say that?" She explained: "A good mother would never want her child to "eat such a big bitterness" (*chi zheme da de ku*)!" And I was left speechless.

Just as the "little class head" would *guanjiao* the class in an adult language that he or she is exposed to and has internalized from early on, children also use such criteria to judge adults, especially their parents. Immersed as they are in the adults' *guanjiao* language at school and home day by day, this language becomes so natural to them that children use it spontaneously and confidently. For example, the threat of ostracism—used by teachers in the two youngest classes—is quickly picked up by the children. These children are really scared by the threat of being sent to the other classroom. And they believe that this would also seem terrible to their parents, so they sometimes burst out, "I'll send you to Teacher Fanglin (or Teacher Jingjing)'s class" to their parents, as an angry response or even a threat to parents' *guanjiao* attempts. My son Wandou himself threatened me with this treatment quite a few times.

Raising a Good Child: Navigating on Shifting Grounds

The preschool period is a standard starting point to study the influence of school discipline on child development, as children at this age enter the new social space of school and have to adjust to a collective lifestyle that they may have never encountered before. Moreover, it is also an ideal developmental period in which to examine parenting values, as parents constantly reflect on child-rearing beliefs and practices in a self-conscious way. *Guanjiao*, molding the two sets of meanings together: govern/control/constrain and to love/care for/edify, is an important theme in Chinese socialization. Instead of assuming *guanjiao* as some self-evident Chinese cultural essence or a monolithic concept as often described in previous literature, this chapter contextualizes it in the multi-agent child-rearing dynamics as caregivers, educators, and children themselves are navigating amid the shifting grounds of China's complex social and moral transformations.

In her book *American Individualisms: Child Rearing and Social Class in Three Neighborhoods* (Kusserow 2004), Adrie Kusserow discovers that "individualism," the key to the American ethos, is not a monolithic construct. She uses the plural form "individualisms" to indicate how the so-called "individualism" in child-rearing experiences varies greatly by social class. Disciplinary approaches are different in the three preschools she studied, reflecting a "tougher" kind of individualism in working-class neighborhoods and a much "softer" kind in upper-middle-class families. Instead of comparing preschools across different social classes, my study, by focusing on a middle-class preschool community, reveals tensions, struggles, and transformations of *guanjiao* beliefs and practices among middle-class caregivers in Shanghai, in the context of China's rapid social change. Such tensions, struggles, and transformations take place between different generations, between school and family, and between adults and children.

These *guanjiao* dynamics are an integral part of raising a good child in China, as socializers have to negotiate diverse child-rearing ideals and models at a critical moment of historical transition. These ideals and models are products of a transitional era, when the "imagined Chinese" and "imagined Western" norms are contrasted, intertwined, and transformed in the rapidly changing social landscapes. The ambivalences and contradictions in *guanjiao* beliefs and practices hark back to the educational dilemmas introduced in Chapter 1 and also resonate with the tensions in children's developmental experiences examined in the other chapters. Taken together, these converging stories suggest risks, uncertainties, and challenges in the future world that Chinese children will face.

Conclusion: Becoming Human in a Time of Moral Crisis

A Journey of Intellectual Pursuit and Personal Reflections

This research weaves together my intellectual pursuit and my personal reflections. Drawing upon interdisciplinary approaches to morality, child development, and Chinese culture and society, this book investigates how Chinese children, born under the one-child policy and often seen as selfish "little emperors," become moral persons, or in other words, learn to "act human" (*zuo ren*) in a time of a perceived moral crisis amidst China's social transformations.

Zuo ren, the making of a moral person, is at the core of being Chinese. It literally means "acting human" or "becoming human," suggesting that cultivating personhood is an agentive practice and a developmental process, through which moral dispositions and potentials develop into full humanity. Philosophers and educators have ruminated on this subject for thousands of years, and it is still a central idea in today's Chinese child-rearing and education. As I grew up, the one precept from my parents that I remember most is: "Before learning to do things (*zuo shi*), you should first learn to act human (*zuo ren*)," or in other words, "how to act human is the foundation of how to do things." For example, the precondition for me to become a good scholar is that I have learned to become a moral person and that, now as an adult, I am a good human being. This central concern of my parents when they raised me is now becoming my central concern toward my own child. Ever since my son was able to communicate with me, even nonverbally, I have been constantly nagging him: "You should act like/become (*zuo*) a 'good baby' (*hao baobao/guai baobao*)."

The idea of *zuo ren* (becoming/acting human) construes moral development as a process of ceaseless interactions between the developing child and the environment, and it also highlights children's inner potentials to become moral persons. One can examine the wealth of plant metaphors from ancient texts to contemporary discourse in Chinese child-rearing in general and moral development in particular. For example, Mencius uses the sprout metaphor and its need for good soil, sun, and water to signify the interaction between humans' inherent goodness and their relationship with environmental factors (Wong 2015). Another example is an old proverb about the importance of moral education: "It takes ten years for a tree to grow to its full height, but a hundred years for a human to grow to its full maturity" (*shi nian shu mu, bai nian shu ren*).[1] Growing up in the 1980s and 1990s, I was bombarded with the message that we (children) were "flowers of the motherland" (*zuguo de huaduo*). This metaphor, originated from the title of a 1955 movie featuring primary schoolchildren's moral life in socialist China, is popular in official discourse even today, that is, President Xi used it in his International Children's Day speech (June 1, 2015) to emphasize the moral education of Chinese children (Xinhua News 2015). These plant metaphors express a fundamental belief about the nature of child development: that children are precious, vulnerable, yet active agents who grow and express their inner potentials; at the same time, the environment is crucial in providing the necessary nutrients and conditions for children's development and growth. My personal experience and intellectual interests are deeply shaped by the idea of *zuo ren*, as I set out to explore the intersection between the developing child as an agent and the evolving environment at a critical moment of social transition in China.

A Story of Moral Development in China

This book tells a story of moral development in contemporary China. Moral cultivation is the ultimate goal in the Chinese tradition of learning: "Learning how to perfect oneself and to become a better person morally and socially is never viewed as a cost or liability to oneself or anyone else. As such, it is viewed not just positively, but as an ultimate good" (Jin Li 2012: 15). My ethnography uncovers new dilemmas of moral education that complicate this tradition amid China's social transformations and documents children's own experiences navigating this complex moral world.

First, this book demonstrates that Chinese socializers are caught up in quandaries that combine extraordinary educational aspirations for their children's future success and tremendous anxieties about the making of the new moral person—their "only hope." On the one hand, the one-child policy and the severe competition in postsocialist China have reinforced the culturally engrained value of educational success deeply rooted in China's historical past. On the other hand, parents are burdened with enormous pressures to cultivate morality among children. They believe that early childhood is critical for a child's moral upbringing, and they hope to better the future society through cultivating moral children. Nonetheless, they perceive that the society at large is not wholesome, especially in the context of Shanghai schools, imprinted with the values of ruthless competition and materialism. The quandaries that result are manifest in various dimensions: disorientation in the face of conflicting values, felt dissonance between ideology and reality, cynicism about moral cultivation, and despair about China's future moral prospects.

Moreover, this book documents how children's sensibilities in multiple moral domains, including empathy and altruism, fairness and ownership, and generosity and strategic sharing, are emerging in the context of these moral education quandaries in China. First, this book explores how socialization processes tune and twist young children's nascent propensity to empathize with and care for others in the Chinese context. The education of empathy is situated in broader perceptions about contemporary China as a callous society, as discussion in the aftermath of the Little Yueyue case demonstrates. These perceptions result in a tension in empathy education, between cultivating emotional sensitivity and directing empathy to others in need, and suppressing empathy in occasions that require vigilance to avoid exploitation.

Second, the book closely examines the emergence of ownership and fairness understandings in children's life. On the one hand, socializers value children's natural and genuine disposition toward claiming ownership and fairness, and they worry that such natural dispositions are contested and even distorted in an unjust social environment, such as the concern that *qian rang* (deference, modesty, and generosity) might generate hypocrisy. On the other hand, they also worry that these "little emperors," if without proper guidance, will become too self-centered and thus cannot properly negotiate property distribution. I demonstrate how, under such competing concerns and constraints, young children gradually develop more complex ownership notions (i.e., the first-possessor heuristic) and then individual ownership and fairness rules (i.e., equality and merit) in daily practices of property distribution, exchange, and dispute.

Third, this book combines ethnographic and experimental methods to investigate the tension between the ideology of egalitarian sharing promoted by teachers and parents, and the children's practice of sharing for strategic favors, such as identifying good social partners, establishing a reciprocal network, and pleasing authority. I further analyze the underlying bidirectional feedback between the cultural dynamics of *guanxi* (connections, relationships) in contemporary China and children's emerging psychological dispositions for mutualistic cooperation.

Finally, the last chapter reveals the tensions among changing notions and practices of *guanjiao* (the Chinese cultural concept of child-rearing and socialization), through the daily interactions between children and adults both at home and at school. I find that middle-class parents in Shanghai today have become more and more critical and self-reflexive about *guanjiao* beliefs and practices that are predicated upon the hierarchical relationship between adults (authority) and children. They negotiate diverse and even conflicting values, based on their own perceptions of the past and the present and the imaginations of the Chinese and the Western. Such negotiations occur simultaneously at the intrapersonal, interpersonal, and intergenerational levels, as a reaction to the increasingly competitive, stressful, and uncertain society in which their children will have to navigate, survive, and excel.

As my book demonstrates, the stakes for Chinese socializers are high because they are facing tremendous uncertainties at a critical phase in child development during a transitional time of Chinese society, when the longstanding tradition of moral education is being challenged under the one-child policy and the perceived "moral crisis." The heightened tension between cultivating morality and securing future success, and the proliferation of negotiating complex and conflicting child-rearing values, doubtlessly, will have profound impacts on what kind of moral persons these children will eventually become and will shape the future trajectories of Chinese society.

In addition to documenting the impacts of the social transformations, cultural environment, and socialization on the moral development of the nation's youngest generation, my book also reveals the creativity and agency of these young children. Jin Ying negotiated with her mom to give some money to an old beggar despite her mom's warning about beggar-liars in today's China. Chengcheng told his teacher that she should give a piece of cake to the director to cultivate favor, but wanted to get a candy for his beloved *Ayi* Zhang from the director. Yaoyao readily updated her ownership rule from "everything is mine" to the first-possessor rule after playing at her friend's house and applied this new heuristic to every single situation to win property dispute battles. My son, Wandou, used his teacher's strategy of social exclusion—"I'll send you to Ms. Fanglin's class!"—to protest against my *guanjiao*. All these examples suggest that Chinese children are constructing their own moral universe that differs markedly from both adult ideals (that is, of a return to classic Chinese values or a switch to imagined Western values) and adult fantasies (of self-centered, selfish "little emperors").

The story of Chinese children's moral development speaks to issues that are fundamental to all human societies: the concern for becoming a moral person, the struggle between fostering morality/cooperation and competition for survival, and the role of children as both cultural learners and innovative agents. This ethnography, focusing on one community at a specific time and space in China, thus provides a unique reference point for future comparison and conceptualization about morality, child development, and culture.

A Quest for the Future

Toward the end of this book, it is time to look beyond the text and into the future. After all, studying children is like peeking into the future because they *are* the future. This book was inspired by my vision of and enthusiasm for the future of cross-fertilization between anthropology and psychology, in the particular area of child development. It is also borne out of my deep concern for the future of China, my motherland and a rising power in the global arena.

This book follows the call to address the "missing psychology in cultural anthropology" by prominent psychological anthropologists (Quinn and Strauss 2006). Recent theoretical works on morality and ethics have highlighted the urgency of looking at both the naturalistic bases (i.e., psychology) and the social histories (anthropology) of moral/ethical life, child development being an important site of investigating how these two approaches can inform each other (Keane 2015). Webb Keane argues, "what links the psychological and historical dimensions of ethical life is the dynamic of everyday social interaction" (Keane 2015: 33). My book provides an empirical account of how psychological and cultural processes together shape early moral development and makes children's everyday social interactions the center of analysis.

By revealing how children's emerging moral dispositions are shaped by Chinese familial, educational, and cultural dynamics, this study addresses an important disconnect between anthropology and psychology. That is, anthropologists and psychologists talk past each other in their study of children's moral development: while one camp ignores the psychological mechanisms of moral development, the other fails to appreciate the everyday practices in cultural dynamics whereby the moral personhood emerges. This book draws on literatures on various topics in moral development, such as empathy, fairness, and ownership, and illuminates how a conversation between anthropology and psychology sheds light on understanding young children's everyday moral experiences in specific cultural context.

In addition to theoretical cross-fertilization, this study integrates ethnographic and experimental methods to examine moral development experiences. Integration of naturalistic observations and controlled experiments is not new in other disciplines, but in cultural anthropology only few scholars have carried it out, and even fewer in the domain of child development (for one brilliant exception, see Astuti, Solomon, and Carey 2004). The following statement by Vanessa Fong, who integrated large-scale survey data with ethnographic interview data in her study of Chinese singleton children's experiences, aptly addresses the value of integrating statistical and ethnographic representations: "Because they are flawed in different ways, though, statistical and ethnographic representations can complement each other and provide a better provisional understanding of a reality that will always be too complex, varied, and subjective to be fully captured on paper" (Fong 2004: 25). My research reveals the great potential of integrating ethnography and experiment to better theorize children's psycho-cultural experiences, for example, the tension between equality and merit in children's fairness understandings, and the tension between egalitarian sharing and strategic sharing. These two methods inform each other cyclically about regularities/patterns (experiment) and meanings/contexts (ethnography) of children's behaviors.

Also, this study bridges the emerging scholarship of moral anthropology (or the anthropology of morality) and moral-domain theories in moral psychology. In-depth ethnographic fieldwork produces insights into moral experiences in everyday life, which might then contribute to our understanding and critique of psychological constructs. In particular, my analysis shows that even a single social interaction in real life often bears signatures of multiple moral motivations: for example, empathy and care for others are often intertwined with respect and submission to authority in children's simultaneously affectionate and strategic approach to their teachers. Detailed ethnographic analysis blurs the boundaries of moral domains. For example, in a society like China's with a strong hierarchical tradition, respect for authority and loyalty to group underlies educational and developmental experiences in various moral domains.

Furthermore, my research highlights the great potential of studying children in order to answer key questions regarding cultural transmission and change. Young children are important agents in transforming the present into the future and creating new possibilities through the transmission of old cultural knowledge. For example, my study reveals that young children are already learning the cultural norm of *guanxi*, but also demonstrates how they are negotiating new rules of property distribution that differ from traditional doctrines, such as that the younger one should give the big pear to his older brother and keep the small pear for himself.

Finally, by exploring how children's moral dispositions develop in contemporary China, a place that is perceived to be detrimental to moral development, this study illuminates how China's crisis of moral values intersects with family-planning policy and translates into educational anxieties and dilemmas. My book thus enriches the literature on China's moral transformations, the one-child policy, and child development. Contemporary Chinese children's lived experiences, as my book describes, differ in many ways from the childhood experiences of their grandparents and parents. In a recent edited volume, *Ordinary Ethics in China* (Stafford 2013b), several anthropologists analyze various dimensions of Chinese ethical life and moral transformations, and the experiences of children and youths constitute an important part of this story. As Charles Stafford, the book's editor, states, empirical studies of children's lived experiences at the micro-level "illuminate not only the transmission and practice of, but also the invention of, ordinary ethics in new social environments" (Stafford 2013a: 21). But he also notices that existing child-focused studies in China fail to directly engage with the psychological literature, although "psychologists and anthropologists clearly have a great deal to learn from each other when it comes to the study of child development in general and children's moral/ethical development in particular" (Stafford 2013a:21). My book fills in this critical gap and illuminates Chinese children's moral development under the one-child policy in a time of China's moral crisis.

China's rise as a global power is accompanied by tremendous costs on the individual, familial, and societal levels, and the rapid social transformation is having a profound impact on Chinese children—the future of the Chinese nation. Children are likely to suffer from the negative ramifications of social change, yet at the same time they bear hope and creative potential for new cultural and historical horizons at a critical phase of life when human beings learn about their social worlds and cultural values. *Wei ji* (crisis) consists of two Chinese characters, *wei* meaning "danger" and *ji* meaning "opportunity." This term suggests the dialectic relationship between danger and opportunity, like that of *yin* and *yang*, that these two generate, complement, and transform each other. In the midst of dangerous and highly uncertain situations, new potentials and opportunities might arise.

For example, a new policy had been announced in China to allow families to have two children (Buckley 2015). This is a significant event in the Chinese and even the world demographic history: it marks the termination of the one-child policy—perhaps the most strict national family planning policy in the whole world. For scholars, parents, educators, and the general public who share a deep concern about Chinese children and the Chinese nation, it might be an opportune time to study how reproductive choices and child-rearing models evolve following the ending of the one-child policy, how traditional moral education ideals interact with new cultural and institutional realities, how these in turn shape children's own developmental experiences, and ultimately how Chinese children's development might reconfigure the future of China and the world. At this point of historical transition, my book might become a valuable historical record of Chinese singleton children's lives before the one-child policy comes to an end. What my book documents will also serve as an important point of reference for examining Chinese children's experiences in the future.

Amid the deep quandaries of cultivating morality in a society perceived to be immoral, new hope still emerges among parents who strive to transform the society through education. For example, Jianxia, a mother and teacher who I met during my fieldwork, harshly criticized the detrimental consequences of the current social environment and the educational approach to children's moral development, but chose not to conform to popular trends in the society. She had the opportunity to enroll her children in a top preschool through personal connections, but she gave up this "unfair" approach and instead chose to homeschool her own children and children from like-minded families. Instead of competing with other family tutors, she initiated cooperation with them through sharing resources and referring new clients. In this homeschool model, these homeschoolers aimed to promote mutual respect and care between teachers and students, treating each child fairly and *guanjiao* the children in respectful ways. More and more parents joined in this project because they thought that the teachers were cooperative and loving and that the children's inner world was well nurtured. For Jianxia, what matters is the transformative power of mutualistic cooperation for the future of education and society. Chinese people today have deep-seated yearnings for better education through which their children can learn how to act as humans (*zuo ren*), resulting in a better society in which these children can live. Such existential yearnings for a better future, which drive these parents' and teachers' life choices, also motivated me to carry out this research.

Glossary

ai xin 爱心 a heart of love

ayi 阿姨 helper/auntie

ban zhang 班长 class president

bian lian 变脸 change one's face

biaoyang 表扬 praise

bu duli 不独立 lack of independence

bu jiang li 不讲理 unreasonable and disrespectful regarding rules

bu shanyu yu ren jiaowang 不善于与人交往 unsociableness

bu tinghua 不听话 disobedience

bu wenming 不文明 uncivil

buneng chengshou cuozhe 不能承受挫折 cannot accept criticism or stand setbacks

ce yin zhi xin 恻隐之心 a heart sensitive to others' sufferings

cheng ren (ch'eng jen) 成人 become human

chengren hua 成人化 adult-like

chi huang liang 吃皇粮 to live off government money

chi ku 吃苦 eat some bitterness, suffer

chi zheme da de ku 吃这么大的苦 eat such a big bitterness

chong ai 宠爱 indulged with excessive love

chun 纯 pure

chun zhen 纯真 pure and genuine

da ai 大爱 great love

da ren 大人 great people

dan chun 单纯 simple and pure

dao de 道德 morality

dao de pin zhi 道德品质 moral character

dong shi 懂事 sensible

dou zhi dou yong 斗智斗勇 battle of wits and courage

duli 独立 independence

duo guan xian shi 多管闲事 meddle in other's affairs

duocai siwei 多彩思维 colorful reasoning

dusheng zinv 独生子女 singleton child

erhu 二胡 a traditional Chinese instrument, also called the Chinese violin

fa zhi 法治 rule of law

fen xiang 分享 sharing; to share

fen xiang yishi 分享意识 awareness of sharing

ganqing 感情 human sentiments

gen shen di gu 根深蒂固 deeply entrenched

gongli 功利 pragmatically and materialistically oriented

gongping 公平 fairness

guai baobao 乖宝宝 good baby

guan 管 discipline

guan zhi 管治 disciplining-rearing

guanjiao 管教 discipline, train

guanxi 关系 connections, relationships

guanxin 关心 care for

guiju 规矩 rules

guzheng 古筝 a traditional Chinese instrument also known as the Chinese zither

hao baobao 好宝宝 good baby

hong bao 红包 red envelope

hongdeng ting, lüdeng xing 红灯停 绿灯行 stop at the red light, walk at the green light

huanwei sikao 换位思考 put oneself in others' shoes

hukou 户口 household registration record

huoche tou 火车头 engine of the train—class line leader

jiang xin bi xin 将心比心 feel into another's heart

jiao bu yan, shi zhi duo 教不严, 师之惰 to teach without severity/strictness, is the teacher's laziness

jiao dao 教导 teaching

jiao hua 教化 transform through teaching/education

jichu 基础 foundation

jiegui 接轨 gear to, integrate

jingying yishi 精英意识 elite consciousness/aspiration

jiti shenghuo 集体生活 collective life

juan yang 圈养 pen-rearing

kan ren lianse 看人脸色 look upon their faces—be at someone's disposal

kan ren xia cai die 看人下菜碟 look at the people before ordering dishes—be snobbish

kong zhi 控制 control

ku zhe ge lian 苦着个脸 wear a long face

la guanxi 拉关系 making a connection and establishing a relationship

lao Shanghai 老上海 old Shanghai

laoshi 老师 teacher

li rang zhi xin 礼让之心 a heart of courtesy and propriety

liyu tiao long men 鲤鱼跳龙门 upward mobility

lu bu shi yi, ye bu bi hu 路不拾遗, 夜不闭户 if you leave your stuff in the street, no
    one will steal it, and doors can be left unlocked

lun li 伦理 ethics

mei diwei 没地位 have no status

mei zhujian 没主见 lack of independence/independent judgment

menwei 门卫 school guard

mianrong bijiao anjing 面容比较安静 peaceful countenance

mimang 迷茫 confused and disoriented

        Min nong 悯农 Sympathy for the Peasants (a poem, below)

    chu he ri dang wu 锄禾日当午 Planting seeds while the noon sun is blazing hot.

      han di he xia tu 汗滴禾下土 Sweat drips together with the seeds.

   shui zhi pan zhong can 谁知盘中餐 Imagine—every grain in our bowls.

     li li jie xin ku 粒粒皆辛苦 Comes from previous hard work!

mo du 魔都 bedeviled city

nainai 奶奶 paternal grandma

Nanfang Zhoumo 南方周末 *Southern Weekly*

pi dou hui 批斗会 struggle session

ping deng 平等 equality

ping tianxia 平天下 bring peace to the whole world

qian gong jing rang 谦恭敬让 deference and modesty

qian guize 潜规则 hidden rule

qian rang 谦让 modesty, deference, and generosity

qianneng 潜能 hidden potential or latent ability

qiao hu 巧虎 *Bright Tiger*, a popular children's program in China

qinlao 勤劳 diligence

qizhi 气质 deportment

qunti yishi 群体意识 group consciousness

qunzhong 群众 the masses

ren 仁 humanity, benevolence

ren xing 任性 headstrong; self-willed

ren zhi 人治 rule of man

ren zhi chu, xing ben shan 人之初性本善 people at birth are naturally good

renqing 人情 a sense of moral obligation

renxin 人心 creativity

san yang/fang yang 散养/放养 cage-free-rearing

san zi jing 三字经 "Three Characters Classic"

shang huo 上火 get inflamed

Shanghai nanren 上海男人 Shanghainese men

shanliang 善良 kindness/caring

shanyu yu ren jiaowang 善于与人交往 sociableness

shazi 傻子 silly people

shi fei zhi xin 是非之心 a heart of right and wrong

shi nian shu mu, bai nian shu ren 十年树木, 百年树人 It takes ten years for a tree to
    grow to its full height, but a hundred years for a human to grow to its full maturity.

shili 势利 snobbery

shili yan 势利眼 snob

song li 送礼 gift-giving

suan ji 算计 calculating

suan le 算了 forget it

suzhi 素质 quality

suzhi cha 素质差 bad/low quality

suzhi jiaoyu 素质教育 education for quality

tao jinhu 套近乎 cotton up to the boss

ti 悌 respect for one's older brother

tian rang zhi bie 天壤之别 different like heaven to earth

tian xing 天性 inborn nature, natural propensities

tian zhen 天真 naive and innocent

tie fan wan 铁饭碗 iron rice bowl—a secure job

tinghua 听话 obedience

tong 通 transparent

tuo ban 托班 nursery class

wei shou wei wei 畏首畏尾 too timid and overcautious

wei wo du zun 唯我独尊 very egoistic

weibo 微博 Chinese version of Twitter

wei ji 危机 crisis (danger and opportunity)

wo zai meiguo zuo mama 我在美国做妈妈 my mothering experience in the United States

wu guiju bu cheng fang yuan 无规矩不成方圆 nothing can be accomplished without norms and standards

wu si yundong 五四运动 the May Fourth Movement, an anti-imperialist, cultural, and political movement growing out of student demonstrations in Beijing on May 4, 1919

wu zhuo 污浊 polluted

wuzhi zhe wuwei 无知者无畏 He who has no prior knowledge knows no fear.

xiao 孝 filial piety

xiao banzhang 小班长 little class head

xiao hei wu 小黑屋 little dark room

xiao huangdi 小皇帝 little emperors

xiao huoche 小火车 small train—class line

xiao pengyou 小朋友 little friends

xiao ren 小人 petty people

xiao ren jing 小人精 a sophisticated young child

xiao zhuchiren ban 小主持人班 little show hostess class

xin ji 心机 scheming

xin ku le 辛苦了 you have been working so hard

xin ling xiang tong 心灵相通 heart to heart; hearts connected

xin Shanghairen 新上海人 new Shanghainese

xin you ling xi 心有灵犀 two hearts beat in unison

xingquban 兴趣班 interest class

xinji 心计 calculation and scheming

xinli 心理 principles of the heart

xinli chengshou nengli 心理承受能力 psychological bearing capacity (the capacity to accept criticism, tolerate failure, and endure hardships)

xinli sushi 心理素质 psychological quality

xinling 心灵 mind/heart

xinling xiang tong 心灵相通 heart to heart/hearts connected

xiushen 修身 self-cultivation

xiu wu zhi xin 羞恶之心 a heart of shame and disgust

xu wei 虚伪 hypocrisy

xue 学 study

xuelei de jiaoxun 血泪的教训 a lesson learned with blood and tears

xun lian 训练 training

ya sheng 亚圣 second saint (Mencius)

yan mian sao di 颜面扫地 face sweeping the ground—be humiliated

yang 养 nurture

yang bu jiao, fu zhi guo 养不教, 父之过 to feed without teaching is the father's fault

yang zhi 养治 nurturing-rearing

yeye 爷爷 paternal grandfather; a general term for elderly men

yi ba xinsuan lei 一把辛酸泪 a handful of tears, sour and bitter

yi lai shen shou, fan lai zhang kou 衣来伸手, 饭来张口 hold out their hands to be dressed and open their mouths to be fed

yi ti 一体 forming one body

yi tianxia wei ji ren 以天下为己任 take the world upon oneself

ying zai qi pao xian shang 赢在起跑线上 win at the starting line

yingchou 应酬 networking

yingfu jiaoyu 英孚教育 EF (Education First), a popular international education agency that offers English lessons in China

you aixin 有爱心 with a loving heart

you chu xi 有出息 promising, full of promise

you xiao xianjie 幼小衔接 K-to-1(kindergarten to first-grade) transition

you zhujian 有主见 independent, with one's own judgment

youxiu 优秀 excellent

yue ren wushu 阅人无数 meet countless people

zao cao 早操 morning exercise

zao shu 早熟 mature beyond one's age

zaojiao zhongxin 早教中心 early education center

zaojiaoban 早教班 early education classes

zhangmuniang 丈母娘 the wife's mother/the husband's mother-in-law

zheng nengliang 正能量 positive energy—positive attitudes and behaviors in social life

zhenjian dui maiming 针尖对麦芒 head to head

zhiye qigai 职业乞丐 professional beggar

zhong yong zhi dao 中庸之道 golden mean

zi yu 自愈 heal oneself

zi jue yu renmin 自绝于人民 cutting oneself off from the people

zili 自立 independence, autonomy

ziran guilü 自然规律 natural laws

zisi 自私 selfishness

ziwo piping 自我批评 self-criticism

ziwo zhongxin 自我中心 self-centered

zuguo de huaduo 祖国的花朵 flowers of the motherland

zuo 作 (Shanghainese dialect) spoiled, demanding

zuo 做 do/act/become

zuo ren (tso jen) 做人 act/become human

zuo shi 做事 do things

zuo zuo 做作 pretentious

Notes

Introduction

1. Specifically, experimental studies reveal a variety of early emerging moral dispositions and cooperative motivations, such as empathy/care, equality, favoritism, proportionality, hierarchy, and ownership. Recent findings in developmental psychology and developmental neuroscience highlight the early ontogeny of empathy (Saby, Meltzoff, and Marshall 2013; Meltzoff 2002), identify its affective and cognitive components (Davidov et al. 2013; Decety and Howard 2013) and clarify the motivational power of empathy for prosocial behaviors (Hepach, Vaish, and Tomasello 2013a, 2013b; Vaish, Carpenter, and Tomasello 2009). Ownership cognition is another important building block of human morality to guide social coordination (Rochat 2011) because mentally representing and distinguishing one's own and others' property are fundamental elements of moral psychology. Experimental studies in recent years piece together a developmental trajectory that develops from identifying the owner of familiar objects in infancy to a more mature understanding of ownership transfer by the end of preschool years (Blake and Harris 2009; Blake, Ganea, and Harris 2012; Friedman and Neary 2008; Friedman 2008; Neary, Friedman, and Burnstein 2009; Kanngiesser, Gjersoe, and Hood 2010; Shaw, Li, and Olson 2012). Recent experimental studies with infants and toddlers have shown the early onset of fairness expectations (for a review, see Sommerville et al. 2013) and detail how preschoolers develop more complex thinking about the different kinds of fairness principles such as equality and merit (Baumard, Mascaro, and Chevallier 2012). At the same time, studies also suggest that children exert subtle judgment in the choice of who should be their cooperative partners in activities such as sharing (Olson and Spelke 2008; Moore 2009; Shaw, DeScioli, and Olson 2012).

2. "*Tso jen*" is the Wade-Giles version of pinyin "*zuo ren*." In the same fashion, "*ch'eng jen*" is the Wade-Giles version of pinyin "*cheng ren*."

3. The May Fourth Movement (*wu si yundong*) was an anti-imperialist, cultural, and political movement growing out of student demonstrations in Beijing on May 4, 1919. The May Fourth era in a broader sense refers to the period 1915–1921 during which intellectuals initiated cultural and literary reforms, which is also called the New Culture Movement.

4. Themes like this are featured in the great modern writer, Lu Xun's novels and essays, according to Jon L. Saari (1990).

5. Although the famous series of studies described in "Preschools in Three Cultures" (Tobin, Wu, and Davidson 1991) and "Preschools in Three Cultures Revisited" (Tobin, Hsueh, and Karasawa 2011) feature two renowned public preschools in China, one in Kunming, Southwest, and the other located in the old center of Shanghai, Biyu Preschool differs from these as a newly built private school located in the newly developed Pudong district, China's financial hub.

6. The term *Shanghainese* can refer to either the dialect of Shanghai or the native Shanghai people.

7. In China, preschool teachers tend to call their students "baby" (*baobao*), an affectionate designation.

8. Frugality as a virtue is taught on many other occasions and through other methods in this preschool. For example, in Class 1A, during lunchtime, before starting to eat, children were required to learn and recite a famous ancient poem on frugality that young children can easily remember, "Sympathy for the Peasants" (*Min nong*).

The poem goes like this:

Planting seeds while the noon sun is blazing hot (*chu he ri dang wu*),
Sweat drips together with the seeds (*han di he xia tu*).
Imagine—every grain in our bowls (*shui zhi pan zhong can*).
Comes from previous hard work (*li li jie xin ku*)!

Chapter 1

1. A colloquial term that refers to the generation of people who were born in the 1970s.

2. Unlike in mainstream American hospitals where pregnant women can enjoy an individual space for child delivery, such one-on-one delivery rooms and maternity wards are highly scarce resources in China, provided only to those who have the financial means or special connections (*guanxi*), and competition for such resources is huge.

3. I included the option "cultivating artistic quality" because it has become a trend that parents send young children to various extracurricular classes for artistic training, such as piano, violin, Chinese music instruments, calligraphy, painting, and so forth.

4. [1]Little Show Hostess Class is a popular Chinese invention that aims to train children on skills and manners needed to fulfill the role of a hostess in shows such as school celebration events. Parents and educators consider it valuable because they believe it can help children cultivate self-confidence and develop good communication skills.

5. Keyu was Siya's classmate in Class 3B.

6. "Math Olympics" is a popular "interest class" for children of preschool age.

7. The details of the topic will be discussed in Chapter 5.

8. "*Lu bu shi yi, ye bu bi hu*" is a phrase originally from the famous historiography, *zi zhi tong jian* ("Comprehensive Mirror to Aid in Government"), published in 1084. It initially referred to a historical period in the Tang dynasty of good social order and moral ethos. It then becomes a popular idiom that refers generally to an imagined society with superior social and moral order.

9. Contrary to parents' assumption that young children don't understand the pragmatics of gift-giving, stories in Chapter 4 reveal that in real life, even three-year-olds have some subtle understandings about these.

10. "Red envelope" (*hong bao*) is a red package with money inside, as a gift given during holidays and social occasions such as weddings. It is also a synonym for bribery.

11. Although Meifang's son in this story had no clue of adults' gift-giving culture, there were other young children who did grow aware of such practices. The details of this issue are explained in Chapter 4.

12. The Chinese *chu xi* literally means "out breathing," and it can be translated as promising, or full of potential.

Chapter 2

1. Although the explicit focus of the "Child-in-the-Well" story is on empathy, Mencius expands it into an analysis of several basic human moral dispositions as part of his thesis on inborn good human nature.

2. These basic points in the Chinese tradition of empathy (i.e., feeling for and into the misery of others is a basic part of human nature and is universal to all humans) resemble Adam Smith's treatise on compassion in the beginning of *The Theory of Moral Sentiments* (Smith 2011): "How selfish soever man may be supposed, there are evidently some principles in his nature, which interest him in the fortune of others, and render their happiness necessary to him, though he derives nothing from it except the pleasure of seeing it. Of this kind is pity or compassion, the emotion which we feel for the misery of others, when we either see it, or are made to conceive it in a very lively manner. That we often derive sorrow from the sorrow of others, is a matter of fact too obvious to require any instances to prove it; for this sentiment, like all the other original passions of human nature, is by no means confined to the virtuous and humane, though they perhaps may feel it with the most exquisite sensibility. The greatest ruffian, the most hardened violator of the laws of society, is not altogether without it" (p. 4).

3. Mencius believes every human being possesses these four basic moral senses: *ce yin zhi xin* (a heart of compassion), *xiu wu zhi xin* (a heart of shame and disgust), *li rang zhi xin* (a heart of courtesy and propriety), and *shi fei zhi xin* (a heart of right and wrong).

4. http://bbs.tianya.cn/post-free-2301432-1.shtml

5. http://v.ifeng.com/quanminxiangduilun/xiaoyueyue/

6. Ibid.

7. Anthropologists distinguish "basic empathy"—"the most basic, nonconscious ways in which the human body orients itself and reacts to the world and to other bodies" from "complex empathy"—"a more conscious awareness of and engagement with other bodies and people" (Hollan 2012: 71).

8. This is a Chinese proverb that uses a metaphor: The hearts of two persons are linked like the white line that runs through the horn of the divine rhino, therefore at just a hint, the hearer understands immediately.

9. The details of which will be presented in Chapter Four.

10. As a venue for teacher-parent communication, the *Family-School Communication* book is a weekly report collection in which teachers record children's weekly performance and parents give feedback and comments.

11. This term refers both specifically to one's grandfather and generally to elderly men.

Chapter 3

1. For detailed description of this incident, the photo of that exam sheet and other people's comments, please see this news report: http://news.163.com/12/0418/19/7VD81S5100011229.html.

2. *Guangming Daily* is a newspaper led by the Central Communist Party that focuses mainly on education.

3. See http://vote.weibo.com/poll/1647961.

4. Moral education thoughts around this specific incident are directly incorporated in discussions of Chinese governance. For example, analysis of this incident was proposed as a question in

one of the practice tests for the 2016 National Exam of Civil Service Admission in China; see http://weibo.com/p/230418a702e3120102wlz6.

5. A classic study (Hook 1993) provides a general account of how children (four- to fifteen-year-olds) gradually grasp a more sophisticated understanding of these rules, but the burgeoning new field of ownership cognition in infancy and early childhood now has produced more precise and nuanced findings.

6. For example, three-year-olds attribute ownership according to who controls permission to use it (Neary, Friedman, and Burnstein 2009). By the age of four, children prioritize verbal statements over physical possession in determining ownership (Blake, Ganea, and Harris 2012); by five years of age, children develop a mature understanding of ownership transfer, such as the difference between giving and stealing (Blake and Harris 2009), and the difference between creative labor (e.g., making something new out of the clay) and minor modification (e.g., cutting off a small piece of the clay) (Kanngiesser, Gjersoe, and Hood 2010); and six-year-olds apply ownership rules, such as first-possession, control of permission, not only to physical property, but also to different types of ideas (e.g., stories, jokes, and songs), but not all kinds of ideas (i.e., a common word) (Shaw, Li, and Olson 2012). Also, by the age of six, children value ideas (design of a picture) over labor (drawing the picture designed by others) in artistic creation (Li, Shaw, and Olson 2013).

7. For a full description of the background, methods, and findings of this study, please refer to the article, *Preschoolers' Understanding of Merit in Two Asian Societies* (Chevallier et al. 2015).

8. This study reveals interesting similarities and differences between Chinese and Japanese children in the same study: while the majority of Japanese children (twenty-eight out of thirty-nine) also favored the big contributor in the final distribution, more Japanese children (twenty-nine out of thirty-nine) chose to give one cookie to each character in the initial distribution. But because my book is to provide a detailed ethnographic documentation about moral development in a Chinese community, instead of a comprehensive cross-cultural comparison of different case studies, I choose not to summarize the comparison of the Japanese and Chinese results in the main text of this chapter.

9. I conducted some other experiments with these children before conducting this cookie-distribution experiment (equality merit in fairness cognition) with them. Some of these experiments involved giving the children candies as rewards and asking them to share candies with hypothetical figures; these experiments are summarized in the next chapter.

10. According to Class 3A rules, each play zone has a fixed number of tickets. This time, Teacher Tang made an exception for Xinbao.

Chapter 4

1. According to the teacher's comments and my own observations, Chengcheng's sophistication in carefully cultivating and managing the relationships with his superiors is visible on other occasions, too. For instance, he liked tattling to gain favor from the teacher by monitoring his peers and reporting their misbehaviors to the teacher. He also would seize any opportunity to talk to the school director, and he later became one of the director's favorite children.

2. Anthropologist Susan Blum's book, *Lies that Bind: Chinese Truth, Other Truths* (Blum 2007) systematically examines the incongruities between ideological norms and strategic reality, from the perspective of truth and deception.

3. Mingming and Lele are common children's names in China.

Chapter 5

1. This kind of gardening/plant metaphor is very common in Chinese understanding of child development and child-rearing. See more in the Conclusion.

2. According to folk Chinese beliefs originated from traditional Chinese medicine system, certain foods are "hot," including tropical fruits such as bananas and mango, the intake of which will cause the human body to "get inflamed" (*shang huo*) and lose its internal balance. Young children are believed to be even more vulnerable to such "hot" foods, as their bodies are "hotter" than adults because they are younger and their inherent "yang" essence is preserved better than in later life.

Conclusion

1. In this proverb, *a hundred years* is a general phrase that refers to the human life span.

Bibliography

Ainsworth, M. S. 1979. Infant–Mother Attachment. *American Psychologist* 34(10): 932–937.

Allinson, R. E. 1992. A Hermeneutic Reconstruction of the Child in the Well Example. *Journal of Chinese Philosophy* 19(3): 297–308.

Anagnost, Ann. 1997. "Children and National Transcendence in China." In *Constructing China: The Interaction of Culture and Economics*, edited by Kenneth G. Lieberthal, Shuen-fu Lin, and Ernest P. Young, pp. 195–222. Ann Arbor, MI: Center for Chinese Studies, University of Michigan.

Anagnost, Ann. 2004. The Corporeal Politics of Quality (Suzhi). *Public Culture* 16(2): 189–208.

Astuti, Rita, and Maurice Bloch. 2010. Why a Theory of Human Nature Cannot Be Based on the Distinction between Universality and Variability: Lessons from Anthropology. *Behavior and Brain Sciences* 33(2–3): 83–84.

Astuti, Rita, and Maurice Bloch. 2012. Anthropologists as Cognitive Scientists. *Topics in Cognitive Science* 4(3): 453–461.

Astuti, Rita, Gregg E. A. Solomon, and Susan Carey. 2004. Constraints on Conceptual Development: A Case Study of the Acquisition of Folkbiological and Folksociological Knowledge in Madagascar. *Monographs of the Society for Research in Child Development* 69(3). Oxford: Wiley-Blackwell.

Baker, Hugh D. R. 1979. *Chinese Family and Kinship*. New York: Columbia University Press.

Bakken, Børge. 2000. *The Exemplary Society: Human Improvement, Social Control, and the Dangers of Modernity*. New York: Oxford University Press.

Batson, C. Daniel. 2009." These Things Called Empathy: Eight Related but Distinct Phenomena." In *The Social Neuroscience of Empathy*, edited by Jean Decety and William Ickes, pp. 4–15. Cambridge, MA: The MIT Press.

Baumard, Nicolas, Jean-Baptiste André, and Dan Sperbe. 2013 A Mutualistic Approach to Morality: The Evolution of Fairness by Partner Choice. *Behavioral and Brain Sciences* 36(1): 59–78.

Baumard, Nicolas, Olivier Mascaro, and Coralie Chevallier. 2012. Preschoolers Are Able to Take Merit into Account when Distributing Goods. *Developmental Psychology* 48(2): 492–498.

Bender, Andrea, Edwin Hutchins, and Douglas Medin. 2010. Anthropology in Cognitive Science. *Topics in Cognitive Science* 2(3): 374–385.

Beng, Kor Kian. 2013. "In China, a New Compact to Foster a Fairer Society." *The Straits Times*. http://www.stasiareport.com/the-big-story/asia-report/china/story/china-new-compact -foster- fairer-society-20131121, accessed December 1, 2016.

Benson, P. 2011. "Altruism and Cooperation among Humans: The Ethnographic Evidence: Introduction Part III." In *Origins of Altruism and Cooperation*, edited by Robert W. Sussman and C.

Robert Cloninger, pp. 195–202. New York: Springer Science & Business Media. http://link
.springer.com/chapter/10.1007/978-1-4419-9520-9_11 (accessed December 1, 2016).

Blake, Peter R., Patricia A. Ganea, and Paul L. Harris. 2012. Possession Is Not Always the Law:
With Age, Preschoolers Increasingly Use Verbal Information to Identify Who Owns What.
Journal of Experimental Child Psychology 113(2): 259–272.

Blake, Peter R., and Paul L. Harris. 2009. Children's Understanding of Ownership Transfers.
Cognitive Development 24(2): 133–145.

Bloch, Maurice. 2005. "Where Did Anthropology Go?: Or the Need for "Human Nature." In
Essays on Cultural Transmission, edited by Maurice Bloch, pp. 1–20. Oxford: Berg. http://
www.bergpublishers.com/Default.aspx?base (accessed December 1, 2016).

Bloch, Maurice. 2012. *Anthropology and the Cognitive Challenge*. Cambridge, UK: Cambridge
University Press.

Bloom, Paul. 2013. *Just Babies: The Origins of Good and Evil*. New York: Random House/Crown.

Blum, Susan D. 2007. *Lies That Bind: Chinese Truth, Other Truths*. Lanham, MD: Rowman &
Littlefield.

Boehm, Christopher. 2008. Purposive Social Selection and the Evolution of Human Altruism.
Cross-Cultural Research 42(4) 319–352. http://ccr.sagepub.com/content/early/2008/07/11/106
9397108320422 (accessed December 1, 2016).

Bourdieu, Pierre. 2008. "The Forms of Capital." In *Readings in Economic Sociology*, edited by
Nicole Woolsey Biggart, pp. 280–291.Oxford: Blackwell. http://onlinelibrary.wiley.com
/doi/10.1002/9780470755679.ch15/summary (accessed December 1, 2016).

Bowlby, John. 1969. *Attachment and Loss*. New York: Basic Books.

Bowlby, John. 1982. *Attachment*. New York: Basic Books.

Bowles, Samuel, and Herbert Gintis. 2011. *A Cooperative Species: Human Reciprocity and Its
Evolution*, reprint. Princeton, NJ: Princeton University Press.

Boyd, Robert, Herbert Gintis, Samuel Bowles, and Peter J. Richerson. 2003. The Evolution of
Altruistic Punishment. *Proceedings of the National Academy of Sciences* 100(6): 3531–3535.

Briggs, Jean L. 1999. *Inuit Morality Play: The Emotional Education of a Three-Year-old*. New Haven,
CT: Yale University Press.

Buckley, Chris. 2015. "China Ends One-Child Policy, Allowing Families Two Children." October
29. *New York Times*. http://www.nytimes.com/2015/10/30/world/asia/china-end-one-child
-policy.html_r=0 (accessed December 1, 2016).

Burns, Monica Patricia, and Jessica Sommerville. 2014. "I Pick You": The Impact of Fairness and
Race on Infants' Selection of Social Partners. *Developmental Psychology* 5: 93.

Cameron, L., N. Erkal, L. Gangadharan, and X. Meng. 2013. Little Emperors: Behavioral Impacts
of China's One-Child Policy. *Science* 339(6122): 953–957.

Chai, Jing. 2013. Yan Yanhong: Wo Bu Renshi Wo Ziji (Yanhong Yan: I Don't Know Myself).
http://blog.sina.com.cn/s/blog_48b0d37b0102eptx.html (accessed December 1, 2016).

Champagne, Susan. 1992. *Producing the Intelligent Child: Intelligence and the Child Rearing
Discourse in the People's Republic of China*. PhD diss. Stanford University.

Chan, Carol K. K., and Nirmala Rao. 2009. *Revisiting the Chinese Learner: Changing Contexts,
Changing Education*. Hong Kong: Springer, Comparative Education Research Centre, the
University of Hong Kong.

Chan, Kara. 2006. Consumer Socialization of Chinese Children in Schools: Analysis of Consump-
tion Values in Textbooks. *Journal of Consumer Marketing* 23(3): 125–132.

Chang, Xiangqun. 2010. *Guanxi or Li Shang Wanglai: Reciprocity, Social Support Networks, Social
Creativity in a Chinese Village*. Taipei, Taiwan: Airiti.

Chao, R. K. 1994. Beyond Parental Control and Authoritarian Parenting Style: Understanding Chinese Parenting through the Cultural Notion of Training. *Child Development* 65(4): 1111–1119.

Cheng, Kaiming. 2000. "Understanding Basic Education Policies in China: An Ethnographic Approach." In *The Ethnography Eye: Interpretive Studies of Education in China*, edited by Judith Liu, Heidi A. Ross, and Donald P. Kelly, pp. 19–50. New York: Falmer.

Cheung, Kwok Wah, and Suyan Pan. 2006. Transition of Moral Education in China: Towards Regulated Individualism. *Citizenship Teaching and Learning* 2(2): 37–50.

Chevallier, Coralie, Jing Xu, Kuniko Adachi, Jean-Baptiste van der Henst, and Nicolas Baumard. 2015. Preschoolers' Understanding of Merit in Two Asian Societies. *PLoS ONE* 10(5): e0114717.

Chinese Communist Party. 2001. *Program for Improving Civic Morality (Gongmin Daode Jianshe Shishi Gangyao)*. http://www.people.com.cn/GB/shizheng/16/20011024/589496.html (accessed December 1, 2016).

Chua, Amy. 2011. *Wo Zai Meiguo Zuo Mama: Yelu Faxueyuan Jiaoshou de Yuerjing (My Mothering Experience in the United States: Parenting Advice from a Yale Law Professor)*, translated by Xinhua Zhang. Beijing: Zhongxin Chubanshe (China CITIC Press).

Cline, Erin M. 2015. *Families of Virtue: Confucian and Western Views on Childhood Development*. New York: Columbia University Press.

Davidov, Maayan, Carolyn Zahn-Waxler, Ronit Roth-Hanania, and Ariel Knafo. 2013. Concern for Others in the First Year of Life: Theory, Evidence, and Avenues for Research. *Child Development Perspectives* 7(2): 126–131.

Decety, Jean, and H. Howard, 2013. The Role of Affect in the Neurodevelopment of Morality. *Child Development Perspectives* 7(1): 49–54.

DesChamps, Trent. D., Arianne E. Eason, and Jessica A. Sommerville. 2015. Infants Associate Praise and Admonishment with Fair and Unfair Individuals. *Infancy* 21(4) 478–504.

Deutsch, Morton. 1975. Equity, Equality, and Need: What Determines Which Value Will Be Used as the Basis of Distributive Justice? *Journal of Social Issues* 31(3): 137–149.

Dillon, S. 2010. "In PISA Test, Top Scores from Shanghai Stun Experts." December 7. *New York Times*. http://www.nytimes.com/2010/12/07/education/07education.html (accessed December 1, 2016).

Duan, Siping. 2012. Shui Ling "Rang Li" Xianru Liannan Jingdi? (Who Makes "Modestly Declining the Pear" a Moral Dilemma)? http://guancha.gmw.cn/2012-04/20/content_4133996.htm (accessed December 1, 2016).

Engelen, Eva-Maria, and Birgitt Röttger-Rössler. 2012. Current Disciplinary and Interdisciplinary Debates on Empathy. *Emotion Review* 4(1): 3–8.

Farrer, James. 2002. *Opening up: Youth Sex Culture and Market Reform in Shanghai*, 1e. Chicago, University of Chicago Press.

Fasig, Lauren. G. 2000. Toddlers' Understanding of Ownership: Implications for Self-Concept Development. *Social Development* 9(3): 370–382.

Fassin, Didier. 2012. "Introduction: Toward a Critical Moral Anthropology." In *A Companion to Moral Anthropology*, edited by Didier Fassin, pp. 1–17. New York: John Wiley & Sons.

Faubion, James D. 2011. *An Anthropology of Ethics*. Cambridge and New York: Cambridge University Press.

Fears, Danika. 2013. Extreme Parenting: "Eagle Dad" Trains Son, 5, to Be World's Youngest Pilot. TODAY.com. http://www.today.com/moms/extreme-parenting-father-encourages-5-year-old-son-be-worlds-8C11089735 (accessed December 1, 2016).

Fehr, Ernst, Helen Bernhard, and Bettina Rockenbach. 2008. Egalitarianism in Young Children. *Nature* 454(7208): 1079.

Fiske, Alan Page. 1991. *Structures of Social Life?: The Four Elementary Forms of Human Relations?: Communal Sharing, Authority Ranking, Equality Matching, Market Pricing.* New York: Free Press; Toronto: Collier Macmillan Canada; New York: Maxwell Macmillan International.

Fiske, Alan Page. 1992. The Four Elementary Forms of Sociality: Framework for a Unified Theory of Social Relations. *Psychological Review* 99(4): 689–723.

Fiske, Alan Page, and Nick Haslam. 2005." The Four Basic Social Bonds: Structures for Coordinating Interaction." In *Interpersonal Cognition*, p. 267–298. New York: Guilford.

Fong, Vanessa L. 2004. *Only Hope: Coming of Age under China's One-Child Policy*, 1e. Stanford, CA: Stanford University Press.

Fong, Vanessa L. 2007a. Morality, Cosmopolitanism, or Academic Attainment? Discourses on "Quality" and Urban Chinese-Only-Children's Claims to Ideal Personhood. *City & Society* 19(1): 86–113.

Fong, Vanessa L. 2007b. Parent-Child Communication Problems and the Perceived Inadequacies of Chinese Only Children. *Ethos* 35(1): 85.

Fong, Vanessa L., Cong Zhang, Sun won Kim, et al. 2012. "Gender Role Expectations and Chinese Mothers' Aspirations for Their Toddler Daughters' Future Independence and Excellence." In *Chinese Modernity and Individual Psyche*, edited by Andrew B. Kipnis, pp. 90–117. New York: Palgrave Macmillan.

Fong, Vanessa L., and Sung won Kim. 2011. "Anthropological Perspectives on Chinese Children, Youth, and Education." In *A Companion to the Anthropology of Education*, edited by Bradley A. U. Levinson and Mica Pollock, pp. 333–348. New York: Wiley-Blackwell.

Freedman, Maurice. 1966. *Chinese Lineage and Society: Fukien and Kwangtung*, 1e. London: Athlone Press.

Friedman, Ori. 2008. First Possession: An Assumption Guiding Inferences about Who Owns What. *Psychonomic Bulletin & Review* 15(2): 290–295.

Friedman, Ori, and Karen R. Neary. 2008. Determining Who Owns What: Do Children Infer Ownership from First Possession? *Cognition* 107(3): 829–849.

Friedman, Thomas L. 2013. "The Shanghai Secret." October 22. *New York Times*. http://www.nytimes.com/2013/10/23/opinion/friedman-the-shanghai-secret.html (accessed December 1, 2016).

Fung, Heidi. 1999. Becoming a Moral Child: The Socialization of Shame among Young Chinese Children. *Ethos* 27(2): 180–209.

Fung, Heidi, and Benjamin Smith. 2010. "Learning Morality." In *The Anthropology of Learning in Childhood*, edited by David F. Lancy, John Bock, and Suzanne Gaskins, pp. 261–286. Walnut Creek, CA: AltaMira.

Gansberg, Martin. 1964. "37 Who Saw Murder Didn't Call the Police." March 27. *New York Times*. http://www.nytimes.com/1964/03/27/37-who-saw-murder-didnt-call-the-police.html (accessed December 1, 2016).

Geraci, Alessandra, and Luca Surian. 2011. The Developmental Roots of Fairness: Infants' Reactions to Equal and Unequal Distributions of Resources. *Developmental Science* 14(5): 1012–1020.

Gintis, Herbert, Samuel Bowles, Robert Boyd, and Ernst Fehr. 2003. Explaining Altruistic Behavior in Humans. *Evolution and Human Behavior* 24(3): 153–172.

Goh, Esther C. L. 2013. *China's One-Child Policy and Multiple Caregiving: Raising Little Suns in Xiamen*, 1e. London; New York: Routledge.

Goh, Esther C.L., and Leon Kuczynski, L. 2009. Agency and Power of Single Children in Multi-Generational Families in Urban Xiamen, China. *Culture & Psychology* 15(4): 506–532.

Greenhalgh, Susan. 2008. *Just One Child?: Science and Policy in Deng's China.* Berkeley, CA: University of California Press.

Gurven, Michael 2004. Reciprocal Altruism and Food Sharing Decisions among Hiwi and Ache Hunter-Gatherers. *Behavioral Ecology and Sociobiology* 56(4): 366–380.

Haidt, Jonathoan 2012. *The Righteous Mind: Why Good People Are Divided by Politics and Religion.* New York: Pantheon.

Haidt, Jonathan, and Jesse Graham. 2007. When Morality Opposes Justice: Conservatives Have Moral Intuitions that Liberals May Not Recognize. *Social Justice Research* 20(1): 98–116.

Haken, H. 2004. *Synergetics: Introduction and Advanced Topics.* Berlin and New York: Springer.

Hamann, Katharina, Felix Warneken, Julia R. Greenberg, and Michael Tomasello. 2011. Collaboration Encourages Equal Sharing in Children but Not in Chimpanzees. *Nature* 476(7360): 328–331.

Han, Yi. 1986. Zhongguo "Xiaohuangdi" (The Chinese "Little Emperor"). *Chinese Writers* (3): 4–24.

Hannon, Paul. 2013. "Europe Lags East Asia in School Performance: Province of Shanghai in China Once Again Produced the Best Results." December 3. *The Wall Street Journal.* https://www.wsj.com/articles/SB10001424052702304355104579235502817791742 (accessed December 1, 2016).

Hansen, Mette Halskov. H. 2013. Learning Individualism: Hesse, Confucius, and Pep-Rallies in a Chinese Rural High School. *The China Quarterly 213*: 60–77.

Hansen, Mette Haslov. 2014. *Educating the Chinese Individual: Life in a Rural Boarding School.* Seattle, WA: University of Washington Press.

Hayashi, Akiko, Mayumi Karasawa, and Joseph Tobin 2009. The Japanese Preschool's Pedagogy of Feeling: Cultural Strategies for Supporting Young Children's Emotional Development. *Ethos* 37(1): 32–49.

Henrich, Joseph, Jean Ensminger, Richard McElreath, et al. 2010. Markets, Religion, Community Size, and the Evolution of Fairness and Punishment. *Science* 327(5972): 1480–1484.

Henrich, Joseph Patrick 2004. Foundations of Human Sociality: *Economic Experiments and Ethnographic Evidence from Fifteen Small-Scale Societies.* Oxford and New York: Oxford University Press.

Hepach, Robert, Amrisha Vaish, and Michael Tomasello. 2013a. A New Look at Children's Prosocial Motivation. *Infancy* 18(1): 67–90.

Hepach, Robert, Amrisha Vaish, and Michael Tomasello. 2013b. Young Children Sympathize Less in Response to Unjustified Emotional Distress. *Developmental Psychology* 49(6): 1132–1138.

Ho, D.Y.F. 1986. "Chinese Patterns of Socialization: A Critical Review." In *The Psychology of the Chinese People*, edited by Michael Harris Bond, pp. 1–37. New York: Oxford University Press.

Hollan, Douglas W., and C. Jason Throop. 2008. Whatever Happened to Empathy? Introduction. *Ethos* 36(4): 385–401.

Hollan, Douglas W., and C. Jason Throop, eds. 2011. *The Anthropology of Empathy: Experiencing the Lives of Others in Pacific Societies.* New York: Berghahn.

Hook, Jay. 1993. Judgments about the Right to Property from Preschool to Adulthood. *Law and Human Behavior* 17(1): 135–146.

Hrdy, Sarah Blaffer 2011. *Mothers and Others: The Evolutionary Origins of Mutual Understanding.* Cambridge, MA: Harvard University Press.

Hsiung, Ping-chen. 2005. *A Tender Voyage: Children and Childhood in Late Imperial China.* Stanford, CA: Stanford University Press.

Hsu, Francis L. K. 1971. *Under the Ancestors' Shadow; Kinship, Personality, and Social Mobility in China*. Stanford, CA: Stanford University Press.

Huang, Bochun, Chuanfang Zhong, Song Zhou, Chen Xu, and Yuan Lin. 2011. Meiti Tanfang 18 Lengmo Luren: Youren Cheng "Bieren Bugan Peng Wo Zenme gan" (Interviewing 18 Indifferent Passers-By: Someone Says "How Did I Dare to Help If Others Didn't." October 18. Yangcheng Wanbao. http://news.ifeng.com/society/special/nianyanvtong /content-4/detail_2011_10/18/9942624_0.shtml (accessed December 1, 2016).

Ivanhoe, Philip J. 2000. *Confucian Moral Self-Cultivation*, 2e. Indianapolis, IN: Hackett.

Ivanhoe, Philip J. 2009. *Readings from the Lu-Wang School of Neo-Confucianism*. Indianapolis, IN: Hackett.

James, A. 2007. Giving Voice to Children's Voices: Practices and Problems, Pitfalls and Potentials. *American Anthropologist* 109(2): 261.

Kanngiesser, Patricia, Nathalia Gjersoe, and Bruce M. Hood. 2010. The Effect of Creative Labor on Property-Ownership Transfer by Preschool Children and Adults. *Psychological Science* 21(9): 1236–1241.

Kanngiesser, Patricia, and Felix Warneken. 2012. Young Children Consider Merit When Sharing Resources with Others. *PLoS ONE* 7(8): e43979.

Kärtner, Joscha, and Heidi Keller. 2012. Comment: Culture-Specific Developmental Pathways to Prosocial Behavior: A Comment on Bischof-Köhler's Universalist Perspective. *Emotion Review* 4(1): 49–50.

Kärtner, Joscha, Heidi Keller, and Nandita Chaudhary. 2010. Cognitive and Social Influences on Early Prosocial Behavior in Two Sociocultural Contexts. *Developmental Psychology* 46(4): 905–914.

Keane, Webb. 2015. *Ethical Life: Its Natural and Social Histories*. Princeton, NJ: Princeton University Press.

Kinney, Anne Behnke. 1995. *Dyed Silk: Han Notions of the Moral Development of Children. In Chinese Views of Childhood*, edited by Anne Behnke Kinney, pp. 1–55. Honolulu, HI: University of Hawaii Press.

Kipnis, Andrew B. 1997. *Producing Guanxi: Sentiment, Self, and Subculture in a North China Village*. Durham, NC: Duke University Press.

Kipnis, Andrew B. 2006. Suzhi: A Keyword Approach. *The China Quarterly* 186: 295–313.

Kipnis, Andrew B. 2007. Neoliberalism Reified: Suzhi Discourse and Tropes of Neoliberalism in the People's Republic of China. *Journal of the Royal Anthropological Institute* 13(2): 383–400.

Kipnis, Andrew B. 2009. "Education and the Governing of Child-Centered Relatedness." In *Chinese Kinship: Contemporary Anthropological Perspective*, edited by Susanne Brandtstädter and Gonçalo D. Santos, pp. 204–222. New York: Routledge.

Kipnis, Andrew B. 2011. *Governing Educational Desire: Culture, Politics, and Schooling in China*. Chicago: University of Chicago Press.

Kipnis, Andrew B. 2012a. "Introduction: Chinese Modernity and the Individual Psyche." In *Chinese Modernity and Individual Psyche*, edited by Andrew B. Kipnis, pp. 1–16. New York: Palgrave Macmillan.

Kipnis, Andrew B. 2012b. Constructing Commonality: Standardization and Modernization in Chinese Nation-Building. *The Journal of Asian Studies* 71(3): 731–755.

Kipnis, Andrew B. 2012c. "Private Lessons and National Formations: National Hierarchy and the Individual Psyche in the Marketing of Chinese Educational Programs." In *Chinese Modernity and Individiaul Psyche*, edited by Andrew B. Kipnis, pp. 187–202. New York: Palgrave Macmillan.

Kipnis, Andrew B. 2012d. *Chinese Modernity and the Individual Psyche*. New York: Palgrave Macmillan.

Kleinman, Arthur. 1999 Moral Experience and Ethical Reflection: Can Ethnography Reconcile Them? A Quandary for "The New Bioethics." *Daedalus* 128(4): 69–97.

Kleinman, Arthur. 2006. *What Really Matters: Living a Moral Life amidst Uncertainty and Danger*. New York: Oxford University Press.

Kleinman, Arthur, and Joan Kleinman. 1994. How Bodies Remember: Social Memory and Bodily Experience of Criticism, Resistance, and Delegitimation Following China's Cultural Revolution. *New Literary History* 25(3): 707–723.

Kleinman, Arthur, Yunxiang Yan, Jing Jun, Sing Lee, and Everett Zhang. 2011. *Deep China: The Moral Life of the Person*. Berkeley, CA: University of California Press.

Kohlberg, Lawrence. 1984. *The Psychology of Moral Development: The Nature and Validity of Moral Stages: Essays on Moral Development*, Volume 2, 1e. San Francisco: Harper & Row.

Kuan, Teresa. 2008. *Adjusting the Bonds of Love: Parenting, Expertise and Social Change in a Chinese City*. PhD diss. University of Southern California.

Kuan, Teresa. 2011. The Heart Says One Thing But The Hand Does Another: A Story about Emotion-Work, Ambivalence and Popular Advice for Parents. *The China Journal* 65: 77–100.

Kuan, Teresa. 2012. The Horrific and the Exemplary: Public Stories and Education Reform in Late Socialist China. *Positions: East Asia Cultures Critique* 20(4): 1095–1125.

Kuan, Teresa. 2015. *Love's Uncertainty: The Politics and Ethics of Child Rearing in Contemporary China*. Oakland, CA: University of California Press.

Kusserow, Adrie. 2004. *American Individualisms: Child Rearing and Social Class in Three Neighborhoods*. New York: Palgrave Macmillan.

Laidlaw, James. 2002. For an Anthropology of Ethics and Freedom. *Journal of the Royal Anthropological Institute* 8(2): 311–332.

Lambek, Michael. 2010. *Ordinary Ethics: Anthropology, Language, and Action*. New York: Fordham University Press.

Lan, Huaien. 2010. Ye Shuo Shanghai Nanren (On Shanghainese Men). http://eladies.sina.com .cn/qg/2010/0203/1733967598.shtml (accessed December 1, 2016).

Levin, Dan. 2012. "In China Schools, a Culture of Bribery Spreads." November 21. *New York Times*. http://www.nytimes.com/2012/11/22/world/asia/in-china-schools-a-culture-of -bribery-spreads.html (accessed December 1, 2016).

Li, Bin. 1993. Moral Education in Transition: The Values Conflict in China. *Studies in Philosophy and Education* 12(1): 85–94.

Li, Fang. 2012. "Haizi Luyu Qigai Gei 5 Yuan, Bei Mama Ma 'Shaoya' " ("A Five-Year-Old Who Gave RMB 5 to a Beggar Was Called Idiot by Mother"). October 31. *Wuhan Chenbao* (*Wuhan Morning Post*). http://hb.qq.com/a/20121031/000795.htm (accessed December 1, 2016).

Li, Jin. 2010. "Learning to Self-Perfect: Chinese Beliefs about Learning." In *Revisiting the Chinese Learner*, edited by Carol K. K. Chan and Nirmala Rao, pp. 35–69. Hong Kong: Springer, Comparative Education Research Centre, the University of Hong Kong. http://link.springer.com /chapter/10.1007/978-90-481-3840-1_2 (accessed December 1, 2016).

Li, Jin. 2012. *Cultural Foundations of Learning: East and West*, 1e. New York: Cambridge University Press.

Li, Jin, Lianqin Wang, and Kurt Fischer. 2004. The Organisation of Chinese Shame Concepts. *Cognition & Emotion* 18(6): 767–797.

Li, Jinlei. 2013. "Shengfen Gongbu Qunian Jumin Shouru, Shanghai Renjun Chao 4 Wan Yuan Jushou" ("Average Income in 17 Provinces: Shanghai the Highest, Exceeding 40,000 Yuan."

January 25. *Zhongguo Xinwen Wang* (*China News*). http://news.163.com/13/0125/07 /8M23352U00014JB6.html (accessed December 1, 2016).

Li, Jun. 2012. Cong "Kong Rong Rang Li" dao "Yuehan Zheng Li" (From "Kong Rong Declines the Pear" to "John Fights for the Apple." http://blog.ifeng.com/article/17396906.html (accessed December 1, 2016).

Li, Vivian, Alex Shaw, and Kristina R. Olson. 2013. Ideas versus Labor: What Do Children Value in Artistic Creation? *Cognition* 127(1): 38–45.

Liang, Shuming. 1984. *Renxin Yu Rensheng* (*Mind and Life*). Beijing: Xuelin.

Liu, Wen, Lin Zhu, Xue Zhang, Yu Zhang, and Ying Liu. 2015. Equity Sensitivity of 2–3 Years Old Children in Distribution Condition (2~3Sui Ertong Zai Fenpei Qingjing Xia de Gongping Minganxing. *Acta Psychologica Sinica* (*Xinli XueBao*) 47(11): 1341–1348.

Long, Yingtai. 1997 "A, Shanghai Nanren" ("Wow, Shanghainese Men"). January 7. *Wenhui Newspaper.*

LoBue, Vanessa, Tracy Nishida, Cynthia Chiong, Judy S. DeLoache, and Jonathan Haidt. 2009. *When Getting Something Good Is Bad: Even Three-Year-Olds React to Inequality.* Oxford: Blackwell. http://dx.doi.org/10.1111/j.1467-9507.2009.00560.x (accessed December 1, 2016).

Luhrmann, T. M. 2006. Subjectivity. *Anthropological Theory* 6(3): 345–361.

Mageo, Jeannette. 2011. "Empathy and "As-If" Attachment in Samoa." In *The Anthropology of Empathy: Experiencing the Lives of Others,* edited by Douglas W. Hollan and C. Jason Throop, pp. 69–93. New York: Berghahn.

Maslin, Janet. 2011. Amy Chua's "Battle Hymn of the Tiger Mother"—Review. January 19. *New York Times,* http://www.nytimes.com/2011/01/20/books/20book.html (accessed December 1, 2016).

Meltzoff, Andrew N. 2002. Imitation as a Mechanism of Social Cognition: Origins of Empathy, Theory of Mind, and the Representation of Action. In *Blackwell Handbook of Childhood Cognitive Development,* edited by U. Goswami, pp. 6–25. Oxford: Blackwell.

Mencius. 1998. *Mencius,* translated by David Hinton. Washington, DC: Counterpoint.

Miller, Peggy J., Angela R. Wiley, Heidi Fung, and Chung-Hui Liang. 1997. Personal Storytelling as a Medium of Socialization in Chinese and American Families. *Child Development* 68(3): 557–568.

Ministry of Education of the People's Republic of China. 2002. Announcement of Implementing Chinese " 'Little Citizens' Moral Cultivation Plan" (Guanyu Shishi Zhongguo "Xiaogongmin" Daode Jianshe Jihua de Tongzhi). http://www.moe.gov.cn/jyb_xxgk/gk_gbgg/moe_0/moe_8 /moe_25/tnull_287.html (accessed December 1, 2016).

Moore, Chris. 2009. Fairness in Children's Resource Allocation Depends on the Recipient. *Psychological Science* 20(8): 944–948.

Munro, Donald J. 2000. *The Concept of Man in Contemporary China.* Ann Arbor, MI: Center for Chinese Studies, The University of Michigan.

Naftali, Orna. 2010. Caged Colden Canaries: Childhood, Privacy and Subjectivity in Contemporary Urban China. *Childhood* 17(3): 297–311.

Neary, Karen R, Ori Friedman, and Corinna L Burnstein. 2009. Preschoolers Infer Ownership From "Control of Permission." *Developmental Psychology* 45(3): 873–876.

Nie, Yilin, and Robert J. Wyman. 2005. The One-Child Policy in Shanghai: Acceptance and Internalization. *Population and Development Review* 31(2): 313–336.

Noles, Nicholaus S., and Frank C. Keil. 2011. Exploring Ownership in a Developmental Context. *New Directions for Child and Adolescent Development* 2011(132): 91–103.

Ochs, Elinor, and Tamar Kremer-Sadlik. 2007. Introduction: Morality as Family Practice. *Discourse & Society* 18(1): 5–10.

Ochs, Elinor, and Merav Shohet. 2006. The Cultural Structuring of Mealtime Socialization. *New Directions for Child and Adolescent Development* (111): 35–49.

Ochs, Elinor, and Olga Solomon. 2010. Autistic Sociality. *Ethos* 38(1): 69–92.

Olson, Kristina R., and Elizabeth S. Spelke. 2008. Foundations of Cooperation in Young Children. *Cognition* 108(1): 222–231.

Osburg, John. 2013. *Anxious Wealth: Money and Morality among China's New Rich*. Stanford, CA: Stanford University Press.

Over, Harriet, and Malinda Carpenter. 2009. Priming Third-Party Ostracism Increases Affiliative Imitation in Children. *Developmental Science* 12(3): F1–F8.

Oxfeld, Ellen. 2010. *Drink Water, but Remember the Source*. Berkeley, CA: University of California Press.

Pan, Tianshu. 2011. "Place Attachment, Communal Memory, and the Moral Underpinnings of Gentrification in Post-Reform Shanghai." In *Deep China: The Moral Life of the Person*, edited by Arthur Kleinman, Yunxiang Yan, Jun Jing, Sing Lee, and Everett Zhang, pp. 152–176. Berkeley, CA: University of California Press.

Piaget, Jean. [1932] 1997. *The Moral Judgment of the Child*. New York: Free Press.

Quinn, Naomi. 2005. Universals of Child Rearing. *Anthropological Theory* 5(4): 477–516.

Quinn, Naomi. 2006. The Self. *Anthropological Theory* 6(3): 362–384.

Quinn, Naomi, and Jeannette Marie Mageo. 2013. *Attachment Reconsidered: Cultural Perspectives on a Western Theory*. New York: Palgrave Macmillan.

Quinn, Naomi, and Claudia Strauss. 2006. Introduction to Special Issue on the Missing Psychology in Cultural Anthropology's Key Words. *Anthropological Theory* 6(3): 267–279.

Rawls, John. 1971. *A Theory of Justice*. Cambridge, MA: Harvard University Press.

Rai, Tage Shakti, and Alan Page Fiske. 2011. Moral Psychology Is Relationship Regulation: Moral Motives for Unity, Hierarchy, Equality, and Proportionality. *Psychological Review* 118(1): 57–75.

Robbins, Joel. 2012. "Cultural Values." In *A Companion to Moral Anthropology*, edited by Didier Fassin, pp. 115–132. New York: John Wiley.

Rochat, Philippe. 2011. Possession and Morality in Early Development. *New Directions for Child and Adolescent Development* 2011(132): 23–38.

Rochat, Philippe, Maria D. G. Dias, Guo Liping, et al. 2009. Fairness in Distributive Justice by 3- and 5-Year-Olds across Seven Cultures. *Journal of Cross-Cultural Psychology* 40(3): 416–442.

Saari, Jon L. 1990 *Legacies of Childhood: Growing up Chinese in a Time of Crisis, 1890–1920*. Cambridge, MA: Council on East Asian Studies, Harvard University Press.

Saby, Joni N., Andrew N. Meltzoff, and Peter J. Marshall. 2013. Infants' Somatotopic Neural Responses to Seeing Human Actions: I've Got You under My Skin. *PLoS ONE* 8(10): e77905.

Sahlins, Marshall. 2011. What Kinship Is: Part Two. *Journal of the Royal Anthropological Institute* 17(2): 227–242.

Sandel, Michael J. 2010. *Justice: What's the Right Thing to Do?* New York: Farrar, Straus and Giroux.

Schmidt, Marco F. H., and Jessica A. Sommerville. 2011. Fairness Expectations and Altruistic Sharing in 15-Month-Old Human Infants. *PLoS ONE* 6(10): e23223.

Settles, Barbara H., Xuewen Sheng, Yuan Zang, and Jia Zhao. 2013. "The One-Child Policy and Its Impact on Chinese Families." In *International Handbook of Chinese Families*, edited by Chan Kwok-bun, pp. 627–646. New York: Springer. http://link.springer.com/chapter/10.1007/978-1-4614-0266-4_38 (accessed December 1, 2016).

Shaw, Alex, Peter DeScioli, and Kristina R. Olson. 2012. Fairness versus Favoritism in Children. *Evolution and Human Behavior* 33(6): 736–745.

Shaw, Alex, Vivian Li, and Kristina R. Olson. 2012. Children Apply Principles of Physical Ownership to Ideas. *Cognitive Science* 36(8): 1383–1403.

Shweder, Richard A, N. Much, L. Park, and M. M. Mahapatra. 1997. "The 'Big Three' of Morality (Autonomy, Community, Divinity) and the 'Big Three' Explanations of Suffering." In *Morality and Health*, edited by Allan M. Brandt and Paul Rozin, pp. 119–169. New York: Routledge.

Singer, Tania, and Claus Lamm. 2009. The Social Neuroscience of Empathy. *Annals of the New York Academy of Sciences* 1156: 81–96.

Siu, Helen F. 2006. China's Century: Fast Forward with Historical Baggage. *American Anthropologist* 108(2): 389–392.

Slote, Michael. 2010. The Mandate of Empathy. *Dao* 9(3): 303–307.

Smith, Adam. 2011. *The Theory of Moral Sentiments*. Mineola, NY: Dover.

Smith, Craig E., Peter R. Blake, and Paul L. Harris. 2013. I Should but I Won't: Why Young Children Endorse Norms of Fair Sharing but Do Not Follow Them. *PLoS ONE* 8(3): e59510.

Snare, Frank. 1972. The Concept of Property. *American Philosophical Quarterly* 9(2): 200–206.

Sommerville, Jessica A., Marco F. H. Schmidt, Jung-eun Yun, and Monica Burns. 2013. The Development of Fairness Expectations and Prosocial Behavior in the Second Year of Life. *Infancy* 18(1): 40–66.

Sperber, Dan. 1996. *Explaining Culture: A Naturalistic Approach*. Oxford, England, and Cambridge, MA: Blackwell.

Stafford, Charles. 2013a. "Ordinary Ethics in China Today." In *Ordinary Ethics in China*, edited by Charles Stafford, pp. 3–25. London and New York: Bloomsbury.

Stafford, Charles. 2013b. *Ordinary Ethics in China*. London and New York: Bloomsbury.

Steinmüller, Hans. 2011. The State of Irony in China. *Critique of Anthropology* 31(1): 21–42.

Steinmüller, Hans. 2013. "The Ethics of Irony: Work, Family and Fatherland in Rural China." In *Ordinary Ethics in China*, edited by Charles Stafford, pp. 133–153. London: Bloomsbury.

Strauss, Claudia, and Naomi Quinn. 1997. *A Cognitive Theory of Cultural Meaning*. Cambridge, MA: Cambridge University Press.

Sykes, Karen M. 2012. "Moral Reasoning." In *A Companion to Moral Anthropology*, edited by Didier Fassin, pp. 169–185. New York: Wiley.

Tang, Yuezhi. ed. 2011. "Hong Huang Paohong Yelu Huayi 'Huma' Cai Meier" ("Huang Hong Harshly Attacks Yale Asian 'Tiger Mother' Amy Chua"). July 2. *Sohu News*. http://learning.sohu.com/20110702/n312265036.shtml (accessed December 1, 2016).

Throop, C. Jason. 2012. "Moral Sentiments." In *A Companion to Moral Anthropology*, edited by Didier Fassin, pp. 150–168. New York: Wiley.

Thurston, Anne F. 1980. "Urban Violence during the Cultural Revolution: Who Is to Blame?" In *Violence in China: Essays in Culture and Counterculture*, edited by Jonathan Neaman Lipman and Stevan Harrell, pp. 149–173. New York: State University of New York Press.

Tobin, Joseph, Yeh Hsueh, and Mayumi Karasawa. 2011. *Preschool in Three Cultures Revisited: China, Japan, and the United States*. Chicago: University of Chicago Press.

Tobin, Joseph J., David Y. H. Wu, and Dana H. Davidson. 1991. *Preschool in Three Cultures: Japan, China and the United States*. New Haven, CT: Yale University Press.

Tomasello, Michael. 2009. *Why We Cooperate*. Cambridge, MA: The MIT Press.

Tomasello, Michael, Alicia P. Melis, Claudio Tennie, Emily Wyman, and Esther Herrmann. 2012. Two Key Steps in the Evolution of Human Cooperation: The Interdependence Hypothesis. *Current Anthropology* 53(6): 673–692.

Tu, Wei-Ming. 1985. *Confucian Thought*. New York: State University of New York Press.

Turner, Victor W. 1995. *The Ritual Process: Structure and Anti-Structure*. New York: Aldine de Gruyter.

de Waal, Frans B. M. 2008. Putting the Altruism Back into Altruism: The Evolution of Empathy. *Annual Review of Psychology* 59: 279–300.

Vaish, Amrisha, Malinda Carpenter, and Michael Tomasello. 2009. Sympathy through Affective Perspective Taking and Its Relation to Prosocial Behavior in Toddlers. *Developmental Psychology* 45(2): 534–543.

Wang, Juefen, and Fang Jiang. 2012.Meiguo Xiaohuo Zai Nanjing Yu Qigai Fenxiang Shutiao (An American Man Sharing Potato Chips with a Beggar in Nanjing). http://news.xinhuanet.com /society/2012-05/09/c_111916738.htm (accessed December 1, 2016).

Wang, Junxiu, and Yiyin Yang. 2013. *Zhongguo Shehui Xintai Yanjiu Baogao 2012–2013 (Annual Report on Social Mentality of China 2012–2013)*. Beijing: Shehui Kexue Wenxian Chubanshe (Social Science Academy Press).

Wang, Ying, and Vanessa L. Fong. 2009. Little Emperors and the 4:2:1 Generation: China's Singletons. *Journal of the American Academy of Child & Adolescent Psychiatry* 48(12): 1137–1139.

Watkins, David A., and John Burville Biggs. 2001. *Teaching the Chinese Learner: Psychological and Pedagogical Perspectives*. Comparative Education Research Centre, the University of Hong Kong.

Weisner, Thomas S. 1997. The Ecocultural Project of Human Development: Why Ethnography and Its Findings Matter. *Ethos* 25(2):177–190.

Whitehead, Charles. 2012. Why the Behavioural Sciences Need the Concept of the Culture-Ready Brain. *Anthropological Theory* 12(1): 43–71.

Wines, Michael. 2011a. "Toddler's Accident Sets Off Soul-Searching in China." October 18. *New York Times*. http://www.nytimes.com/2011/10/19/world/asia/toddlers-accident-sets-off-soul -searching-in-china.html (accessed December 1, 2016).

Wines, Michael. 2011b. "Chinese Toddler Who Was Run Over Twice Dies." October 21. *New York Times*. http://www.nytimes.com/2011/10/22/world/asia/chinese-toddler-who-was-run-over -twice-dies.html (accessed December 1, 2016).

Wong, David B. 2015. Early Confucian Philosophy and the Development of Compassion. *Dao* 14(2): 157–194.

Woronov, T. E. 2003. *Transforming the Future: "Quality" Children and the Chinese Nation*. PhD diss. University of Chicago.

Woronov, T. E. 2009. Governing China's Children: Governmentality and "Education for Quality." *Positions* 17(3): 567–589.

Wu, David Y. H. 1996. "Parental Control: Psychocultural Interpretations of Chinese Patterns of Socialization." In *Growing Up the Chinese Way*, edited by Sing Lau, pp. 1–26. Hong Kong: Chinese University Press.

Xinhua News. 2015. Let the Flowers of the Motherland Blossom under Sunshine (Rang Zuguo de Huaduo Zai Yangguang Xia Zhanfang). http://news.xinhuanet.com/2015- 05/31/c_1115464048.htm (accessed December 1, 2016).

Xu, Binzhong. 2012. "Shanghai Jinnian Jiang Zaixian Rutuo Nan: Youeryuan Jinliang Kai Tuoban" ("Shanghai Nursery Class Enrollment Tightened: More Nursery Class Preschools Demanded"). *Xinwen Chenbao (Shanghai Morning Post)*, March 22. http://www.eol.cn /shanghainews_5281/20120323/t20120323_756980.shtml (accessed December 1, 2016).

Xu, Jing. 2014. Becoming a Moral Child amidst China's Moral Crisis: Preschool Discourse and Practices of Sharing in Shanghai. *Ethos* 42(2): 222–242.

Yan, Yunxiang. 1996. *The Flow of Gifts: Reciprocity and Social Networks in a Chinese Village*, 1e. Stanford, CA: Stanford University Press.

Yan, Yunxiang. 2002. "Unbalanced Reciprocity: Asymmetrical Gift Giving and Social Hierarchy in Rural China." In *The Question of the Gift: Essays across Disciplines*, edited by Mark Osteen, pp. 67–84. London: Routledge.

Yan, Yunxiang. 2003. Private Life under Socialism?: Love, Intimacy, and Family Change in a Chinese Village, 1949–1999. Stanford, CA: Stanford University Press.

Yan, Yunxiang. 2009. The Good Samaritan's New Trouble: A Study of the Changing Moral Landscape in Contemporary China. *Social Anthropology* 17(1): 9–24.

Yan, Yunxiang. 2011. "The Changing Moral Landscape." In *Deep China: The Moral Life of the Person* 1e, edited by Arthur Kleinman, Yunxiang Yan, Jun Jing, Sing Lee, and Everett Zhang, pp. 36–77. Berkeley, CA: University of California Press.

Yan, Yunxiang. 2012. Food Safety and Social Risk in Contemporary China. *The Journal of Asian Studies* 71(3): 705–729.

Yan, Yunxiang. 2013. "The Drive for Success and the Ethics of the Striving Individual." In *Ordinary Ethics in China*, edited by Charles Stafford, pp. 263–291. London: Bloomsbury, London School of Economics Monographs on Social Anthropology.

Yang, Mayfair. 2002. The Resilience of Guanxi and Its New Deployments: A Critique of Some New Guanxi Scholarship. *The China Quarterly* (170): 459–476.

Yang, Mayfair Mei-hui. 1994. *Gifts, Favors, and Banquets: The Art of Social Relationships in China*. Ithaca, NY: Cornell University Press.

Ye, Weimin, and Ying Shen. 2011. "Chen Xianmei: Shan Zai Fushi Zhijian" ("Chen Xianmei: Benevolence in a Small Step." December 30. *Nanfang Zhoumo (Southern Weekly)*. http://www.infzm.com/content/67063 (accessed December 1, 2016).

Yin, Jianli. 2009. *Hao Mama Shengguo Hao Laoshi* (*A Good Mother Is Better than a Good Teacher*). Beijing: Zuojia Chubanshe (Writers' Press).

Yu, Jing. 2013. "Qie Man Xuanran "Gaibang Nanjing Fenduo" Chengyuan de Xingfu" ("Caution at Publicizing the Happiness of Nanjing Beggars." June 4. *Nanfang Dushi Bao (Southern Metropolis Daily)*. http://star.news.sohu.com/20130604/n377910295.shtml (accessed December 1, 2016).

Yu, Yongping. 2010. "Fada Diqu Ying Gao Zhiliang Puji Xueqian Jiaoyu" ("Economically Advanced Regions Should Popularize High-Quality Early Education." October 13. *Zhongguo Jiaoyubao (China Education Daily)*. http://www.cnsaes.org/homepage/html/resource/res03/2466.html (accessed December 1, 2016).

Zhang, Jingya. 2013. "Jia Qigai Rang Zhengnengliang Hanxin: Liulanggou Cheng Daoju" ("Fake Beggar Chills Positive Energy." February 28. *Beijing Chenbao (Beijing Morning Post)*. http://society.people.com.cn/n/2013/0228/c1008-20626383.html (accessed December 1, 2016).

Zhang, Li. 2008. China's Ascent as a Theoretical Question. *Anthropology News* 49(8): 13–13.

Zhang, Li, and Aihwa Ong, eds. 2008 *Privatizing China: Socialism from Afar*. Ithaca, NY: Cornell University Press.

Zhang, Qianfan. 2011. "Xiaoyueyue Shijian Rang Mengzi Mengxiu" ("The Death of Little Yueyue Leave Mencius Dumbstruck"), October 25. http://view.news.qq.com/a/20111025/000017.htm (accessed December 1, 2016).

Zhu, Jianfeng. 2008. *Winning the Competition at the Start Line: Chinese Modernity, Reproduction and the Desire for a "High Quality" Population*. PhD diss. University of Minnesota.

Zigon, Jarrett. 2008. *Morality: An Anthropological Perspective*. London: Bloomsbury Academic.

Index

Note: Page numbers in *italics* indicate figures; page numbers followed by "*t*" indicate tables.